Business Development in Licensed Retailing

Business Development in Licensed Retailing

A unit manager's guide

Conrad Lashley and Guy Lincoln

OXFORD AMSTERDAM BOSTON LONDON NEW YORK PARIS
SAN DIEGO SAN FRANCISCO SINGAPORE SYDNEY TOKYO

Butterworth-Heinemann
An imprint of Elsevier Science
Linacre House, Jordan Hill, Oxford OX2 8DP
225 Wildwood Avenue, Woburn MA 01801-2041

First published 2003

British Library Cataloguing in Publication Data
A catalogue record for this book is available from the British Library

Library of Congress Cataloguing in Publication Data
A catalogue record for this book is available from the Library of Congress

ISBN 0 7506 5334 5

For information on all Butterworth-Heinemann publications
visit our website at www.bh.com

Composition by Genesis Typesetting, Rochester, Kent
Printed and bound in Great Britain by MPG Books Ltd, Bodmin, Cornwall

Contents

Foreword

JD Wetherspoon Plc operates almost 600 pubs throughout the United Kingdom. It is the fastest growing company in the UK and the ninth fastest in Europe.

The company has created more than 10,000 jobs in its pubs and head office during the past four years and aims to create an additional 3000 jobs each year for the next ten years.

It is vitally important to our business that all of our outlets consistently offer the highest standards of service and customer at all times.

Our managers and associates who serve the customers on a day-to-day basis are essential in ensuring that Wetherspoon continues to build a loyal customer base and to grow the business on a year-by-year basis.

The company's overall performance is dependent on the quality and effectiveness of all our employees in every one of the pubs.

Management and staff training has always been, and continues to be, a main priority for the company.

It therefore gives me great pleasure to write the Foreword to this book by Conrad Lashley and Guy Lincoln.

It is my opinion that *Business Development in Licensed Retailing* will be a valuable reference for any management development programme.

The book has been written and organized in a manner that explains all of the underlying management principles involved in running a busy and successful licensed operation.

At the same time it gives a wide range of practical examples and guidance on how to achieve success.

These principles of effective recruitment, induction, training, leadership and retention are at the heart of Wetherspoon and provide the foundations for the service, quality and consistency to all our customers.

Tim Martin, Chairman – JD Wetherspoon

Preface

The licensed retail sector is undergoing dramatic change. The impact of attempts to increase competition by limiting the number of licensed outlets that any one firm can directly manage has been profound. Since the late 1980s, the major brewers have had to refocus their operations. They have been forced to divest most of their direct holdings of pub and bar outlets, and those few firms still in the brewing business now concentrate on the direct management of high volume, branded properties that have much in common with traditional retail units. As a direct consequence of divestment by the major brewers, a significant number of large non-brewing pub retailers have entered the marketplace. The skills needed to run these businesses are increasingly similar to those required of more traditional retailers. Each unit is frequently a significant business in its own right.

This book focuses on the key skills needed to manage bar, pub and restaurant units, irrespective of whether the business is largely 'wet' or largely 'dry'. We recognize that the boundary between pubs and restaurants is becoming increasingly blurred. Many pubs and bars that are chiefly places where people go to drink have significant food sales. In other cases, what might be considered 'restaurants' now encourage customers to buy drinks before and after their meals. In reality these distinctions are less relevant to unit managers than understanding who the customers are and why they are using the establishment. Thus we use examples of businesses that combine food and drink sales in multi-unit locations. The skills needed at unit level are similar, irrespective of the balance of food and drink sales in the business.

Flowing from this, to illustrate our points we use examples from best practice in retailing. These are not always traditional bar and pub locations, but the point is that the sector can learn from professional approaches in sectors that are similar. In particular we use examples from J.D. Wetherspoons, Harvester Restaurants, TGI Fridays and, occasionally, McDonald's Restaurants, because these provide examples of management practice that could be adopted by the licensed retail sector. In the first case the company is chiefly 'wet' led but also has a significant food business; in the second and third cases, both companies have a considerable minority of total sales arising from the sale of drinks. In the case of the fast-food operator, the company's professional approach to brand management, monitoring business performance and commitment to service quality management provides an example that could benefit many licensed retailers.

The unit manager and the staff directly involved with customers have a particular significance in delivering customer satisfaction. Satisfied customers are much more likely to return, and building a strong base of loyal customers is a key source of competitive advantage, leading ultimately to sales and profit growth. Although many licensed retail organizations express these sentiments in official documents and in public pronouncements, detailed investigation of what they actually do in practice reveals this as a somewhat rhetorical set of claims. Many are guilty of claiming that people are their most important asset, yet treating them as a cost to be minimized.

At this stage, many British mangers are still developing their understanding of what is needed to manage bars, pubs and restaurants, but one emerging shared truth is that the unit manager is key to the success of each business unit. The performance of the restaurant, bar or pub is most fundamentally influenced by the skills, talents, priorities and personality of the immediate unit manager. Studies comparing different levels of profitability, sales, staff turnover, customer satisfaction and employee satisfaction in different units in the same group show how important the performance of the unit manager is to the success of the unit. Indeed, industrial experience in many licensed retail organizations shows that a change of managers in the same unit can result in dramatic changes in the unit's business performance.

This book aims to provide a resource for both unit management programmes in licensed retail organizations and for academics preparing students for careers in licensed retail management. It is deliberately written in a way that addresses a *'how to do agenda'* by offering a practical guide to the skills and knowledge needed by those who will be managing bars, restaurants and pubs in fast-moving licensed retailing contexts. The book is deliberately presented in a non-academic style, without the referencing and quotations typical of academic texts. Within a higher education context, it is assumed that the book will be largely used at Level Two in programmes of study. Traditionally, this stage of hospitality, leisure and tourism management programmes focuses on the practical techniques involved in managing operations. Similarly, the book is written in a way that goes beyond the simple checklist of many distance-learning materials found in in-company management development programmes.

At root, the book assumes that managers running what are substantial businesses in their own right need to be *'reflective practitioners'*. The very nature of the task-driven practical immediacy of their work means that they have to be capable of active management and practical solutions to unit management situations. That said, they also need to be capable of standing back and reflecting on their actions so as to be more effective in future. The problem is that many unit managers in hospitality retail operations are by inclination *'Activist'* learners (Honey and Mumford, 1986) – that is, they are mostly people who are comfortable in action and 'sorting things out', but less so with standing back and thinking about what they are doing and why. We recently came across a pub manager who had recruited 287 people in a six-month period – the normal establishment was fifty employees. He was recruiting over ten new staff every week. Indeed, the replacement of staff dominated his work for that period. Instead of spending time developing sales, addressing customer satisfaction and increasing profits, he was almost permanently engaged in recruitment. Had he stood back and reflected on the situation, he might have come up with some more useful ways of spending his time. This case is not untypical; many managers feel comfortable keeping busy, and spend little time in active self-critical reflection.

Given the learning needs of both current and would-be managers, the text attempts to combine theoretical concepts and practical advice in a way that uses theory as a tool but is not overly theoretical. Where appropriate, the text is illustrated by examples from different licensed retail operations. In the main, these are set within a context that assumes that hospitality retail operations are not all the same. Using a model developed with Steven Taylor (Lashley and Taylor, 1998), we suggest that there are three types of licensed retail offers to customers; uniformity dependent, choice dependent and relationship dependent. Each of these offers involves a different set of customer expectations, critical success factors, definitions of service quality and requirements for frontline staff performance. Hence this text assumes that there is no one best way of managing hospitality retail units, but there is likely to be a match between the offer to the customer and the way service employees are managed.

Finally, the content of the book is informed by research with a number of key licensed retail operators. It is much closer to a programme of manager training and development in industry than a traditional single-disciplined book. Hence the content asks, what does a manager of one of these units need to know? It therefore contains a number of key themes that are rarely found in one text.

Given that managers of licensed retail organizations have little strategic control over marketing, people or financial matters, the text focuses on providing an understanding of these matters and showing how they shape the manager's immediate tactical role. Fundamentally, the manager has to understand that people are the key asset of the business, and a large part of the book focuses on understanding and working with people. Understanding what makes them tick, team leadership, successful recruitment and staff training are all essential in controlling the hidden cost of staff turnover. Traditionally, many of these businesses have been happy to live with levels of staff turnover that mean each job is filled twice or three times per year. Apart from the high direct costs to the business, high staff turnover creates barriers to building customer loyalty and competitive advantage through quality service delivery.

A second key theme in the book explores the nature of service difference and different offers made to customers, together with the implications this has for service quality and service quality management. In addition to the variations in key service offers discussed above, customers use a variety of licensed retail operations on different occasions. The same customer may have different expectations of the products and services within the same bar or restaurant depending on the 'occasion' of the visit. Unit managers need to have a thorough understanding of service quality management and the critical success factors that will shape customer assessment of quality of the visit.

Thirdly, the book explores a number of issues associated with managing the unit as a commercial venture. At an immediate tactical level, managers need to understand how to manage their own time effectively and how to ensure that other team members are working towards the various aims and objectives set. The business planning process is therefore a core aspect of effective unit operation. It is through this device that team member efforts are directed towards global goals to manage costs and ensure that revenue exceeds expenditure and generates profits for the organization. Within the framework the book argues for and demonstrates an alternative approach to managing people compared with traditional management approaches in the field. The approach takes for granted that people are the key asset in delivering improved business performance and shows that an investment in people through improved salaries and training budgets can boost the bottom-line performance of the business.

Further reading

Honey, P. and Mumford, A. (1986). *Manual of Learning Styles*. BBC Books.
Lashley, C. and Taylor, S. (1998). Hospitality retail operations types and styles in the management of human resources. *J. Retail. Cons. Serv.*, **5(3)**.

Conrad Lashley
Professor of Hospitality Retailing
Leeds Metropolitan University

Guy Lincoln
Senior Lecturer in Licensed Retailing
Leeds Metropolitan University

Figures

Tables

CHAPTER 1

What business are you in?

After working through this chapter, you should be able to:

- highlight the key features of licensed retail service

- identify different types of licensed service operations

- explain the key drivers of licensed services types

- contrast and compare service management techniques.

Bar and pub services management

In the past, many people thought that the key to successful pub business was 'location, location, location' – in other words, the location of the pub or bar was the most important factor in determining its success. However, there are many successful bars and pubs that are in poor locations yet still manage to build sales and good profits. It's not so much where your pub or bar is located, *but what goes on inside it* – in particular, how the landlord and staff deal with customers.

This chapter aims to show that although licensed retail services are different, customers expect the quality of product and services to match their expectations. Good unit management understands what customers want, and recognizes that employees – their selection, training, motivation, reward and management – are key to customer satisfaction.

Licensed retail services

Licensed retail organizations provide drink and/or food and/or accommodation in a service context. In most cases, these services are both produced and consumed on the premises. In the case of the 'off trade', the product is consumed away from the premises in a manner much closer to general retail services. Whilst reference will be made to the off-licence dimensions of the business, this book is largely concerned with the management of on-site licensed retailing because these businesses are more complex and involve a more detailed service transaction than simply retail. It is important to recognize that bars, pubs and restaurants offer services that have a deep-seated meaning to customers that touch on the domestic and cultural meanings of hospitality. These meanings will be briefly touched on later in the chapter, but the host and guest relationship, where the licensee/landlord is in effect inviting customers into his or her home, is an important element of the service being provided.

This book is aimed at licensed retail operations where bars or pubs are directly managed as part of a chain. Licensed retailing involves an increasing focus of bar and pub services on brands that make a clear offer to an identified profile or segment of customers and the occasions on which they use pub and bar services. Whilst much of the book applies to the management of all bars and pubs, and can be applied both in the free house and in the 'tied trade', the book is specifically concerned with identifying issues associated with licensed retail units that are managed as part of a chain (Table 1.1).

Licensed retail organizations that operate through chains provide these services in a way that is increasingly:

1 *Branded*: services are usually sold under a brand name, traditionally a brewery or beer brand. Brands are chains of bar, café and pub outlets that trade under the same name. The brand may represent a cluster of attributes or benefits to customers, who have an idea of what to expect when entering the premises. Traditionally this was the brewery beer brand, although increasingly brands are trading names that shape customer expectations and cluster round similar service offers.

2 *Customer focused*: a consequence of branding is to shape the nature of the products and services that make up the brand to particular customer types, needs and

Brand name	Licensed retail service	Number of units	Owner corporation	Main service predominance
J.D. Wetherspoons	Pubs with significant food offer	500	J.D. Wetherspoons	Wet led
Chef & Brewer	Pub and restaurant service	95	Scottish & Newcastle Retail	Food led
TGI Fridays (UK)	American restaurant and cocktail bar	40	Whitbread Restaurants	Food led
Harvester Restaurants	Traditional restaurant and pub	130	Bass Leisure Retail	Food led
John Barras	Community pub and restaurant	155	Scottish & Newcastle Retail	Wet led
Brewers Fayre	Pub and restaurant services	273	Whitbread Restaurants	Food led
Brewsters	Pub and restaurant services	120	Whitbread Restaurants	Food led
All Bar One	Cosmopolitan bars serving food	54	Bass Leisure Retail	Wet led

Table 1.1 A selection of major licensed retail brands as at May 2001 (source: *Martin Information Guide to Pub, Bar & Nightclub Brands* (2001)

experiences. Issues such as age, gender, social class, income, region, family and lifecycle, consumption patterns and service needs help retailers to focus the brand and the messages required by customers.

3 *Standardized*: though this will vary according to the nature of the brand and business, standardization follows from the requirement of customers for consistency and predictability. Typically, the range of food and drink items, the prices charged, decor and building layout are standardized across all units.

4 *Consistent in quality*: management of the experience has to be concerned with ensuring that customers get the experience they expect. That is, not only the physical products but also the type of service they get from staff must be consistent and in line with customer expectations. Thus service quality, staff training and performance appraisal become important tools in unit management.

5 *Managed via operating systems*: consistency and standardization across hundreds of units frequently require that all operate to a centrally designed system that guides the way in which products are purchased, assembled and served. In many cases these systems also lay down how training, recruitment and other staff management issues are to be handled.

6 *Sales driven*: using techniques from the retail goods sector, licensed retail businesses are concerned to ensure that communication with customers is clear. The nature of the product and services on offer are stated in a way that allows minimal confusion and misunderstanding. Point-of-sale material and staff

training in 'up-selling' techniques, together with an array of other techniques, attempt to maximize the sale to each customer.

7 *Mass marketed*: to generate customer identification and to shape clear communications with customers, licensed retailing organizations increasingly use mass advertising through television and newspapers, as well as other promotional techniques, to inform customers about the brand and services on offer.

8 *Location defined*: these managed pubs and bars have a distinct set of location characteristics that define their typical size and high street, suburban or trunk road locations, property types, age characteristics, parking facilities, or proximity to transport links, etc.

Table 1.2 illustrates some brand features of a sample of licensed brands.

Brand	Style/target customer	Ideal sites	Locations
J.D. Wetherspoons	Traditional basic pub, no frills style, but food growing in importance	Empty buildings, not usually pubs, in good positions; 5 500 sq ft	Nationwide from London origins, most major cities
Chef & Brewer	More up-market pub restaurants; a long established brand	Minimum 3 000 sq ft front house, 1 750 sq ft back	Suburban, country and 'city village' sites
TGI Fridays (UK)	Licensed from USA; smaller units (200 seats) being developed; some next to Travel Inn	7 000 sq ft	Early, city centre sites; now more major roads and suburban
Harvester Restaurants	Country farmhouse-style eating places; casual family dining	Off major motorways and roadside sites	Mostly located in South East and Midlands
John Barras	Victorian-style community pubs	On main road and community sites	Most located in Northern England
Brewers Fayre	Pub restaurant aimed at the adult market	Out of town, 1–3 acre sites by towns with 50 000+ population	Suburban, within short distance of motorways
Brewsters	Pub restaurant aimed at the family market; some re-branded from Brewers Fayre	Out of town, 1–3 acre sites by towns with 50 000+ population	Suburban, within short distance of motorways
All Bar One	Cosmopolitan bars, quality food and restaurant-style service	High street locations, vary in size	Affluent urban areas, major cities

Table 1.2 Some brand features of a sample of licensed retail brands

Over the past few decades, branded licensed retail services have taken an increasing share of bar, café, restaurant and hotel business in the UK and other western countries. The consistency of service, lower costs through the scale of their operations, and appeal of a variety of brands to target markets have ensured wide success.

As a unit manager working in one of these branded businesses you are required to understand the nature of the brand in which you are working – that is, what is it that customers are buying into? With this understanding you are able to focus on customer expectations and what has to be done to ensure that customer expectations are met.

Most importantly, as a unit manager in branded business you are required to understand and work within the disciplines of the brand. Customers who experience different facilities, prices, quality and service in different establishments in the same brand will become confused about what the brand represents. Their expectations become less clear and more uncertain, and a likely consequence is that they will seek out a competitor who is more consistent.

Active learning point

In the table below, fill in the details of a bar brand known to you.

Brand	Comments
Brand name/owner/number of outlets/geographical location	
Food/drink/accommodation offer Number of products/price	
Service attributes/quality/ positioning/the service experience	
Staffing/types/numbers/contact with customers	
Evidence of product/service consistency	
Marketing and sales drives/pricing and promotional strategies	
Description of typical customers – age, gender, income group, consumption patterns, service needs	

The downside of licensed retail branding!

Whilst these branded services have been very successful in capturing an increased share of licensed retail service business, they face some difficult management issues. Many of the features of these operations that have brought about their success also lead to problems, and hence the need for this book.

Management skills

In the past, successful management in the pub business was often defined as about being 'a nice couple who keep a good pint'. In other words, being a welcoming and friendly host and maintaining good product quality standards were deemed to be key determinants of success. Nowadays the high-volume businesses that are directly managed in brand formats require different skills. The tightly defined brand supported by operating systems, quality management techniques and policies derived at Head Office can lead organizations to adopt a 'command and control' style that allows little scope for individual manager or employee initiative. Managers at unit level are expected to work to the 'one best way'. As we shall see, for some businesses this is consistent with the offer to customers, but sometimes it creates unnecessary difficulties because you may feel stifled and discouraged from being creative in your work.

This book shows that there are a number of ways in which your skills as a unit manager can be tapped and developed to the benefit of the brand.

Employee dissatisfaction

The operating systems, tight product specification and 'one best way' job design allow little scope for individual flair and creativity. Employees experience jobs that are tightly controlled, routine and monotonous. On top of this, the uneven pace of work in many bar and pub services, together with the difficulties inherent in serving customers, add extra stress to licensed retail service work. Consequently, many licensed retail operations face high labour turnover. It is not unusual for licensed retailers to experience average labour turnover of over 150 per cent per year across the whole brand, with some jobs and units recording labour turnover of over 500 per cent per year. Apart from the direct costs of replacing staff – which can be considerable in themselves – you as the manager will face difficulties through the sheer volume of recruitment, selection, and training that you have to undertake.

Service inconsistencies

Problems with service consistency can occur for several reasons. First, the very scale of these organizations means that they are attempting to deliver consistent customer experiences through a very large number of units. Hundreds of unit management personnel and thousands of staff must all share an understanding of the brand, and be prepared to work within the rigidities of operating procedures. With so many people involved, there are clearly many opportunities for things to go wrong.

The second problem relates to the labour turnover. When there is a high rate of labour turnover, a constant stream of new employees are joining and leaving the organization. In these circumstances, it is difficult to communicate and train employees to the desired standards.

The very nature of service contact means that both employees and customers may react inconsistently with each other. Customer perceptions of different employees will shape the way they evaluate the service and employees as people. It may be unrealistic to expect employees always to act with good grace and with a desire to delight the customer. Now and again tiredness, boredom, and frustration with management can cause service problems.

Customer service needs ● ● ●

Whilst customers are attracted to the certainties of the branded service operation, they often dislike being treated as a number. Customer expectations vary in different brands. In some cases the individual wants more consistency and standardization, and in other cases the customer wants the service to be more personal. The same individual may want different experiences from the same hospitality operation, depending on his or her mood, the time of day and the occasion (Figure 1.1).

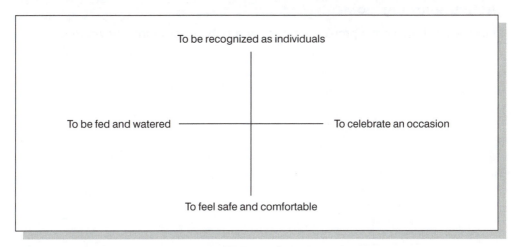

Figure 1.1 Typical pub customer service needs

Furthermore, customer service needs are dynamic. As more people experience pubs and their services, their expectations are moving and shifting. Licensed retail service organizations constantly have to review and audit customer expectations; they can never sit back and assume they know what customers want.

Local and regional tastes ● ● ●

National branded services may come across tension in the need to maintain the standardized national brand through which customers learn to know what to expect, owing to local or regional tastes that cut across the standard brand. That is, customers may expect to be able to order certain drinks or products in the local restaurant or pub, but the brand does not normally stock these items, and instructs managers not to provide services 'out of brand'. This can be a particular problem where customers have a sense of belonging with their local. Unit managers have to understand that local tastes in beer brands, menu items and even in pub games may need to be provided for local customer tastes. There is therefore likely to be some limit on the degree of standardization that can be imposed across the estate.

The 'big is ugly' syndrome • • •

As we have seen, the scale and coverage of these licensed retail operations brings advantages through cost reduction and standardization, but large organizations can be unwieldy and slow to change. In fast-moving consumer markets such as the licensed retailing sector, very standardized operating systems and centralized controls can be a disadvantage. The narrow span of control and tall hierarchies that help the organization to manage consistency over a lot of units makes for long lines of communication and slow decision-making processes. It is therefore very easy for these organizations to miss changes in consumer taste and be unresponsive to variations in the customer base.

Active learning point

In the box below, list the problems faced by a pub or bar brand known to you.

The answer . . .

Many licensed retail organizations recognize the various problems that they face and are looking to alternative ways of managing their businesses. This book assumes a more empowered approach to unit management.

Unit management and staff have the key role in delivering licensed retail services; they need to be empowered in its true sense to manage the unit and service encounters in a way that:

1 Gives them the authority to do whatever it takes to deliver the service that customers want. Within the limits of the brand, there should be flexibility to meet customer needs.

2 Ensures that all concerned are given the skills to do the job. Adequate training and being allowed to be effective is the basic building block of personal initiative.

3 Ensures that managers and staff are recognized and rewarded for their contribution to successful service. Removing barriers to taking initiative and developing a sense of personal effectiveness is the defining feature of empowerment. Through this, all concerned share a sense of ownership with customer satisfaction and the success of the venture.

4 Develops organization control systems that need to be both 'tight and loose'. In other words, the organization system needs to control those issues that are essential for business success – standardizing the essentials but also allowing for local responsiveness.

5 Manages the organization through a flat structure that minimizes the number of management levels in the organization, thereby enabling short lines of communication and quick decision-making.

6 Encourages initiative and creativity. A learning organization should be prepared for people to make mistakes, providing people are able to think about their errors and learn from the experience.

7 Encourages upward communication from the units to brand and operations managers so that information can be provided on effective processes, successes and best practice and can be shared across all pubs and bars in the brand.

The following chapters in this book discuss this approach further and provide a course of sessions that will help you as a unit manager to be more effective in managing hospitality retail service operations. Before that it is important that you understand the nature of licensed retail services and variations between the different types and levels of service offered.

About services . . .

At the beginning of the chapter we said that licensed retailing involved the supply of food and/or drink and/or accommodation in a service context. That said, the nature of the food, drink and accommodation supplied varies. Clearly bars, cafés, inns and taverns all represent different types of cluster of the three activities. However, the distinction between establishments is becoming less and less clear as restaurants, for example, encourage diners to come to their establishments and drink, and bars increasingly offer their customers food as well as alcohol. As shown in Table 1.1, many pubs and bars make a considerable food offer to customers, whilst for others food is part of the offer but the business is essentially 'wet led'.

Whilst the type and quality of products on offer to customers is important, the key feature for unit managers to understand is the precise nature of the service experience that is being supplied, and what customers are expecting of the service encounter. Customer expectations are best understood by building a picture of the key features of service. This shows how different brands offer different bundles of service experiences to customers. That is, there are service experiences that are of different types, over and above the nature of the food, drink or accommodation offered.

Drivers of service types

Almost all services, including licensed retail services, can be said to have four features that make them different from manufactured products:

1 Time
2 Face-to-face interaction
3 The product–service dimension
4 The predictable–personal dimension.

The first two are of lesser importance in shaping service types, although they are important in service management. The latter two are key factors in building an understanding of the variations in licensed retail services.

Time ▪ ▪ ▪

In most cases a service involves an instant interaction between the customer and employee. The service instant is over and gone the moment it has occurred; it cannot be produced in advance, nor can it be taken back and reworked if a problem occurs. The bar person's smile cannot be re-enacted if it strikes the customer as mechanical and less than genuine.

Clearly, this *perishable* feature of the service encounter means that licensed retailers have to get it right first time. Service operation systems, communications and staff training are essential in assisting in the delivery of consistent service quality that gets it right every time.

Face-to-face interaction ▪ ▪ ▪

In all licensed retail situations, the service received by customers involves face-to-face interactions. Customers and staff can see each other, and customers are evaluating the performance of the employee through a whole range of conscious and subconscious cues. Thus body language, tone of voice, words used, appearance and personal hygiene help build a picture of the employee that establishes the customer's impression of the organization and its service.

This means that your employees should be well trained in the various techniques used to develop the appropriate feelings of welcome and the importance of customers as individuals. In addition, employee satisfaction and dissatisfaction become crucial. As F.W. Marriott is quoted as saying, 'It takes a happy worker to make happy customers'.

Customer loyalty is likely to be most successfully built on the basis of contacts with staff who make them feel welcome and cared for, and with sentiments that appear to be genuinely felt by the person concerned.

The product–service dimension ▪ ▪ ▪

All licensed retail services involve the customer being supplied with a combination of physical products and service based on contact with customers. In a pub, the physical elements will obviously involve the food and drink supplied as well as the décor and other features of the physical amenities – toilets, parking, smoking and non-smoking areas etc. In addition customers are being supplied services by staff, and the friendliness with which they are approached, the speed of service and the on-going relationship with service staff are significant.

These *tangible* and *intangible* aspects of the services cover a wide range of issues that can be arranged in a list according to the extent that each is tangible and measurable or intangible and difficult to measure. The portion size is a tangible and measurable aspect of the customer's meal experience; operating systems and manuals can specify the size of portion supplied to customers. However, although the décor of the bar or pub may involve a physical assessment of the state of repair and cleanliness, there is also a psychological dimension in its impact on customer mood and impression, and this is difficult to measure.

Similarly, the intangible service aspect of the customer's experience involves some factors that are clearly difficult to measure. The impact of an employee's smile and the body language of the staff behind the bar both create an impression, but are difficult to define and measure. However, role models, best practice and core values can be shared through training. On the other hand, some aspects of the service elements can be measured. The time it takes for a customer to receive the starter after having placed the order, or the time it takes to be acknowledged whilst waiting at the bar, for example, can be identified and measured against a standard. These aspects contribute to the customer's evaluation of service quality, and can be subject to specific targets and measures in time.

Figure 1.2 provides an example of some of these tangible product and intangible service aspects of the customer's experience for a licensed retail outlet in a bar.

Whilst all licensed retail services involve combinations of these product and service aspects in the offer to customers, not all are equally weighted. In some cases, the tangible product aspects are more important sources of customer satisfaction, while in other cases the intangible service factors become more important. Figure 1.3 shows a continuum of hospitality service businesses that have different bundles of product and service benefits to customers.

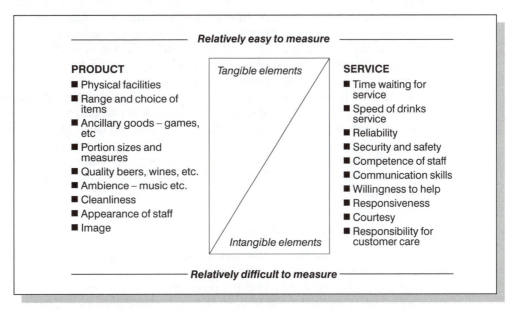

Figure 1.2 Tangible and intangible elements of customer service for a bar

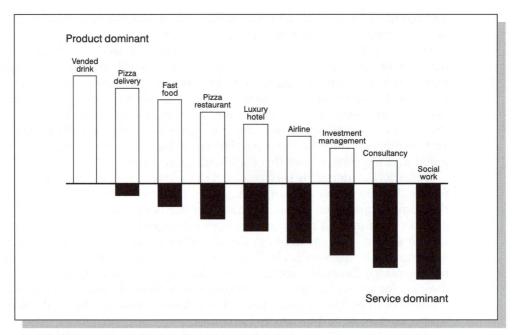

Figure 1.3 Continuum of product and service benefits

In some cases the same brand may represent a different cluster of benefits, depending on the means by which the customer is supplied with the product and service. For example, The Dog and Duck supplies service to customers in three formats that show how service interactions with customers vary (Table 1.3). The restaurant operation involves traditional service interactions between customer and staff. The bar service requires limited interactions, but staff need to build a relationship with customers. Issues to do with acknowledgement of the customer, waiting time and service speed as well as product quality will be important in these fields. The off-licence sales involve customers buying pre-packed items in a simple retail operation that involves minimum staff interaction.

It can be seen from the above that the range and complexities of licensed retail services will vary. The source of customer satisfaction will also vary. In some cases satisfaction will largely be product derived – e.g. product taste, variety, size, temperature etc. In other cases these factors will be important, but the range and quality of contact with service will also be important. Following from this, the management of employees will vary according to the complexity and predictability of service needs.

The predictable–personal dimension ● ● ●

Given the personal nature of the service interaction, customers are faced with a difficulty in predicting the quality of the service they will get. For the reasons outlined under the first two points above, they cannot judge the quality of an experience until they've had it. In part, this customer difficulty explains the success of the branded standardized service businesses in licensed retailing. They attempt to

Restaurant	Bar service	Off-licence
1 Greet & seat customers give out menus	1 Acknowledge/greet customer	1 Acknowledge waiting customer
2 Take drinks order	2 Take order	2 Accept order
3 Serve drinks	3 Supply order and request payment	3 Fulfil order
4 Take food order	4 Accept payment	4 Tell customer of charge
5 Serve first course	5 Receipt	5 Accept payment
6 Check back – starter OK?	6 Salutation	6 Salutation
7 Clear starter plates	7 Talk with customer when not serving	
8 Serve main course	8 Clear empty glasses, etc.	
9 Check back – main course OK?	9 Serve drinks, take money etc., as requested	
10 Clear main course plates		
11 Offer sweet menu		
12 Take order for sweets		
13 Check back – sweets OK?		
14 Offer coffee		
15 Serve coffee		
16 Offer refill		
17 Present bill		
18 Payment		
19 Provide receipt		
20 Salutation		

Table 1.3 Customer contact with service staff at The Dog and Duck

make it clear to each customer what can be expected, and they spend a lot of time and energy attempting to ensure that these expectations are met.

Not all services can be *standardized* in this way; some have to be *customized* to the needs of the individual. Professional services like dentistry and medical care provide the most obvious examples. In licensed retailing there are clearly limits on the degree to which services can be totally customized, because the operating systems and standardized offer that make customers attracted to the brand also limit the opportunity for giving each customer a totally individual service. It is possible in many ways to personalize the nature of the customer's experiences; for example, a service can be provided that either allows a wide choice through which the service is personalized, or through the service interaction it is possible to encourage the customer to feel important as an individual. Traditional pubs are able to create a sense of customer uniqueness because of the high levels of repeat visits that are associated with the 'local', and the use of personalized glasses, or standing location at the bar, etc.

It is possible to detect a services continuum that places different types of service experiences according to the way in which the customer is offered a fairly predictable service, and variations in the degree to which different services personalize the customer experience. As with the product–services continuum, most services involve some elements of personalization because of contact with service

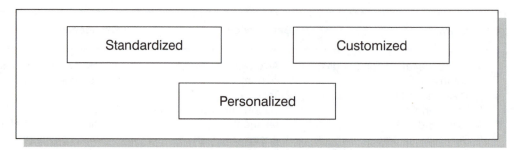

Figure 1.4 Continuum of predictable and personal service benefits

personnel, but the degree to which predictability or personalization is important varies between services. Figure 1.4 provides some examples of variations in the mix of predictable and personalized benefits from different licensed retail services.

These two sets of factors interplay to create a number of *ideal service types*. These ideal service types are useful because they show that not all service firms are making the same offer to customers. The extent to which services are standardized or customized for individual customers, and the importance of the tangible and intangible aspects of service, vary between services.

Whilst it may be true that few licensed retail brands represent any one of these types, they each represent a position closer to one or other of the ideal types, and the model is helpful in establishing the essential features of the customer offer.

Figure 1.5 shows three ideal types of service depending on the nature of the offer on these dimensions. As we have seen, most licensed retail services supply customers with a set of service elements that are at the same time standard and shaped to the customers' needs, and they offer service benefits that supply physical products to them. By bringing these two sets of factors together we can reveal a number of ideal service types, three of which have particular relevance to licensed retail services.

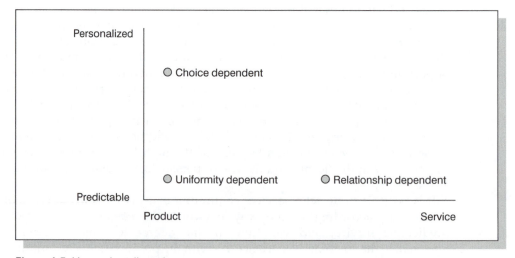

Figure 1.5 Licensed retail service types

Uniformity-dependent hospitality services

Uniformity-dependent services are based on customer expectations that the goods and services supplied by the brand will be consistent. In many ways they are buying into the certainty that they will be able to predict the experience, the product and even the price they will pay for their hospitality service. Customer satisfaction is more dependent on the food, drink and accommodation received – the tangible dimension of service. The intangible service aspects are important, but customers are more concerned with speed and are prepared to accept simpler and shorter contacts with service employees. Many fast-food and self-service restaurant operations are typical of this type of licensed retail brand. In retail supermarkets, the introduction of self-billing techniques are in part a response to this kind of customer need.

Customers judge the quality of their experience with this kind of brand by the extent that it continues to be consistent and predictable. Quality measurement is based on monitoring consistency and uniformity. Operational standards rigidly define the product (size of portion, service presentation etc.) and service aspects (service times or contact, words to be used in very precise ways etc.).

In this type of licensed retail operation, pub and bar management is chiefly concerned with managing the delivery of the standard product and service. Managers spend a large part of their time monitoring production of the food and drink and the accommodation to ensure they meet the standards set. Staff training is concerned with learning the 'one best way' by which goods are produced and served. Staff are managed and monitored to make sure that they are working to the standard set. Staff appraisal, pay and rewards are frequently linked to service consistency. Managers and staff are encouraged to work in the set way and not to use initiative and flair. Box 1.1 provides an example.

Box 1.1   *J.D. Wetherspoons*

J.D. Wetherspoons is the largest single pub concept, and also the fastest growing. Although senior managers deny it is a brand, it meets many of the criteria of a brand. It has a clear image with customers, which helps assure customers of what to expect. Internal controls are designed to ensure consistency and meet customer expectations. The units are based round a format that can be replicated and rolled out across the nation. As of May 2001, the company managed 500 pubs, and had opened more new units in the past twelve months than any other pub brand. Economies of scale together with centralized controls ensure cost benefits as well as consistent quality. The pubs are chiefly 'wet led', but food sales represent a significant income stream – on average between 20 and 30 per cent of total revenue.

In many ways, Wetherspoons is an example of a uniformity-dependent service and has some similarities with McDonald's, the fast-food company. Work organization and job design are in many ways examples of the service factory and are informed by techniques developed in manufacturing. *Efficiency* is an important consideration, and jobs are designed to maximize the use of labour through technology and simplified job design. The second dimension is that Wetherspoons offers services that can be easily quantified and *calculated*. Targeting service times, product range and pricing strategies ensure that regular customers can specify what they are likely to get, and the time it will take. Tight job design and productivity levels allow managers to be more certain of the level of outputs from a given level of labour inputs. Customers are able to *predict* products, services and prices. Customers have a reasonable idea of what they will be offered in different Wetherspoons pubs and bars, and even the prices to be charged. From an employment perspective, employee performance and the need for labour hour by hour can be predicted with reasonable accuracy. Finally, customers, through the impact of these other dimensions, can experience a sense of personal *control*. From an employment perspective, the design of jobs and the management hierarchy aim to ensure maximum control of employee performance.

Standardization and the accompanying psychological benefits are important features of the offer made by the company to its customers, and this shapes much of its management of human resources. Its 'brand values' are tightly drawn and closely managed, although not openly described as such. The service dimension is largely shaped by concepts and practices developed in manufacturing industry. The approach draws on principles and techniques such as the division of labour, *scientific management* and the use of technology to minimize the need for much employee discretion.

Choice-dependent services

Choice-dependent services have many similar features to uniformity-dependent services in that customer satisfaction is largely based on the tangible nature of the food, drink and accommodation supplied. Customers have a high expectation of consistency in the product and service, but they also want to be able to give their experience a personal touch. In this case the product range is sufficient to allow customers a wide choice of the food and drink that they consume. In some instances the service aspect also allows them to be given the kind of service they want. Staff are trained to give one of a number of service performances, depending on the customer type or occasion.

Customers judge the quality of their experience through a combination of product consistency and feeling that they have been recognized for themselves as individuals. Being able to predict and recognize these service needs becomes important, but through branding and the identification of the customer service types the service is 'customized'. In many ways these organizations supply services that are similar to customized cars. Mass production techniques ensure uniformity and lower operating costs, but customers are able to personalize their experience. Operational standards are like those in the uniformity-dependent services. Product specifications define the way that food and drink is to be prepared and served, with portion sizes and the product range all laid down by the national brand manual. Service methods and service time targets are also defined and measured as an assessment of quality management. However, the importance of making the customer experience more personal, with service tailored to developing feelings of individuality, requires the staff to give a range of performances that cannot be so tightly defined or scripted. Staff performance is vital to ensuring that the customers feel important as individuals.

Management is also concerned with monitoring consistency in production and service. They have to be able to evaluate the quality of customer experiences. This means applying judgements that cannot be so easily systematized. Given the importance of employee performance, managers spend a considerable amount of time and effort recruiting employees who will 'naturally' summon up the feelings and emotions needed to give the customer the service needed. Training and providing staff with role model examples are key activities. Training in particular has a core significance. All employees are trained to advise the customers about their choice. Knowing the contents and production methods of menu items, for example, is essential in guiding customers. Pay and rewards are typically associated with sales and staff performance. Box 1.2 provides an example.

Box 1.2 *TGI Friday Restaurants*

There is much about TGI Friday Restaurants that also involves attributes of efficiency, calculability, predictability and control. Customers are encouraged to expect certain service standards, which allow for efficient service. Service standards require that starters are served within seven minutes of receipt of the order and main courses are served within twelve minutes of the order being presented to the kitchen. Information technology is used to ensure that these service targets are met. Like J.D. Wetherspoons, menus are fixed and determined centrally, as are prices and production methods. Menus are standardized throughout the country, so customers visiting different restaurants know what to expect. The layout of the restaurants, the staff uniforms, type of employees, décor, etc. are also standardized. Through the various tangible and supporting intangible standards to the service, customers optimize their control of the meal experience. They can calculate how long the meal will take, the approximate cost, and the style of service they will receive. Standardization enables predictability and control.

Though there are clearly similarities with Wetherspoons, the nature and degree of standardization is different. For all its standardized approach, TGI Fridays does allow customers more opportunities to customize their eating and drinking experiences. The food menu, for example, contains over 100 items, and the cocktail menu is similarly extensive. This allows customers a wider range of choices over how they construct the experience. Similarly, regarding the intangibles, employees are encouraged, whilst operating to the service standards, to provide customers with a service experience that is special to them. Thus, if customers wish to linger over their meal, or celebrate a special occasion (birthday, etc.), employees alter the service pace or create a celebratory atmosphere accordingly. If the Wetherspoons offer is best typified as being about mass production, the TGI Fridays experience is best typified as being about mass customization. Like the use of model and range types in car manufacture, TGI Fridays offer allows target market groups to be served in a way that meets predictable service needs – so groups out to celebrate a party, or couples out for quiet night, can each receive the service style that they look for.

Relationship-dependent services

Relationship-dependent services are those in which the customer is buying into a standardized and predictable offer, but which involves a more elaborate service. There are more frequent contacts between the customer and the service staff, and customers give priority to the quality of the service as a source of satisfaction. That is not to say that the tangible products (food, drink etc.) are not important; they are, and customers have expectations about these. However, the nature of the service they receive becomes of particular importance. Many licensed retailers are attempting to compete through the quality of their service offer to customers, and thus there is movement in the way the organization delivers service to its clients.

The nature of the service interactions may require service staff to be flexible. They may need to make some decisions in response to the customer's service requirement. Typically employees would be empowered to make some decisions, within prescribed limits, to meet customer service needs or deal with customer complaints.

The service organization is concerned with maintaining the standard products and service targets as well as ensuring that staff take ownership of the service encounter. Empowered employees need to be trained sufficiently to be able to make the decisions needed to give customer satisfaction. Management styles are likely to be more participative because managers are not able to sanction every detail of the service encounter and employees need to be left to make the decisions needed. Employee motivation, training and rewards are particularly important in that they need to match with the forms of participative management being applied. Box 1.3 provides an example.

Box 1.3 *Harvester Restaurants*

Harvester Restaurants have features in common with both McDonald's and TGI Fridays. In many ways brand attributes offer efficiency, predictability, efficiency and control, but there are additional psychological, intangible elements to the offer that suggest havens of homeliness and tradition in a fast-changing and confusing world.

The core concept is of a family restaurant and pub. The décor conveys a rustic image, with menus based on traditional 'English' fare, and the pricing strategy pitches the offer in the mid-price range. Although menus offer a reasonable choice of dishes, preparation techniques are based on simple routine tasks and relatively limited skill levels are required to complete them. Restaurant-style service is through waiting staff taking orders and serving plated meals. The bar area is designed in a pub style, is stocked with a typical range of beers, wines and spirits, and offers bar meals.

Service standards reflect the ethos of 'treating customers as though they were guests in your own home'. The style of service has an informal formality that also reinforces brand values of homeliness, hospitality, tradition and naturalness. Thus the brand can be defined as being standardized in the tangibles. Customers know what to expect and how much it will cost. Whilst the brand also defines core values in customer service, the nature of the business is such that the intangible elements of the brand cannot be standardized in the same way as with tangibles, and are therefore reliant on the efforts of front-line staff.

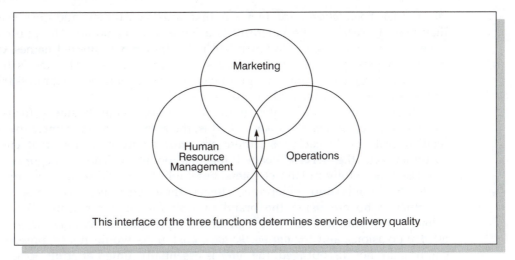

This interface of the three functions determines service delivery quality

Figure 1.6 Functional interdependence of service management

John Barras, a Scottish and Newcastle local pub brand, is another firm that is making a clear pitch based on a relationship-dependent strategy. Their chain of 'locals' is unusual for a large multi-unit operation. Most of the major brands are either high-volume city centre bars and cafés, or are in trunk road type locations. The John Barras pubs aim to build relationships with local customers and thereby maximize customer loyalty repeat visits. Although they haven't gone down the route of empowering staff in groups, they are specifically recruiting pub managers who have a profile capable of building relationships with customers and the local community.

Other customers are also an important aspect of building relationships across the customer base. Establishing strong group bonds, offering competitions and activities that meet customer social needs, is a key dimension of the pub and bar business. Unit managers have to understand this aspect of the service offer to customers. For many pubs and bars this relationship-dependent feature of their service enables a competitive advantage when compared with others.

These three examples have shown how the different service offers to customers result in different approaches to managing licensed retail operations. The idea of '*fit*' is important – in other words, the nature of the service that customers buy needs to match with marketing strategies, the way in which employees are managed, and the work that managers do in managing the licensed retail operation. Figure 1.6 shows how these functional aspects of hospitality service management overlap with each other.

As a unit manager, you need to understand the nature of the service you are supplying to customers so that you are able to manage the operation, the staff and service quality with consistency.

Working with customers

As we have seen, licensed retailing has increasingly used branding as a way of telling customers what to expect. In some cases the business has been focused on a service offer without being formally branded through common logo, décor, menu, etc., but has been *'blueprinted'* in a way that targets customers and the services that they want to receive. The blueprint is a loose form of brand. The pub company appears to operate a set of independent pubs; they have different names, different décor and perhaps even different drinks and food menus. The key is that they represent a targeted strategy that produces a type of experience that meets the needs and expectations of a focused group of customers.

A useful starting point for giving a licensed retail business focus is the consideration of *customer occasions* – that is, the reasons why customers use licensed retail operations. In each case, there are critical success factors that ensure the customer gets the service needed for that occasion. These categories will be discussed more fully in later chapters, but Table 1.4 provides some examples.

Clearly, brands and blueprints cluster these customer occasions to attract customers who are using the brand or unit for similar reasons. For example, Whitbread Restaurants' *Brewers Fayre* brand represents *special meal out, feed me* and *pit stop* occasions, and the *out on the town* customers would not be present. Whilst children are not discouraged, the offer is essentially aimed at adult occasions. The same company's *Brewsters* brand also offers occasions that cover *feed me* and *pit stop*, but they are also aimed at *family outings*, and include children's play areas. Again, the *out on the town* customers are not compatible.

This consideration of customer occasions recognizes that people use licensed retail operations in different ways, and the same individuals may be visiting different pubs and bars for different occasions. This focus allows you, in your capacity as

Customer occasion	Description	Critical success factors
Feed me	Customers want feeding with minimum effort and formality	Quick, friendly service, good value for money
Family outing	Visits with children (under 10 years); may be single parents in the week and two adults at the weekends	Child-friendly service, value for money, children's menu, female friendly, children's facilities
Pit stop	Shoppers, business people and tourists having a break – usually lunch-time and early evenings	Quick service, easy communication of the menu and drinks, female friendly, smoke-free atmosphere
Special meal out	Couples and groups, spend time over the meal, several courses, high expectations of service and quality, some shared special occasions (Valentine's Day)	More paced service, multi-course offer, drinks to support the occasion, table ordering, good quality environment
Out on the town	Typically Friday and Saturday evening, groups and couples, students, having a good time, involves drinks	Lively informal atmosphere, music and atmosphere of something happening, rapid drinks service, fashion drinks

Table 1.4 Examples of customer occasions in licensed retailing

either the brand manager or the unit manager, to concentrate on the factors that are critical for success, and to consider what other occasions might be explored that are compatible with the brand core occasions. Equally importantly, it also helps to identify customer occasions that do not sit well with the core brand occasions – in other words, customer who might upset the core business.

About hospitality

The nature of pub and bar management often involves acts of hospitality, because customers often regard the pub as a sort of home from home and the landlord as *'mein host'*. The nature of hospitality needs to be carefully considered by licensed retailers who are attempting to operate chains of pubs and bars, because the provision of genuine hospitality can be an important way of building competitive advantage over those who do not understand its true meaning.

To understand the commercial applications of hospitality better, it is necessary to explore hospitality in its widest sense. In times past, hospitality and the need to be hospitable were highly valued in Britain. Being genuinely hospitable to travellers and less fortunate members of the community was seen as a good thing and was highly valued. In Britain today, hospitality and the expectation of being hospitable are not afforded anything like the same status as in the past and as in some other societies. That said, there are lessons that commercial operators can learn from a study of hospitality in private, domestic settings.

Importantly, being hospitable in a private setting involves the host being responsible for the guest's happiness. There is a special link, and the guest is in a mutual pact. The host becomes the guest and the guest becomes the host on another occasion. In private domestic settings, hospitality:

- involves mutual giving and obligation
- is generous and open-handed
- is unselfish
- is welcoming
- is warm.

Most importantly, hospitality is based on appropriate motives and is more than hosting. A good host may be effective at keeping glasses full, food on the table and the room temperature comfortable, but may be acting for ulterior motives – perhaps to win favour, for seduction or for vanity. Good hospitality requires the right motives:

- the desire for the guest's company
- pleasure in entertaining
- the desire to please others
- concern for the needs of others
- awareness of the duty to be hospitable.

Hospitable people are those who possess one or more of these motives for entertaining.

This raises the difficulties faced by many licensed retail organizations. The commercial rationale in which they operate often distorts the relationship with their guests. The commercial rationale sells hospitality as a commodity; guests become customers, and both the host and guest develop a reduced sense of mutual obligation. A consequence is that many organizations report difficulties in retaining customers and want to develop more repeat visits.

Clearly, individual licensed retailers cannot change society's sense of hospitality or run their operations as though they were private domestic hosts, but they might be better able to build a more robustly loyal community of customers if they better understand hospitality in these contexts. For example, genuine hospitality is closely linked to values of generosity, beneficence and mutual obligation. Without wishing to suggest that profit-driven organizations would be willing to give away products, consideration of how regular customers can be rewarded with extra benefits that celebrate their importance and uniqueness as individuals could be successful. The key here is making the giving seem like an act of genuine generosity rather than the formulaic *'give-away'* typical of many branded hospitality businesses.

Hospitality retailers also need to consider the recruitment, selection and training of hosts who are capable of being hospitable, and who display characteristics of hospitality.

Conclusion

This chapter has attempted to provide an overview of some of the key concerns and issues relating to unit management in licensed retail services. These are described as multi-unit businesses that supply various combinations of food and drink, and accommodation in a branded format where customers are given clear messages as to what to expect of the products and services making up the brand. Licensed retail service operations have grown in significance and in market share over the last twenty years. They have been able to focus the service offer on particular customer segments, and to offer customers standardized service quality through the use of tightly managed operating systems. Customers have in turn increasingly used these brands to predict the service experience.

Whilst there have been substantial benefits to both customers and licensed retail organizations, these organizations are not without difficulties. The highly standardized service offer can be restrictive, inflexible and slow to change with customer tastes. Furthermore, many licensed retail organizations experience high labour turnover of employees, who find the restricted operation monotonous and boring. High levels of labour turnover create problems for delivering service quality, increase costs, and put pressure on managers, who have to spend a high proportion of their time recruiting replacement staff.

Although there are some common features to licensed retail services, not all services are the same. Apart from the obvious variation in the food, drink and accommodation offered in different businesses, the nature of the service experience also varies. In particular, the product-services and the standardized–customized dimensions interact to create three service types that apply to licensed retail services. Customers who buy uniformity-dominant services are buying services that are highly standardized and predictable, and more product-dependent. Choice-dependent services allow customers a wide choice through which to build their own service experience. In this case, customers are buying into services that are product-dependent but are capable of being adapted to their personal needs. Relationship-dependent services involve services that are standardized but require more significant service interactions. Customer satisfaction is most influenced by the nature of the service experience that they receive. In reality, most licensed retail brands involve some combination of these types, or reflect a different balance between the three service types. Unit managers can benefit from understanding the key element of the service offer so as better to understand the priorities that have to be managed.

To varying degrees, each of these service types faces the problem of customer loyalty and the need to build a loyal customer base. A common feature is that customers, who may well be called guests, are well aware of the commercial relationship with hospitality supplier/host. Licensed retailers need to consider carefully the human activity of hospitality, and the qualities that make hospitable behaviour.

Reflective practice

Answer the questions to check your understanding of this chapter.

1 List the key features of licensed retail service
2 Describe different types of licensed retail service operations
3 Describe the key drivers of licensed retail services types
4 Contrast and compare service management techniques
5 Highlight the potential management difficulties of each approach
6 Describe hospitality and the characteristics of being hospitable.

Further reading

Heal, F. (1990). *Hospitality in Early Modern England*. Clarendon Press.

Heskett, S. H., Sasser, W. E. and Hart, C. W. (1990). *Service Breakthroughs: Changing the Rules of the Game*. Free Press.

Lashley, C. (2001). *Empowerment: HR practices for Service Excellence*. Butterworth-Heinemann.

Lovelock, C. (1981). Why marketing needs to be different for service. In: *Marketing of Services* (J. H. Donnelly and W. R. George, eds.). American Marketing Association.

Telfer, E. (1996). *Food for Thought: Philosophy and Food*. Routledge.

Schmenner, R. W. (1995). *Service Operations Management*. Prentice Hall.

Looking for more than breath on the mirror in recruitment

Learning objectives

After working through this chapter, you should be able to:

- identify the main sources of recruits
- plan and organize staff recruitment
- plan and organize staff selection
- conduct a selection interview.

Recruiting and selecting staff for effective service

Staff recruitment and selection is important in licensed retail service organizations. The ability to attract and recruit people who have a 'natural' affinity with customers is particularly important for 'frontline' staff. Although staff performance can be improved by customer care programmes, the essential qualities are related to the individual's personality and commitment to providing good service.

Careful recruitment and selection is also important to reduce staff turnover and disciplinary problems and to improve employee satisfaction. You need to take the time to select the right person to match the needs of the job, and one who will fit in with the rest of your team. Staff recruitment and selection can occupy a large part of a unit manager's time, particularly where there are high levels of staff turnover. Under time pressures, it is tempting to reduce the effort put into recruitment and selection, but this is often a false economy because it creates problems.

Before starting the recruitment and selection process it is necessary to think about the job and the person needed to do it. Many managers in licensed retail operations make problems for themselves because they fail to understand the importance of careful planning when recruiting employees, and to consider the needs of the new recruits. The first step involves thinking about the duties and responsibilities of the job and the skills needed to be successful in it. The second involves considering new recruits, their motives for becoming an employee, and their needs both in the early stages of employment and beyond.

Flexible employees

The demand for licensed services varies through time. In some cases these variations can be predicted; for example, different days of the week and different months have different sales levels – Monday is quiet and Saturday is busy, January has a low level of sales, but in December sales are high. It is not unusual for these variations to be very dramatically different, with perhaps 50 per cent of the weekly sales occurring on Friday and Saturday, or 50 per cent of annual sales in November and December. In other cases the variations are difficult to predict – for example, changes in the weather can result in higher or lower than normal sales.

In all cases, you need to be able to call on sufficient staff to meet the demand. That means being able to get more staff in busy times, and to have fewer staff when sales are lower.

Planning future needs is essential, and this will be discussed more in Chapter 7. However, recruiting for the future and deciding on how flexible labour will be managed is essential. Traditionally, licensed retail managers have managed this problem by having a 'numerical flexibility' – lots of staff available who can be brought in when needed. Typically, full-time staff numbers are kept to a minimum and restricted to the more 'skilled' employees, who are supported by extra employees as needed. Staff may therefore include:

- regular part-time staff – staff who work regularly for the pub or restaurant for a varied number of hours each week depending on the needs of the business
- temporary/short-term staff – staff who usually work on a full-time basis for a fixed term in order to meet the demands of a busy period or planned staff absence

- casual staff – infrequent employees who work during the busiest periods and in some cases are used for specific types of demand (e.g. banquets or parties)
- agency staff – people who work for an agency or contractor that supplies staff to meet planned or unplanned shortages.

These varied types and sources of staff allow managers to meet staffing needs whilst limiting the financial commitment when demand for the unit's services are low. However there are some difficulties caused by this approach:

- employee commitment to the service, customers and organization may be lower
- employee incomes may vary and create dissatisfaction, leading to higher labour turnover
- skill levels may be low because of limited investment in training
- service quality may suffer
- there may be reduced productivity and sales per hour
- there may be reduced customer repeats because of increased customer dissatisfaction.

One way round some of these problems is to recruit more full-time employees, but create a more flexible workforce through wide skills training. 'Functional flexibility' results in a more flexible workforce where staff can be employed in a variety of roles as the demand for the business varies. This will be discussed more fully in Chapter 6.

The key point here is that, whatever the form of the employment relationship – full-time, part-time, temporary or casual – the selection and recruitment process needs to be planned and the steps laid out in this chapter carefully followed. *Ultimately your customers will judge the quality of service on the basis of their experience – they are unconcerned with the employee's terms of employment.*

The local market for labour

Irrespective of the form of employment relationship, recruitment does not take place in a vacuum. Licensed retail employers are usually competing with other service sector employers for labour, and any one business may be recruiting similar people to work in supermarkets, shops and stores, other licensed retail outlets, offices, call centres etc.

Licensed retailers who do not at least match the terms and conditions of their competitors for labour may contribute to *'push factors'*, which lead to employee dissatisfaction with your employment. Similarly, if you are aware of local competitor conditions it is possible to draw up a reward package that creates *'pull factors'* to help you attract staff.

Active learning point

Choose a hospitality retail unit known to you and in the table below list the other local organizations competing for the same potential employees.

Competitor organization	Approximate annual recruitment	Training and development provided	Pay and benefits provided
1			
2			
3			
4			
5			
6			
7			
8			
9			
10			

The supply of employees

As with all markets, the market for labour in any local area will be affected by the laws of supply and demand. Thus your ability to attract enough staff of the right quality and characteristics depends on the competition from other firms *and* on a cluster of factors that influence the total supply of labour in that market.

1 *Levels of unemployment and employment* represent a major factor in licensed retail services' labour markets. In areas where unemployment is low, recruitment into licensed retail organizations can be difficult.

2 *The industry profile of the area* may result in fewer or more potential recruits being available even within any given level of unemployment. It has been difficult to recruit people into licensed retail operations where employment has been based

on 'heavy' industry. Understanding the potential difficulties can help you to be more focused in your efforts to recruit people in these circumstances.

3 *The participation rate* of people in the local labour market varies between areas and regions of the country. Where more women and young people participate in employment as well as men, the potential supply of labour will be greater. The participation rate also varies over the year, as some people want to take on a second job to earn extra money for Christmas or summer holidays. Recognizing the ebb and flow of interest in second jobs can help you to attract people for fixed terms to meet particular difficulties.

4 *Where people live in relation to the unit* and the associated ease of transport to the site will be a factor. Late-night working in a remote part of town may restrict potential recruits to those with personal transport. Mapping the major housing estates and transport systems can help build a picture.

5 *Educational establishments* such as secondary schools, further education colleges and universities can all provide useful sources of part-time, temporary and casual labour. Making contacts with significant staff members in schools and colleges can help to improve communications between you and potential employees.

The importance of planning ahead

The more planned and carefully undertaken the recruitment and selection process, the more likely you are to be successful in selecting employees who stay with you and who make a contribution to the unit. Hurried recruitment invariably leads to difficulties later.

As the unit manager, you need to think forward over the next few weeks to consider your recruitment needs. Planning ahead means that you will have the employees in place, trained with the right skills, when they are needed. Here are some of the points to build into the plan:

- *future peaks in demand* – the Christmas build up, or some other period when sales are above the norm and extra staff are needed
- *holiday arrangements* – when staff take planned annual holidays you will need cover for absent employees
- *staff turnover* – this creates an ongoing demand for replacement staff, and often it is more cost effective to recruit replacement staff in batches to match the predicted loss (although, as Chapter 5 shows, staff turnover is costly and wasteful)
- *planned retirements, maternity leave, etc.* – these are predictable and will create some vacancies that have to be filled.

It is important to consider the process of recruiting new employees and the time taken to develop an effective performer. Issues such as the time taken to recruit, the number of applicants needed on average, the number of interviews needed, the induction period and training programme all need to be considered. The more time these steps take, the more time you have to put into the process of planning for the future.

Successful recruitment is unhurried and systematic. The following sections take you through the key steps of considering the job and the type of person needed, how to attract applicants, selection and induction.

Describing the job to be done

Even in the smallest units it is necessary to consider the work to be done by the recruits. By thinking carefully about the job and what has to be undertaken, you will be in a much stronger position to recruit a person who will be able make an effective contribution.

The job description

This starts with the job, not the jobholder, or the terms and conditions under which he or she will be employed. The job description should include the following broad headings:

- job title, department and location – this gives the job a name and position
- job function – what the job is about
- job superior – who will the candidate answer to?
- job subordinates – which jobs will the holder supervise?
- relationships with others – non-hierarchical relationships
- main duties – what is to be done
- occasional duties – what is to be done now and then
- limits to authority – what the jobholder can/can't decide.

Table 2.1 provides an example. The duties and other details are written in a way that describes the job and the relationship between it and other jobs. When preparing

Job title, department and location	Kitchen Assistant, kitchens of The Dog and Duck
Job function	Simple food preparation in the kitchen
Job superior	Head Chef
Job subordinates	None
Relationships with others	Delivery staff (food and dry goods), food service staff
Main duties	1 Assist daily in the initial preparation of the kitchen 2 Prepare cold food as required by the chef 3 Assist with preparation of meals 4 Wash-up or return to stores any equipment used in food preparation. 5 Clean and tidy food stores 6 Assist with unloading kitchen supplies
Occasional duties	1 Check the quantity and quality of goods received 2 Assist the chef with stock-taking 3 Assist with service as required
Limits to authority	The jobholder is not authorized to sign for goods Deficiencies or damaged goods must be reported to the chef

Table 2.1 Example of a job description for a Kitchen Assistant

Hospitality, Leisure & Tourism Series

these documents it is important to consider the job and what you want the jobholder to do. The main duties are described as active verbs. It is a good idea to show the job description to a current jobholder to check whether the job description describes the job as it is being done; organizations are dynamic and jobs change.

Finally, in all cases you should consider *empowerment*. Could the jobholder be more empowered? In the above example, could the employee be empowered to sign for goods and consult with the chef over damaged goods and deficiencies?

Describing the ideal recruit

Many managers make mistakes in the recruitment of staff because they do not carefully consider the ideal person to be able to undertake the job as outlined in the job description. A well thought-out job description helps you to think about the person needed – background and prior experience, education and training, personality and characteristics.

Drawing up a *staff specification* helps to prepare for the recruitment process. This should be written down, although care must be taken not to apply prejudices to the processes – that is, to make assumptions that are unfounded. In some cases you may not be able to recruit the ideal person, but will need to build the necessary profile through training and further development. The following are some of the categories to be considered:

Physical make-up	Age
	Appearance
	Build
	Health
	Speech
	Eyesight
	NB: It may be possible to justify a specific sex
	(e.g. lavatory attendant), but be careful
Education and training	School qualifications and grades
	Further or higher education
	Recognized skills programme – NVQs
	Other qualifications or training
Work experience	Experience in industry
	Specific industry or sector
	Similar type of work
	Work in related sector with transferable skills
	Responsibility for people or money
Personality	Sociability and extroversion
	Empathy
	Honesty
	Stability
	Leadership, etc
Personal circumstances	Requirement to work
	Requirement to work shifts
	Requirement to live in/out

Whilst compiling this list of factors it is important to remember the requirement, in law and in practice, for equal opportunities. Openly discriminating on the grounds of gender, ethnicity or religion is illegal. However, a good unit manager works beyond the legislation to ensure that all employees and potential employees are treated equally and fairly. When selecting criteria for inclusion in the staff specification, you must be sure the criteria are genuine requirements of the job to be done. It is possible to be guilty of *indirect discrimination* – that is, to specify job requirements that by definition exclude people who are capable of effective performance.

Not all the desirable qualities are of equal importance, and it is useful to list them under headings that show how *desirable* or *essential* they are (see Table 2.2). It is possible to build up knowledge and skills through training and development. Again, careful consideration of the *essential* requirements helps you to be focused in the selection process.

The key point when drawing up the staff specification is to think carefully about those requirements that really are essential for the job. You want to end up with a list that both helps you to define the sort of person who can do the job and also does not exclude people who in reality could be effective.

	Essential	Desirable
Physical make-up		
Age	Over 18	20–45
Appearance	Clean	Smart and well groomed, hair and hands important
Health	No record of notifiable diseases	
Education and training		
Schooling	Able to read and write and do simple calculations	Able to check invoices and delivery notes
Skills training		NVQ I & II in food preparation and cookery, or equivalent
Work experience		
In licensed retail industry	Worked in food preparation, with over 2 years' experience	Worked in food preparation in licensed retailing operation
Personality		
Stability	Polite, not easily flustered	Cheerful disposition
Honesty	Evidence of high standards of honesty from past employers	
Personal circumstances	Able to work to full range of shift duties through the year	

Table 2.2 Staff specification for a Kitchen Assistant

Hospitality, Leisure & Tourism Series

Thinking about the sort of person needed also leads to thoughts about:

- how you will check the person's qualities and abilities
- the selection process and
- the best sources of this type of applicant.

Active learning point

Using what you know about the operations featured in this book, make a list of the source of employees and the recruitment processes most likely to recruit frontline employees in J.D. Wetherspoons Limited, TGI Fridays, Harvester Restaurant.

Licensed retailer	Source of recruits and the recruitment process
J.D. Wetherspoons	
TGI Fridays	
Harvester Restaurants	

Attracting candidates

Once you have decided on the duties of the job to be filled and the sort of person required, you need to consider the best source of likely candidates before considering the processes involved in selecting them. The aim of attracting applicants is to interest a sufficient number so you can make an appointment of the ideal candidate(s):

- too many applicants is as problematic as too few
- the aim must be to attract suitable applicants.

Sources of applicants

Candidates will be attracted from the local labour market, and the following lists represent some common means of communicating with potential applicants to inform them of job vacancies. As with all advertising, the more targeted and accurate the message, the more it will appeal to the most suitable applicants. Vague, misleading and dishonest descriptions of the job or person needed are *always* counterproductive.

Internal sources • • •

Here, candidates come from within your unit. Sources include:

1 Internal promotions. These help to build staff morale and show that employees can progress if they stay with you.
2 Present staff on temporary, casual or part-time contracts who wish to become full-time employees. As above, this has a motivational benefit, but also you will have a better knowledge of the person than of an external applicant.
3 Individuals recommended by current staff (family/friends). Again this might lead to a better knowledge of the new recruit. It is cheaper because advertising costs are reduced, though there is usually an introduction fee to the staff member. There is a danger of setting up cliques in the workforce.
4 Candidates attracted by notices and posters on your premises. This is a relatively inexpensive method, although there may be issues about the impression created by ongoing staff turnover. Also, some units discourage customers to be employees, whereas others see it as a benefit.
5 Previous applicants. It is not unusual for the recruitment process to attract more suitable candidates than there are vacancies, and it is a good idea to keep the details of these applicants on record so that you can contact them when another vacancy comes up. Consistent interest in working in the unit might be an indicator of future stability.

External sources • • •

Here, candidates come from outside your unit and are recruited in the following ways:

1 Newspaper advertising. Advertising is likely to be in local newspapers, though some management and skilled craft jobs may recruit from a national labour market. The key benefit is that the advertisement will be seen by a large number of people who might be interested in the job. They can take the form of box advertisements, or classified ads. The box advertisements are more expensive and are best reserved for a major recruitment campaign.
2 Local radio. This gives good coverage and could be used for a major recruitment campaign – as when opening a new unit – but is likely to be too expensive for ongoing recruitment for one unit. This is an approach that a branded licensed retailer with several units in one radio area might use.
3 Job Centres and other state employment agencies. These can provide a constant and generally low-cost source of applicants. Commercial recruitment agencies are used in some cases, but are usually regarded as too expensive for most frontline staff.
4 Posters and notices in shop windows or local clubs. These are usually low cost and are visible to people who live in the immediate area.
5 Direct mail shots to local housing estates. These are again local to the unit and are relatively cheap; they are often used for openings and re-launches.
6 Universities and colleges. Further education establishments in your locality are a good source of employees. Students on licensed retail, hospitality, leisure or tourism programmes are worth prioritizing, but students in general are a valuable

source of potential recruits. Course Leaders, Careers Officers and the Student Union are worth contacting.

7 Schools careers teachers. These are also a good source of recruits, both for young people finishing their schooling and looking for permanent employment, and for continuing students who want part-time, casual and temporary employment. Work experience sessions can also be a good source of recruits – many courses have two- or three-week periods to gain work familiarization. Licensed retail managers can use these sessions to promote careers in their organization.

Time spent in cultivating contacts with significant people in these local organizations will prove to be a valuable investment for the future. This is a particular need in licensed retail organizations experiencing rapid staff turnover. As we have seen, high staff turnover is expensive but is a fact of life in some units, and ensuring that you have a strong supply of potential labour is important.

Advertising

Many of the sources of recruitment available to you as unit manager will be outside the unit. In some cases, material will be supplied from head office, and you will not be able to spend much money on advertising. Whatever the medium, it is advisable to consider some general pointers to successful job advertising.

1 *Attract* the attention of the potential applicant. Usually this is by boldly showing the job title (*Kitchen Assistant*) or the person type you are looking for (e.g. *Bright Young Person*). Make sure that this key factor is prominent and cannot be missed.

2 *Interest* the person once you have attracted his or her attention. Give details – who, what, where – of the job. Name the company and briefly describe the purpose of the job and where it is located. Provide a brief outline of the person needed, the salary and opportunities for advancement. You want to attract suitable applicants and non-suitable people can be turned away.

3 *Desire*. You are trying to make the advertisement stimulate a desire to do something about following up the advertisement. It is here that many go wrong. In some cases advertisements are just plain boring, and in others there is a strong temptation to oversell the job and provide inaccurate information.

4 *Action*. Provide instructions as to how to follow up the job – a telephone number, or address to apply for an application form. This is an obvious point, but is a common error in many advertisements.

Figures 2.1–2.3 provide examples of a display advertisement, a classified advertisement and a semi-display advertisement respectively.

Gathering information about applicants

The advertising process will invite interested people to apply formally for the position. In most cases information about candidates is gathered via an application form, because this provides details about each candidate that will assist in filtering those candidates who appear to meet the staff specification requirements.

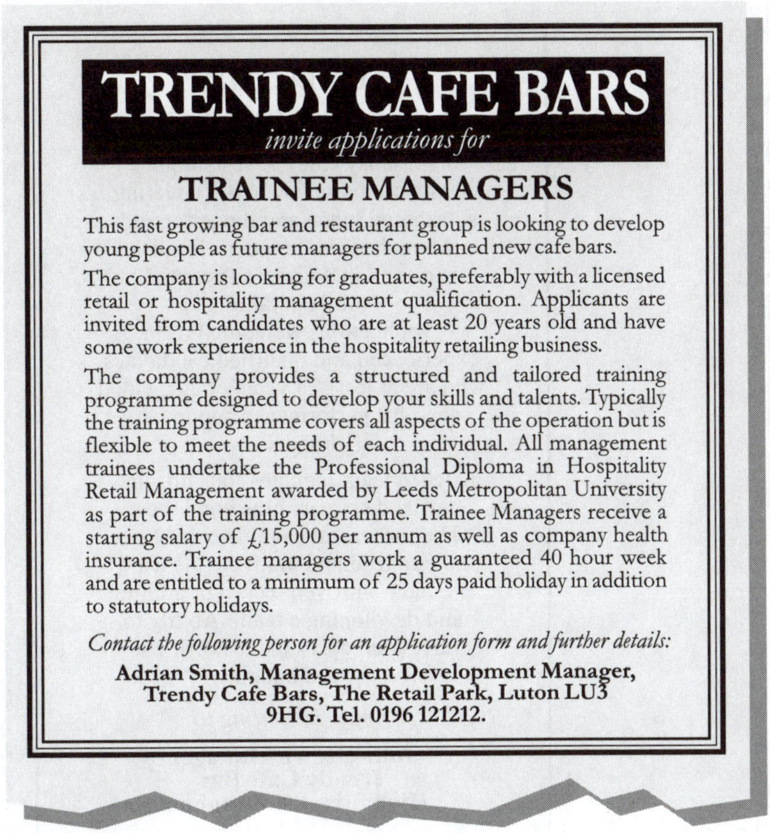

TRENDY CAFE BARS

invite applications for

TRAINEE MANAGERS

This fast growing bar and restaurant group is looking to develop young people as future managers for planned new cafe bars.

The company is looking for graduates, preferably with a licensed retail or hospitality management qualification. Applicants are invited from candidates who are at least 20 years old and have some work experience in the hospitality retailing business.

The company provides a structured and tailored training programme designed to develop your skills and talents. Typically the training programme covers all aspects of the operation but is flexible to meet the needs of each individual. All management trainees undertake the Professional Diploma in Hospitality Retail Management awarded by Leeds Metropolitan University as part of the training programme. Trainee Managers receive a starting salary of £15,000 per annum as well as company health insurance. Trainee managers work a guaranteed 40 hour week and are entitled to a minimum of 25 days paid holiday in addition to statutory holidays.

Contact the following person for an application form and further details:

Adrian Smith, Management Development Manager, Trendy Cafe Bars, The Retail Park, Luton LU3 9HG. Tel. 0196 121212.

Display advertisement

Figure 2.1 A display advertisement for licensed retail staff

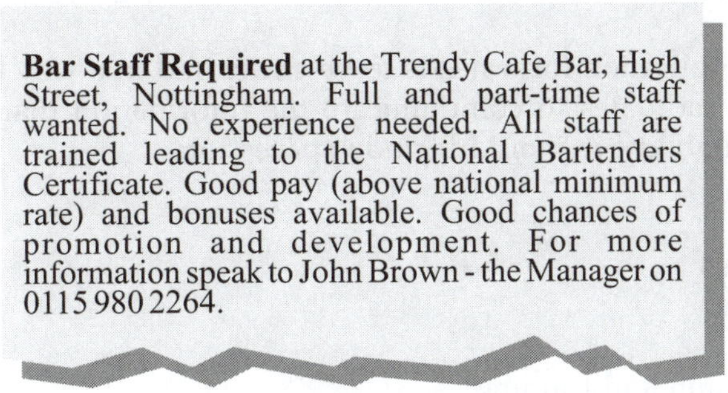

Bar Staff Required at the Trendy Cafe Bar, High Street, Nottingham. Full and part-time staff wanted. No experience needed. All staff are trained leading to the National Bartenders Certificate. Good pay (above national minimum rate) and bonuses available. Good chances of promotion and development. For more information speak to John Brown - the Manager on 0115 980 2264.

Classified advertisement

Figure 2.2 A classified advertisement for licensed retail staff

HEAD CHEF
required

For busy cafe bar restaurant.
Restaurant seats over 100 covering
substantial lunch and dinner periods.
Menu based on modern English
cuisine and includes a substantial pub
food operation.
Applications welcomed from
experienced and qualified candidates
who are at least 24 years of age. Good
pay plus performance and loyalty
bonuses.

Kitchen team includes four full-time
staff and six part-time employees.
The successful candidate must be
able to lead and motivate the team
and have a proven record in training
and developing a team. Ability to
control food costs and to work within
agreed budgets.

Apply in writing to

John Brown Manager
Trendy Cafe Bar
High Street Nottingham

Semi-display advertisement

Figure 2.3 A semi-display advertisement for licensed retail staff

The application form needs to be structured in a way that is simple to fill in and allows candidates to communicate the information that you require to decide on their suitability. It should include spaces for:

- name
- address
- gender
- age
- education and training
- past work experience
- other interests
- personal circumstances
- names and addresses of references.

The application form needs to be laid out so that the information required to decide to progress with the application is easily seen and, most importantly, has been provided by the applicant. A clear layout that asks the candidate unambiguous questions is essential. A common mistake in application forms is that they do not allow space for applicants to fill in the answers, and ask vague questions.

The application only provides part of the information, and in most cases the final selection is based on an interview and other selection techniques that help you to understand the applicants sufficiently well to make a selection.

Making a short-list

The applications received need to be considered so that you can decide on those candidates who match, or nearly match, the staff specification. The applications can be sorted systematically by comparing each application with the staff specification criteria using a matrix. This allows you to see how each candidate compares with the requirements outlined in the staff specification, and also allows comparison between candidates. Table 2.3 provides an example of applications received for a post, and shows how the matrix can assist in making a short-list. The example here suggests a code system, with + indicating whether the candidate meets the 'essential requirements' and ++ the 'desirable requirements'.

Candidates	Age, etc.	Education and training	Work experience	Personal circumstances
Brown	+	++	++	+
Green	++	++	+	
White	+	+		+
Black	+		++	+
Pink	++	++	++	+
Grey	++	++	++	+
Olive	+	+	+	+
Purple	+	+	++	

Table 2.3 Example of a short-listing matrix for a Kitchen Assistant

In the above example, Pink and Grey are clearly worth interviewing, as they are both qualified, have the work experience, are of the preferred age group and are able to work shifts. Brown might also be worth interviewing because the candidate matches all but the desired age criteria. The candidate might be a little younger than desired but may have other strengths. Similarly, Black is under-qualified but meets other criteria. This candidate might be worthy of further consideration, perhaps holding on the reserve list?

Making the selection

The aim of the selection process is to continue finding out about the candidates so that the judgement whether to recruit or not is based on as sound a basis of information as possible. Usually, the selection of staff to work in bars and pubs is based on a simple interview with the manager, but there are alternatives that might be worth considering.

Types of interviews

One-to-one interviews • • •

The unit manager, or a deputy, interviews the candidates one by one on his or her own. There is less cost in management time, but the weakness is that just one person's judgement is involved. It is possible for the interviewer to miss an important aspect of the interviewee's performance or apply personal prejudices.

Two or more interviewers • • •

The interview is conducted with one or more interviewers – e.g. unit manager plus deputy. Here the purpose is to bring in a wide range of perceptions and skills on which to base the selection. In some cases, one person asks questions while the other person observes and makes notes. This method is more costly in management time, but there are some safeguards against individual prejudices. Managers involved in the selection process are more likely to support the selection made. Interviewees can find this type of interview more intimidating, particularly if there are more than three interviewers. This form of interview may be subject to collective prejudice, particularly where one of the interviewers is forceful.

More than one interview • • •

In some cases, where there are many suitable candidates, managers may conduct a first round of interviews from which a short-list of candidates is selected for a second round of interviews – frequently on another day. This form of selection is costly in management and candidates' time, and is applied in the selection of skilled staff or management personnel. The benefit is that more applicants are seen, and the selection is ultimately made on the basis of candidate's performance on two occasions. In other cases more than one interview might be arranged on the same day, with a different purpose to each interview or a different person performing the interview. Again the benefits are increased exposure to the candidates, and more manager opinions are involved in the selection process.

Role-plays

In role-plays the intention is to invite the candidate to deal with a situation, or give a performance, which helps to reveal more about the person in non-interview situations. Popular examples involve asking the person to deal with a customer complaint in which the manager acts as disgruntled customer. In other cases, candidates are invited to sing a song or tell a joke. The organization of role-play and evaluation of the performance usually involves more than one manager. This approach is more costly, because candidates still go through an interview process as well as the role-play. The key benefit is that this approach provides a wider set of behaviours and information about the candidate.

Personality/aptitude tests

Personality tests and aptitude tests both aim to supply further information about the candidates. Personality tests vary, but some of the issues explored in Chapter 4 can be measured by using them. For example, it is possible to measure the various dimensions of *extroversion and introversion*, and *stability and instability*, through personality tests. Similarly, aptitude tests are designed to measure a person's general abilities and suitability for certain types of work. The problem with both these sets of measures is that whilst they both appear to be 'scientific', they are not foolproof predictors of future work performance. It is possible for performance to be affected by other factors outside of the individual, and it is also possible for a person who knows the tests to give answers that do not provide a true reflection of his or her personality or abilities. However, used in support of other selection techniques they can be a valuable aid to decision-making.

References

References supplied by previous employers or character witnesses are an important part of the selection process. The case study in Chapter 5 reveals a frequently made error – that of not following up the references of selected candidates prior to employment. In the case quoted, several people were recruited who had poor records with previous employers. Clearly, written references can be somewhat bland, but even so they are better than nothing and can be supported by a telephone conversation with the former employer. The most common practice is to follow up references after the selection interview, although some managers do ask for references before the interview. In the latter case, existing employers may be unaware of the applicant's intention to apply for a position with another firm, and this can cause difficulties. However, information from references can be useful when making a selection between candidates.

Whilst references are generally invaluable, some caution needs to be practised because they can be subject to bias:

- in the majority of cases, employers are loath to give explicitly damning criticism of employees
- in some cases, they may even provide overly complimentary comments about an employee whom they wish to get rid of
- in other cases, the negative feelings created when an employee leaves may lead the employer to be unfairly critical of the employee.

The selection interview

As shown earlier, the selection interview aims to fill out details regarding candidates so that you are able to make the selection on a wide range of information. In many ways people feel more comfortable with the judgements that they make in an interview than is justified by experience. There are several flaws with the interview:

- you are making judgements about people after only a short time
- people give performances in a formal interview that may not be a true reflection of their work performance
- the formal situation may make interviewees nervous and limit their performance
- the interview relies on subjective judgement, and may involve the 'halo effect' or prejudice.

Some of these difficulties can be addressed through including several colleagues in the interview process, and by making the judgement using a wide range of sources of information.

Prior to the interview:

1 Identify and invite all other managers who will be involved in the interviews
2 Identify the interview process, test and role-plays to be used in the selection of applicants
3 Read through all the candidates' application forms and identify issues that need to be explored with each candidate
4 Identify a quiet room for interview that will be free from interruptions
5 Allocate sufficient time for each interview and invite the candidates to attend at the appropriate time
6 Consider the room layout and style of interview to be used.

During the interview:

1 Stick strictly to the time allocated – poor timekeeping creates a bad impression
2 First introduce yourself and other interviewers – help the interviewee to relax
3 Explain the interview and selection process, and in particular tell interviewees when they will hear the result
4 Adopt a relaxed and friendly manner
5 Start with easy general questions
6 Ask open-ended questions – these encourage interviewees to talk
7 Listen carefully to answers and pick up on issues that arise
8 Always create the impression that you are interested in the candidate and are genuinely concerned to give the candidate a fair chance
9 Provide an opportunity for the candidate to ask questions
10 Recognize that the interview is a two-way process and that you want to leave each candidate with a good impression of the organization
11 Close the interview on time and in an orderly manner, ensuring that the candidate understands what will happen next.

After the interview:

1 Make notes on the candidate – again, a scoring system can be used to help make the selection
2 If more than one interviewer is involved, confer with others to decide on the candidate selected

3 If you have not called for them earlier, take up references; when these have arrived confirm the candidate (or re-consider in the light of the references)

4 Write to the successful applicant confirming the appointment and including joining instructions.

The selection and recruitment process has to be conducted in a fair and legal manner, and the following list of Acts includes some of the legislation that can apply during the whole process. This is not an exhaustive list, but includes some of the key legislation:

- Asylum and Immigration Act 1996
- Disability Discrimination Act 1995
- Equal Pay Act 1970
- Employment Protection (Consolidation) Act 1978
- Employment Act 1980
- Race Relations Act 1976
- Sex Discrimination Act 1975.

Once the selected candidate starts, you need to plan an induction programme so that he or she is eased into the new job and helped to become effective quickly.

New employee induction programmes

A surprising number of employers fail to provide induction training for new employees. The case study in Chapter 5 is in many ways typical of many firms in the licensed retail industry – poor selection and recruitment practices, with no induction, no training, low quality working practices and high levels of staff turnover. Induction training, in particular, can help to overcome one important feature of staff turnover; the *induction crisis* – the tendency for many new recruits to leave within a short period of joining the firm.

For the new employee, an induction programme:

- helps to overcome the early learning phase where the new employee feels incompetent
- assists the new employee in being accepted by existing staff and making friends
- helps the new recruit to feel part of the organization.

The benefits of providing induction training to the unit are that it:

- helps reduce customer service problems when new employees are learning
- increases productivity levels as new employees become effective more quickly
- demonstrates statutory duties for safe and hygienic working practices.

All new employees, irrespective of whether they are working full-time, part-time, temporarily or on a casual basis, need an induction programme. As individuals they still have the same need to be accepted by the organization quickly, and as new employees they need assistance so that they can become effective as quickly as possible. When planning the induction programme it is necessary to consider the

Hospitality, Leisure & Tourism Series

information and experiences needed to help employees to settle in, and how best the information should be given. Generally, induction programmes are best planned over a period of time. It is a mistake to provide too much information on the first day.

1 *Before the new employee starts work*: The interview starts the process, because candidates should be told of the processes involved in recruitment – when the job will commence, where they will be working, the type of job, the hours, pay and conditions. All this can then be confirmed in writing in a letter of appointment. Many firms also provide staff handbooks that provide useful information and details of the company's various policies – health and safety, training and employee development, etc.

2 *On the first day of work*: It is important to remember that all new recruits are likely to feel hesitant about starting a new job, and the main aim is to ensure that they feel comfortable in their job. Too much pressure and inadequate preparation for work stresses are key reasons for staff turnover. Make sure that the person knows where to find the main facilities that he or she will need. It is a good idea to provide the recruit with a 'buddy', to help the new member fit in and show them how things work. A basic programme on health and safety practices and simple hygiene is also useful at this stage. Although practice varies, induction is most effective when the new employee is timetabled as surplus to requirements for the first few days. It maybe that the recruit is working alongside more experienced employees, but it is important to reduce the immediate work pressure in this early learning phase.

3 *Within the first week*: In many cases these initial training programmes will take several days, and the new recruit will continue to be timetabled alongside the experienced employee. Best practice involves a 'buddy' who, rather than just being an experienced employee, is trained to train new staff. Chapter 6 deals more fully with the business benefits of training, but at this stage it is important to recognize that induction training helps the new employee to reach job competence more quickly, and formal training is more effective than learning by trial and error. An interview with the new recruit during the first few days can help to identify any problems or difficulties and gives you the opportunity to communicate the individual's importance and value to the unit.

4 *Within the first few weeks*: The induction programme may continue over several weeks. Apart helping the person to settle in to the organization, this process will continue to build up knowledge and skills needed for effective performance. As a general rule it is a good idea to continue the induction process over a period of time, providing information in small amounts rather than cramming it all into the first few days. Another interview with the new recruit can again check on progress and begin to look forward to the individual's development needs and plans.

In summary, careful recruitment and selection involves planning the needs of the job before thinking about the sort of person most likely to be able to be successful in the post. Once you have though about the job to be done and the person who will do it you need to think about where you are most likely to find the person needed, and the means by which you will invite interested applicants to apply. The selection process must be compatible with the person you are trying to recruit. Finally, a well-designed induction programme is required so as to ensure that the new recruit is quickly absorbed into the firm as an effective member of the team.

Approaches to recruitment and selection

As indicated earlier, there is no one set way to go through the recruitment and selection process in licensed retail operations. The type of person needed for different licensed retail jobs varies according to the type of service offer being made to customers. In addition, the process of recruitment and selection varies to match the person required and the skills necessary for their contribution to the service encounter.

In licensed retailing operations it is possible to identify three types of frontline staff needed in different operations, leading to three different processes, which match with the ideal types. In Chapter 1 we identified the ideal types of service operations:

- uniformity-dependent
- choice-dependent
- relationship-dependent.

Uniformity-dependent licensed retail services

These involve tasks that are simple but highly structured. Work practices involve 'one best way', and employees exercise a limited amount of discretion in completing production tasks. Service encounters are also short and limited in scope, although service staff have to practise some skills and judgement in collating orders, taking money, socially interacting with customers and dealing with complaints. The job description lists simple production and service duties, and work is structured in such a way as to prevent few barriers to potential recruits. In these cases, applicants should meet general requirements for employability and have no health or legislative limitations on them. The interviewing process is generally simple and typically involves few sophisticated selection techniques because training and development programmes and the management approach minimize the significance of individual skills and aptitudes.

An illustration is provided in Box 2.1.

Box 2.1 *J.D. Wetherspoons*

J.D. Wetherspoons recruits staff through a process typical of uniformity-dependent organizations. The jobs require few inherent skills, other than those of general employability, discipline, and basic levels of numeracy and literacy. Some attention is paid to customer service skills when the staff are being recruited for 'counter' duties, but only a small number of employees are rotatable. The majority are employed for and are trained in all elements of their job, whether 'production' or 'service' roles. In most pubs, numerical flexibility is achieved through the use of part-time staff. Typically, part-time staff work for sixteen hours per week although some, particularly school students, might be employed only for busy weekend periods. Approximately 60 per cent of employees work on part-time contracts.

Vacancies are advertised within the restaurants and at Job Centres. In some cases, local managers make contacts with local schools and colleges to ensure supplies of recruits. Although significant recruitment has been from amongst young people in the past, the company has increasingly been recruiting middle- and 'third' age employees.

The selection process involves one interview with a single management person – in some cases an assistant manager, in others the unit manager. Levels of staff turnover in the company are low for this sector.

All new employees, irrespective of their employment tenure, receive induction training that involves:

- basic orientation – a short taught programme on health and safety and basic food hygiene practices
- a probation period during which they typically spend one to three weeks on basic induction training timetabled surplus to requirements.

Once through this initial period, all employees are both trained and evaluated in their job performance.

Choice-dependent licensed retail services

These also involve simple tasks, but there are likely to be more of them. Production jobs may involve 'one best way' practices, although the service encounters are personalized to individual customers. Service employees have to be able to provide the service performance required by each customer, and thus have to possess a range of personality and character traits that will enable them to be effective in 'performing' in front of customers. In these circumstances the job description will list simple duties, but the staff specification might be much more elaborate in describing the personality required. Selection and interviewing techniques are more complex, as managers are looking for people with the 'personalities and skills' necessary.

Box 2.2 provides an example.

Box 2.2 *TGI Friday Restaurants*

Production jobs in TGI Friday Restaurants are similar to those in J.D. Wetherspoons in that the recipes and dishes to be prepared are cooked to set recipes and produced to 'one best way' methods. Some aspects are also laid down and trained out as a way of standardizing service targets and performance. That said, frontline staff have to be able both to advise customers about dishes and cocktail items, and to provide the specific performance required by each customer or party. Frontline staff in the bar and restaurant need to be able to relate well with customers. In the words of the company, 'They need to be extroverts, but not too much'.

Most employees are recruited and trained for specific kitchen, restaurant or bar jobs. There is little functional flexibility where employees move between departments. Over 80 per cent of the employees are full time, and functional flexibility is achieved by timetabling people through a set number of busy and quiet shift periods. Often part-time employment is used as a way of getting to know an individual prior to long-term employment.

Vacancies are usually advertised through Job Centres and contacts with existing employees. Selection processes involve several interviews – sometimes as many as four – and some role-plays where applicants may be asked to tell jokes or give a performance. Many recruits have undergone higher education, and most recruits are under 30 years of age.

All employees are trained prior to starting work in either a production or service capacity. They attend a one-week course that outlines the company's products and culture, and have to pass a test on the subjects taught. All staff are then trained in their respective roles and eased into their work situation. Usually they work alongside a more experienced employee, and restaurant staff, for example, will be given a quiet section of the restaurant to work for the first few shifts.

Relationship-dependent licensed retail services

These involve simple but more frequent contacts between customers and frontline staff. Production jobs may range from basic 'one best way' approaches to more traditional food production operations. Service relationships need to be matched to customer social and ego needs, and hence service employees have to be capable of building a relationship with customers. The job descriptions may appear simple, but the staff specification will identify characteristics that focus on extroversion and stability. In some cases, the development of social relationships with customers is based on the establishment of sound social relationships amongst employees. Selection and recruitment procedures would typically be concerned with a person who fits in with other staff members and is the sort of person who can build relationships with customers. Word-of-mouth advertising through existing employees would typically help in building a team spirit and a shared culture.

Box 2.3 provides an example.

Box 2.3 *Harvester Restaurants*

Harvester Restaurants have some features in common with both J.D. Wetherspoons and TGI Fridays in that there are standardized branded aspects to the customer offer that restrict and limit job autonomy. Whilst there are elements of 'one best way' in the kitchen, bar and service jobs, frontline staff need to develop good relationships with customers. Hence there is a need to select people who can relate to the chain's customer base. In addition, the organization of employees in empowered autonomous workgroups means that new recruits must fit in with the existing workforce.

Employees are selected and trained for one of the three key departments – kitchen, bar or restaurant – and there is little functional flexibility. Approximately 40 per cent of employees are full time, and numerical flexibility is achieved through the use of part-time staff, who account for 60 per cent of employees.

Advertising is through Job Centres and, most importantly, through existing employees who recommend that family and friends apply for vacant posts. Interviews tend to be with several managers, although typically only one interview is used. In some cases, an existing employee is involved in the interview and advises managers on applicants. Most employees recruited tend to mirror the customer profile – traditional British with conservative tastes, and more then 30 years old.

All employees go through an induction programme, although this is conducted concurrently with work on shift. Usually the new recruit works alongside a more experienced employee.

Conclusion

This chapter has outlined some of the important steps needed in recruiting and selecting employees to work in licensed retail operations. Effective recruitment starts with consideration of the types of tenure required by the job. Recruiting people to full-time, part-time, temporary or casual employment has implications for both the sources of recruits and the levels of commitment that can be expected from jobholders. In situations where demand for licensed retail services varies, and has peaks and troughs, it is often necessary for you to plan ahead so employees are in place in time for the increased demand.

The first step in the recruitment process requires you to have a definition of the job you are trying to fill. A formal job description is useful, because it helps you to think clearly about what the job entails and, leading from this, the type of person capable of doing it. Again, it is worth formalizing your thoughts by drawing up a staff specification. The staff specification helps you to identify the person and the qualifications and experience that will be lead to success in the post.

Consideration of the ideal candidate helps you identify where that person may be found. Often internal recruitment can be useful, because you may have prior knowledge of the applicant. Recruiting from outside the existing workforce can have the benefit of bringing in new people and ideas. Whatever the source of applicants, the selection process needs to be planned so as to give you enough information to make a sensible and realistic choice. It is likely, therefore that there will be different approaches to recruitment and selection that are best matched to the type of employees you are trying to recruit.

Reflective practice

Answer the following questions to check your understanding of this chapter.

1 Contrast and compare forms of numerical and functional flexibility in licensed retail operations. What are the key benefits and limitations of each?
2 Describe critically the main steps in recruitment selection of staff in licensed retail operations.
3 Contrast and compare the use of internal and external sources of recruitment for a typical 'frontline' post in a licensed retail operation.
4 Using a licensed retail operation known to you, devise a selection procedure for both production and service staff. Explain your answer.
5 Discuss critically the different approaches to recruitment and selection in licensed retail operations. To what extent can there be 'one best way' of recruiting staff?

Further reading

Beardwell, I. and Holden, L. (1994). *Human Resource Management: A Contemporary Perspective*. Pitman.

Biddle, D. and Evenden, R. (1993). *The Human Aspects of Management*. Institute of Personnel Management, London.

Boella, M. (2000). *Human Resource Management in the Hospitality Industry*. Stanley Thornes.

British Hospitality Association (1998). *Creating Hospitality's Virtuous Circle of Employment*. British Hospitality Association.

Maghurn, J. P. (1989). *A Manual of Staff Management in the Hotel and Catering Industry*. Heinemann.

Mullins, L. J. (1998). *Hospitality Management: A Human Resource Approach*. Pitman.

It takes happy workers to make happy customers

After working through this chapter, you should be able to:

- identify different styles and approaches to team leadership

- predict the likely impact of management styles on team member performance

- discuss critically the impact of hierarchy on views about team members

- identify stages in team development needs.

Team leadership and motivation

F. W. Marriott's famous quotation provides the title of this chapter, and is a reminder of the importance that many firms place on ensuring that the unit team is well motivated under the leadership of enthusiastic managers. Managers need to understand their own approaches to managing the team, and know how to adjust their approach when needed. They must appreciate the benefits that team membership can generate as well as understanding the motives and perspectives of team members.

That said, many licensed retail managers find that managing people is their most difficult task. There are many examples of very similar bars and pubs where the only difference between success and failure is the local unit manager's ability to motivate and enthuse the team of employees working in the unit. In one establishment, staff are happy, committed to serving customers, and clearly enjoy their work; in the next unit, employees are grumpy, unmotivated and clearly desperate to escape. Most frequently, the attitudes and assumptions of and the style with which people are managed by their immediate manager are the only noticeable variables. This chapter suggests some approaches both to analysing management style and to understanding the actions of team members.

Active learning point

Table 3.1 lists ten sources of job satisfaction; first rank these in order of importance for yourself, and then rank them in order of importance for a group of employees known to you.

Exercise 3.1: Satisfaction at work • • •

Table 3.1 is a list of possible attractions of a job. Please read them all and rank them 1–10 in order of their importance to you, with '1' indicating the most significant. Thus if you consider 'Pensions and other old-age security benefits' as being most important to you, write '1' by it and so on until all ten factors are numbered. Don't think about your present job, just about what you think is desirable.

Major sources of satisfaction	Important to you	Important to your subordinates
Steady work and steady wages		
High wages		
Pensions and other old-age security benefits		
Not having to work too hard		
Getting along with the people I work with		
Getting along well with my supervisor		
Good chance to turn out good quality work		
Good chance to do interesting work		
Good chance of promotion		
Good physical working conditions		

Table 3.1 Sources of job satisfaction

When you have completed the table for yourself, rank the factors that you think are important to your employees, or people you have recently worked with.

At this stage the two lists are important in establishing the similarities and differences between managers and subordinates. We shall return to the findings later, but at this stage it is important to establish that the list contains two types of factors:

1 *Extrinsic* sources of job satisfaction, which are more material rewards:
   - high wages
   - steady work and steady wages
   - pensions and other old-age security benefits
   - not having to work too hard
   - good physical working conditions
2 *Intrinsic* sources of job satisfaction, which make the person feel better
   - good chance of promotion
   - getting along with the people I work with
   - getting along well with my supervisor
   - good chance to turn out good quality work
   - good chance to do interesting work.

Looking at your responses to the sources of satisfaction survey in Table 3.1:

1 Pick out the top three factors that you have identified for yourself; are they more extrinsic or intrinsic?
2 Pick out the top three factors that you have identified for your subordinates; are they more extrinsic or intrinsic?
3 Make some notes that explain your answer, and keep them close by because we shall return to this exercise.

The relationship between team members and you, the manager, as team leader is important, and there are different ways that you can choose to manage your team. Even empowerment has a variety of forms that can be more directive, consultative, or participative. Each involves employees differently – acting on instructions, making suggestions or working without the direct involvement of the manager. These differences are important in team leadership, and we shall return to them later. First, we need to show how different managers hold different assumptions about their subordinates and have different priorities about the job and the team.

What kind of leader?

Management at all levels involves a social relationship between the manager and the managed. In modern branded licensed retail businesses, the relationship between the manager and the team are key to a successful bar, hotel or restaurant. The following four tests are designed to highlight different elements of the relationship and provide the basis for more discussion later.

Active learning point

Complete the following exercises as accurately as you can. Use your current job or a recent job as the context for your responses.

Exercise 3.2: How close or distant? • • •

To gauge the sociability of the person (you or your boss), score the individual on each of the dimensions given in Table 3.2. Add the scores together and divide the answer by seven.

Indicator	1	2	3	4	5	6	7
Use of first names	Never			Only boss uses them			Always/ mutual
Shares break times	Never			Sometimes			Often
Shares leisure outside work	Never			Sometimes			Often
Exchanges pleasantries	Rarely			Usually			Very often
Shares jokes/humour	Never			Sometimes			Often
Exchanges domestic information	Never			Mostly from subordinates			Often/ mutual
Formality	Very formal			Varies			Very informal
Description	**Psychologically and socially distant aloof from subordinates**	**Remote**		**Friendly**			**Psychologically and socially close friendship with subordinates**

Table 3.2 Gauging sociability

One aspect of the bar, pub or restaurant manager's style concerns the way that he or she relates socially to team members. As stated earlier, the relationship is personal and involves social relationships with team members. Do you remain psychologically aloof, or try be one of the boys/girls? Many managers find this aspect the most difficult to judge, particularly when they first take up a responsible post. An aloof and distant relationship can be perceived as cold and uncaring. The distance between team leader and team can create a barrier that cuts the manager off from the team and thereby prevents effective communication. On the other hand, an overly friendly manner can be misunderstood and lead to disciplinary difficulties (Table 3.3).

In many ways the sociability style adopted by you as the team leader will be determined by a combination of your own personality, your experience, and the context in which the team is working. Some managers are by nature closer to or more distant from subordinates. In these cases, it is difficult to suppress your personality traits, and all things being equal you will perform to your natural inclination. More experienced managers tend to have the confidence to be relaxed and informal with employees. Many new managers believe that it is easier to be formal at first and more relaxed later. Some service situations require a formal service situation, in other cases, informality is required.

Hospitality, Leisure & Tourism Series

Psychological distance	Psychological closeness
Benefits	
Disciplinary action easier	Better knowledge of team members
Formality better matched to formal situations	Good communications with team members
Disciplined working methods	Better knowledge of the immediate situation
People 'know their place'	Better able to build strong group bonds
Better able to tap the creativity of the team	
Limitations	
Distance acts as barrier to good communication	Disciplinary difficulties
Remoteness can breed misunderstanding	Team member behaviour inappropriate in
Team members fearful and hide the facts	formal settings
Leads to conflict with the group	Sloppy working methods
	Poor follow-through on instructions

Table 3.3 Benefits and limitations of distance and closeness

Exercise 3.3: Getting along with others • • •

Read the following reactions by a manager and identify the one that is closest to the way you would react. Also identify the one that is least like the way you would react.

An employee arrives forty-five minutes late for work. The bar manager says:

- 'What, late again, can't you ever get here on time? You are just too unreliable.'
- 'Oh dear, what happened to you, was the bus late again? Let me help you catch up with your work.'
- 'Please come and see me later. I would like to talk to you about your lateness so that it can be avoided in future. In the meantime, do you need any help to make up the lost work?'
- 'I do wish you would get here on time, you know how I rely on you. You have let me down.'
- 'Why does this always happen to me? Whenever I'm on early shift someone comes in late. It really isn't fair.'

These statements are useful in that they each represent different ways that individual managers might feel and act in a given situation. Each makes different assumptions about the position of the manager and the employee, and each represents a different focus for the reaction. The study of *transaction analysis* can assist managers in understanding the basic modes of behaviour that individuals take up in their relationships with other people. Transaction analysis establishes different kinds of transactions and how to deal with them. You need to understand these as a way of understanding your own behaviour and the behaviour of subordinates, and the psychological games that individuals sometimes play.

Ego states • • •

The above statements each start from different *ego states* – that is, assumptions about the communicator (manager) and the relationship with the receiver of the message (the employee who is late).

The parent ego state

This implies a position of power over the receiver. Usually it is learnt from parents, teachers and other authority figures. This may involve an open expression of power – 'do this', 'do that' – or be more implied – 'let *me* help *you*'. It may be critical or nurturing:

1 *The critical parent ego state* is openly dominant, critical and controlling, and involves putting others down and minimizing their problems.

Typical words used	Bad, should, ought, must, always, ridiculous
Tone	Critical, condescending, disgusted
Non-verbal characteristics	Pointing finger, frowning, anger
Underlying attitudes	Judgemental, moralistic, authoritarian

In the example given above – 'What, late again, can't you ever get here on time? You are just too unreliable' – the manager reaction is typical of the critical parent ego state. The reaction is blaming and judging without knowing the circumstances of the employee's lateness.

2 *The nurturing parent ego state* is openly supportive, understanding, sympathetic, affectionate, loving and helping behaviour.

Typical words used	Good, nice, I love you, beautiful, splendid
Tone	Tender, loving, comforting, concerned
Non-verbal characteristics	Open arms, smiling, accepting
Underlying attitudes	Understanding, caring, giving

In the example above – 'Oh dear, what happened to you, was the bus late again? Let me help you catch up with your work' – the reaction of the manager is typical of the nurturing parent ego state. The reaction is concerned, accepting and understanding, without knowing whether the employee was responsible for the lateness.

The adult ego state

This is not related to age. It is concerned with objectively appraising reality and uses information from all sources to make statements and adopt courses of action. It is even-handed and avoids being judgemental before all the information is gathered.

Typical words used	Correct, how, what, why, practical, quantity
Tone	Even
Non-verbal characteristics	Thoughtful, alert, open
Underlying attitudes	Straight, even-handed, evaluation of facts

The third statement – 'Please come and see me later. I would like to talk to you about your lateness so that it can be avoided in future. In the meantime, do you need any help to make up the lost work?' – is typical of an adult ego state. The manager is registering the fact the employee has arrived late and will want to explore the reasons later, but for now is offering whatever assistance is needed to meet the immediate situation. The manager is communicating an even-handed approach that has avoided making a judgement without more facts.

The child ego state

This is again not related to age; it is an expression of the feelings and urges that come to a person. These feelings can be expressed directly or indirectly:

1 *The natural child ego state* involves reactions that are spontaneous expressions of feelings and emotions. It is the ego state that people are in when they are having fun or being affectionate and impulsive. It demonstrates authentic and unfettered emotions that are expressed without concern for the reaction of others, and includes selfishness, anger and jealousy as well as fun and affection.

Typical words used	Wow, fun, want, won't, ouch, hi
Tone	Free, loud, energetic
Non-verbal characteristics	Uninhibited, loose, spontaneous
Underlying attitudes	Curious, fun-loving, changeable

The fourth response – 'I do wish you would get here on time, you know how I rely on you. You have let me down' – is typical of a manager expressing the natural child ego state. The statement expresses the manager's raw emotion, and the focus is on the expression of emotions and the self.

2 *The adapted child ego state* is again concerned with the self and emotions felt by the individual, although this time they are not directly expressed. The concern is to manipulate others into feeling sorry for them or feeling guilty, or to 'suck up' to others.

Typical words used	Can't, wish, try, hope, please, thank you
Tone	Whining, defiant, placating
Non-verbal characteristics	Pouting, sad, innocent
Underlying attitudes	Demanding, compliant, ashamed

The fifth example – 'Why does this always happen to me? Whenever I'm on early shift someone comes in late. It really isn't fair' – is typical of the adapted child ego state. The manager is again expressing emotions and feelings, although in this case is attempting to generate feelings of guilt and sympathy in the employee. The focus of the communication is not the employee, but the manager and his or her feelings.

Understanding ego states

Most people will adopt a mixture of ego states during the normal progress of their working, domestic and social lives, although some individuals may adopt one style more than others, and some situations might encourage individuals to adopt one style more than others. It is important to understand ego states for two reasons:

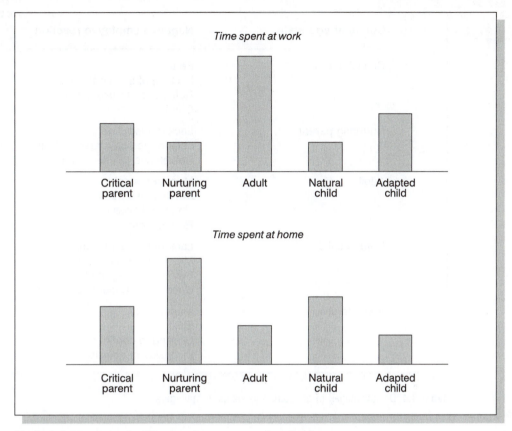

Figure 3.1 Time spent in different ego states at work and at home

1 Managers who adopt a dominant style need to understand the potential difficulties it might cause
2 Managers need to understand the potential reactions to different ego styles.

It is possible to identify the ego state that an individual is engaging from the words used, tone of voice, non-verbal characteristics and underlying attitudes implied in a particular conversation (transaction) between individuals. As stated above, different contexts may mean that individuals use one ego state more than another. Figure 3.1 shows how the same person may use different combinations of ego states at work and at home.

It is not unusual for individuals to adopt a favoured ego state at work, and the danger then is that the individual cannot adapt to the situations that present themselves. It is also possible that if you as the manager have a constant ego state it will create negative reactions amongst your team members (Table 3.4).

In addition to the problems caused by managers adopting a constant ego state, you need to understand the patterns that can be analysed both in the way you communicate with team members and in the reaction of team members. Analysis of the words, tone, non-verbal characteristics and underlying attitudes used by you as team leader and by team members can fit into a number of patterns.

Constant ego state	Negative employee reaction
Critical parent	Fear Lacking of self-confidence Reluctance to use initiative Conflict
Nurturing parent	Lack of discipline Lack of personal responsibility Reluctance to use initiative
Adult	Manager is cold Emotionless boss Unnatural boss Remoteness
Natural child	Lack of respect for manager Matched childishness Sloppy working methods Uncertainty about boss' moods
Adapted child	Manipulated Guilty Lacking in confidence Inconsistent decisions

Table 3.4 Disadvantages of constant ego states in managers

In the examples above, the employee who is late might respond in a way that matches, or corresponds to, the manager's initial ego state. For example, when the manager says, 'What, late again, can't you ever get here on time? You are just too unreliable', the late employee might make one of the following responses:

- 'Don't you speak to me like that, the bus broke down, you are very unfair' – a paired critical parent reaction
- 'It was such a lovely day I decided to walk, it was fun' – a paired natural child reaction
- 'Yes, I'm afraid I am late; I'll start work straight away and make up the lost time' – a cross adult reaction.

In the first two cases, the employee response matches the initial ego state of the manager, either by dropping into the same ego state or by creating a paired reaction – child to parent. In the last case the employee crosses over from the matched response by reacting in an adult ego state. Obviously, these different patterns of response can work in all directions – adult to child, child to parent, etc. You need to be able to understand these patterns of communications, because they can provide a useful device for reducing conflict. For example, where a colleague or team member is adopting a parent or child ego state, adult responses can help to reduce the potential conflict.

Active learning point

Complete the following exercises as accurately as you can. Complete the exercise yourself or give it to a colleague to complete.

Exercise 3.4: Management priorities ● ● ●

Respond to each item in Table 3.5 according to the way you probably act as the leader of a work group. Circle the response that most accurately describes the way you would behave – always (A); frequently (F); often (O); seldom (S); or never (N).

1	I would most likely act as spokesman for the group	A	F	O	S	N
2	I would encourage overtime	A	F	O	S	N
3	I would allow members complete freedom in their work	A	F	O	S	N
4	I would encourage the use of uniform procedures	A	F	O	S	N
5	I would permit the members to use their own judgement in solving problems	A	F	O	S	N
6	I would stress being ahead of competing groups	A	F	O	S	N
7	I would speak as a representative of the group	A	F	O	S	N
8	I would needle members for greater effort	A	F	O	S	N
9	I would try out my ideas in the group	A	F	O	S	N
10	I would let the members do the work the way they think best	A	F	O	S	N
11	I would be working hard for promotion	A	F	O	S	N
12	I would tolerate postponement and uncertainty	A	F	O	S	N
13	I would speak up for the group when visitors were present	A	F	O	S	N
14	I would keep the work moving at a rapid pace	A	F	O	S	N
15	I would turn the members loose on a job and let them go to it	A	F	O	S	N
16	I would settle conflicts when they occur in the group	A	F	O	S	N
17	I would get swamped by details	A	F	O	S	N
18	I would represent the group at outside meetings	A	F	O	S	N
19	I would be reluctant to allow the members any freedom of action	A	F	O	S	N
20	I would decide what should be done and how it should be done	A	F	O	S	N
21	I would push for increased production	A	F	O	S	N
22	I would let some members have authority, which I would keep under review	A	F	O	S	N
23	Things would usually turn out as I had predicted	A	F	O	S	N
24	I would allow the group a high degree of initiative	A	F	O	S	N
25	I would assign group members to particular tasks	A	F	O	S	N
26	I would be willing to make changes	A	F	O	S	N
27	I would ask members to work harder	A	F	O	S	N
28	I would trust the group members to exercise good judgement	A	F	O	S	N
29	I would schedule the work to be done	A	F	O	S	N
30	I would refuse to explain my actions	A	F	O	S	N
31	I would persuade other members that my ideas are to their advantage	A	F	O	S	N
32	I would permit the group to work at its own pace	A	F	O	S	N
33	I would urge the group to beat its previous record	A	F	O	S	N
34	I would act without consulting the group	A	F	O	S	N
35	I would ask the group members to follow standard rules and procedures	A	F	O	S	N

Table 3.5 Management priorities

Scoring the questionnaire

1 Circle the question numbers for the following questions: 8, 12, 17, 18, 19, 30, 34 and 35 – circle the actual number (e.g. 12)

2 Write a number 1 in front of the circled item number if you responded S (seldom) or N (never)

3 Write a number 1 in front of questions not circled if you have answered A (always) or F (frequently)

4 Using a different colour, circle the number 1s that you have written in front of the following question numbers: 3, 5, 8, 10, 15, 18, 19, 22, 24, 26, 28, 30, 32, 34 and 35.

5 Count the *circled* number 1s. This is the score for 'concern for people' (P). Record the score in a space marked 'P' at the end of the questionnaire.

6 Count the *uncircled* number 1s. This is the score for 'concern for tasks' (T). Record your score in a space marked 'T' at the end of the questionnaire.

7 Take the smaller number away from the larger number, e.g. T8 - P4 = T4.

8 Record your answer on the scale given below.

Management styles: people–things priorities

Record your T score below   Record your P score below

24	16	8	0	8	16	24
100% task-centred			50/50			100% people-centred

An equal balance of people and task concerns

Mainly technical/task priority	Mainly people priority
Priority is task, systems, solutions, planning or action related to systems, operational methods, rules and procedures	Focus on the personal needs or problems of others, decisions, solutions, planning or actions related to morale, conflict and motivation problems
Priority is monitoring and measuring task and the work of others	Priority is people-related activities – interviewing, selecting staff, appraisal, counselling.
Priority is things-focused – finance, strategy, planning, control, work study	Enjoys communicating with individuals and groups
Enjoys paperwork and systems	Can find figures and systems difficult
Can have a problem with understanding people	

Table 3.6 Priorities – technical/tasks, or people

Exercise 3.5: A question of balance • • •

As in Exercise 3.4, respond to each item in Table 3.7 according to the way you probably act as the leader of a work group. Rank the following paragraphs as a

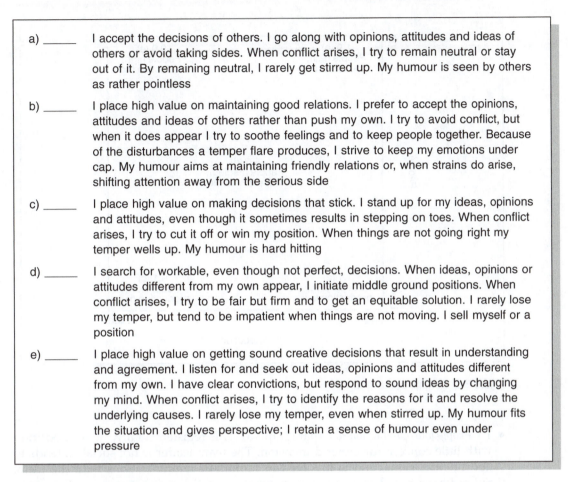

a) _____ I accept the decisions of others. I go along with opinions, attitudes and ideas of others or avoid taking sides. When conflict arises, I try to remain neutral or stay out of it. By remaining neutral, I rarely get stirred up. My humour is seen by others as rather pointless

b) _____ I place high value on maintaining good relations. I prefer to accept the opinions, attitudes and ideas of others rather than push my own. I try to avoid conflict, but when it does appear I try to soothe feelings and to keep people together. Because of the disturbances a temper flare produces, I strive to keep my emotions under cap. My humour aims at maintaining friendly relations or, when strains do arise, shifting attention away from the serious side

c) _____ I place high value on making decisions that stick. I stand up for my ideas, opinions and attitudes, even though it sometimes results in stepping on toes. When conflict arises, I try to cut it off or win my position. When things are not going right my temper wells up. My humour is hard hitting

d) _____ I search for workable, even though not perfect, decisions. When ideas, opinions or attitudes different from my own appear, I initiate middle ground positions. When conflict arises, I try to be fair but firm and to get an equitable solution. I rarely lose my temper, but tend to be impatient when things are not moving. I sell myself or a position

e) _____ I place high value on getting sound creative decisions that result in understanding and agreement. I listen for and seek out ideas, opinions and attitudes different from my own. I have clear convictions, but respond to sound ideas by changing my mind. When conflict arises, I try to identify the reasons for it and resolve the underlying causes. I rarely lose my temper, even when stirred up. My humour fits the situation and gives perspective; I retain a sense of humour even under pressure

Table 3.7 A question of balance

description of your behaviour as a team leader, starting with the statement that is most typical of your behaviour (rank 1) and continuing until the least typical is ranked 5.

Exercises 3.4 and 3.5 both identify management priorities regarding concern for people and tasks. Whilst some managers will have registered a balanced score between the concerns for people and concerns for task, most managers will be prone to prioritize either people or tasks (Table 3.6).

Exercise 3.5 also identifies different management priorities, although it is more concerned with balance between degrees of concern for each. The exercise shows five potential positions and maps these on a grid that uses both a high and a low degree of concern for people, and a high and a low degree of concern for task/ production (Figure 3.2).

The *managerial grid* shows how the balance between concern for production and people can vary between managers. These positions are likely to have different impacts on subordinates and on the team's morale.

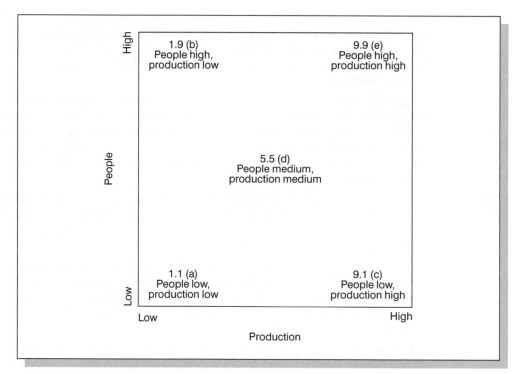

Figure 3.2 The managerial grid

- 1.1 *People low–production low* (paragraph a). This registers a fairly neutral position with little concern for either dimension. The team leader is not sociable, tends to abdicate decisions, and is involved in minimal communications with the team. Subordinates are likely to react in an equally negative manner; many will move to a corresponding low concern for both people and task, morale will be low, and staff turnover will be high.
- 1.9 *People high–production low* (paragraph b). The team leader is concerned with maintaining social relationships and is less formal. Close to the team, the manager would avoid conflict, and places production and tasks as a second priority. Subordinates are likely to be committed to the individual manager. The work atmosphere is happy, but the output is low. Conflict within the team is stifled rather than resolved. Creativity may be stifled. Staff turnover may be pulsed, when the manager or other key team members leave.
- 9.1 *People low–production high* (paragraph c). The team leader prioritizes production, output levels and tasks. Low sociability and more directive styles of decision-making are typical. The manager is more comfortable with systems and rules, and sets standards for the team to work to. Subordinates are likely to react unfavourably to the manager's assumptions that they cannot be trusted. Low commitment is typical. Often, team members work steadily when the team leader is there but slacken off when not being directly supervised. Conflict is generated, and may be individual or organized in collective forms.
- 5.5 *Moderate people–moderate production* (paragraph d). Priorities are balanced between concerns for people and concerns for production. The manager is

moderately sociable, and decision making will tend to be a mix of directive and consultative – tell and sell, tell and test. Subordinates are likely to be more instrumental and put in not too much effort but enough to satisfy the leader. Quality of work and output are not outstanding, and standards are not as good as they might be. Conflicts are never fully resolved.

- 9.9 *High people–high production* (paragraph e). A high priority is placed on both production and the team, and the team leader recognizes the significant role that team members play in achieving high levels of high-quality output. The leader is sociable and adopts more participative styles of leadership and decision making. Subordinates are highly motivated and staff turnover levels are low. Conflict is low, and the employees are committed to service and production goals. The quality of work is good, and both employee and customer satisfaction are high.

Variations in employee involvement in empowerment are linked to variations in the way managers and team members make decisions. In principle, there are only three basic approaches (Table 3.8):

1 Directive – managers make the decisions with little input from employees, who merely act on instructions
2 Consultative – managers make the decisions, but with suggestions or information provided by employees
3 Participative – managers involve employees in making decisions jointly, or delegate decision-making to them.

In practice, the day-to-day management of a bar, pub or restaurant may involve managers and employees in using a combination of styles, though one may be more dominant. The following exercise provides a chance to map these different styles in a workplace known to you.

Style	Directive		Consultative		Participative		None
	Tell	Tell and sell	Tell and test	Seek	Joint problem-solving	Delegates	Abdicates
Manager involvement	Makes decisions and instructs	Makes decisions and instructs with reasons	Makes decisions but reviews after seeking views	Defines problem and seeks employees' view before deciding	Defines problem and makes decision jointly with employees	Defines scope of decision-making authority –monitors decisions	Provides limited direction or support to employees
Employee involvement	Acts on instructions	Acts on instructions and explanation given	Gives views on boss's proposed decision	Discusses alternatives and makes suggestions	Joins in the decision-making process	Makes decisions within boundaries set by boss	Employees decide for themselves and react to events

Table 3.8 Making decisions

Active learning point

Complete the following exercises as accurately as you can. Use your current job or a recent job as the context for your responses.

Exercise 3.6 Mapping decision-making styles • • •

Using a manager well known to you – your boss or a colleague – categorize, using Table 3.9, the proportion of their time spent making decisions in the various styles we have identified.

Mode	Directive		Consultative		Participative		None
Style	Tell	Tell and sell	Tell and test	Seek	Joint problem-solving	Delegates	Abdicates
% time							

Table 3.9 Mapping decision-making styles

On the basis of the exercise, you will be able to identify a more predominant style from amongst the range of possibilities. In each case there are limitations and benefits to over-use of the style, particularly if the style is at odds with the setting and the people who are being managed (Table 3.10).

Mode	Benefits	Limitations
Directive	Works best where there are few options to the tasks to be done – 'one best way', standardized, limited discretion, safety, high-risk situations, where a task has to be done now	Discourages personal initiative, often results in poor morale and poor communications. Can be inflexible and unresponsive to change. Frequently output levels are high under direct supervision, but drop when the manager is not present
Consultative	Works best where managers want to gain from the knowledge and immediate experiences of the workforce. The manager retains control of decisions. Can be useful for overcoming service quality problems or making suggestions for achieving goals	Limited where managers continue to make decisions with little or no reference to employee suggestions. Manager control of decisions can be de-motivating. The processes of consultation can be time consuming and directly costly, and the benefits more difficult to cost financially
Participative	Works best where managers need to allow employees to make immediate operational decisions, or where employees possess better knowledge and experience. Can be useful for gaining employee commitment to service quality, customer and other business goals. Employees have a better sense of 'ownership' if they make the decisions	Difficult for many managers because it involves letting employees make decisions and can represent a loss of control. If employees make decisions, they may make decisions that managers do not like. The processes of participation can be time consuming and directly costly. The benefits may be difficult to cost financially

Table 3.10 Benefits and limitations of decision-making styles

A matter of choice?

We have seen that as a team leader you can behave in a variety of ways – your closeness or distance to the team; the ego states you adopt, decision-making style, and the priorities of concern for the team or concern for production and tasks can all be varied. Your personality, experience and training clearly influence the approach, but are these issues solely a matter of choice?

Licensed retail services vary in the offer made to customers, and these variations require staff to exercise different amounts of discretion to meet customer service needs. The way you manage the service team needs to correspond to the service offer:

1 *Uniformity-dependent*. This is where customers are buying into a highly standardized product and service encounter, so managers may have limited scope to involve employees because 'one best way' approaches to job design reduce the scope for discretion. Management styles will tend towards being directive with some consultation. Some customer service jobs and supervisory jobs might even allow some participation in the form of delegation and joint decision-making, but for most team members, involvement is limited. That said, managers in these units can still be sociable and adopt ego states that treat the employees as adults and with dignity. The team leader and team may be restricted by the operating system, but as the team leader you need to give high priority to both the people and production.

2 *Choice-dependent*. In many cases licensed retail services that offer a wide choice in a branded context are offering mass customization – that is, the customers are being offered standardized products and services but these are personalized by the customer's choice opportunities, or they are offered bundles of products and services that create predictable variations of customization. Employees have to act as consultants and advise customers. In these cases, some aspects of the process will be directive but the service requires more consultation and participation. Team member involvement may require formal mechanisms for tell and test, seek, and joint problem solving. In some cases, the service encounter needs employees to be delegated to do whatever is needed to create guest satisfaction, and it includes some aspect of participation, although this might be limited to managing the service encounter. If you are a manager in one of these units, you need to be sociable and adopt ego states that treat the employees as adults and with dignity. The team leader and team needs to adopt generally consultative approaches, and you as the team leader need to give high priority to both the people and production.

3 *Relationship-dominant*. These licensed retail services may also require a degree of standardization, but the service encounter involves many more stages and staff contact takes on increased significance as a source of customer satisfaction or dissatisfaction. Again there may be some elements of standardization required of the national brand, but employees need to be delegated to meet customer service needs – dealing with unusual requests, responding to service failure, acting in a way that exceeds customer expectations. Joint decision-making as well as the more consultative approaches may be advisable in this type of service. As with the other approaches, you need to consider your sociability, adopt the adult ego state and treat employees with dignity. The team leader and team need to adopt

generally participative approaches, and as the team leader you need to give, as always, high priority to both the people and production.

Active learning point

Complete the following exercise as accurately as you can, using the sources of satisfaction survey earlier in this chapter.

Exercise 3.7: Measuring employee sources of satisfaction • • •

This exercise uses the sources of satisfaction survey featured in Exercise 3.1. Give a copy of this to one or more subordinates of the post for which you made the assessment.

When you have completed the survey of employees, collate the results, and note the differences or similarities with your own assessments of sources of satisfaction:

Major sources of satisfaction	Important to you
Steady work and steady wages	
High wages	
Pensions and other old-age security benefits	
Not having to work too hard	
Getting along with the people I work with	
Getting along well with my supervisor	
Good chance to turn out good quality work	
Good chance to do interesting work	
Good chance of promotion	
Good physical working conditions	

Table 3.11 Sources of job satisfaction

1 Were your top three responses more intrinsic than extrinsic?
2 Compare these with the top three responses of subordinates in your survey.
3 Compare this with you own assessment of the subordinates' sources of satisfaction.

In many organizations, the hierarchy creates a situation where managers higher up the organization believe that their subordinates are more extrinsically motivated than they are themselves. Yet when the same test is given to lower level of management the same results are found. The respondents mostly rank the intrinsic factors higher than the extrinsic factors, and they too rank their subordinates as having more extrinsically driven sources of satisfaction, and so on down the organization.

Misunderstandings as a consequence of organization hierarchy

Misunderstanding as a consequence of organization hierarchy can:

- lead managers to make errors when judging the motives and drives of subordinates
- result in reward packages being aimed at sources of satisfaction that are less important to the employee
- cause employee dissatisfaction
- lead to conflict
- result in poor quality work and customer dissatisfaction.

Working in teams

Organizing employees and managers in teams can bring important benefits in all service organizations. The major benefits are:

- improved communications between all managers and employees ensure that the unit's objectives and goals are understood and shared by all team members
- there will be improved commitment through a greater sense of ownership
- better suggestions and ideas
- more creative ideas available
- people learn from each other
- improved morale and motivation because people are included
- communications are improved by being involved in the decisions.

Types of teams

Working with the management team will involve each individual team member having specific areas of responsibility. In many licensed retail units, junior managers will have responsibility for a specific area of the operations – kitchen, bar, restaurant, accommodation. These functional departments have to work to common goals, and it is up to the unit manager as team leader to ensure that all sections work in a cooperative way. A common problem in many licensed retail operations is that these divisions, based on departments, can produce a 'them and us' culture, with a lack of cooperation or even conflict between teams. Building a strong management team across the unit is an essential feature of effective management.

Setting up multifunctional teams is another way of developing the culture of cooperation and reducing tensions between teams. Often these are based on the identification and resolution of common problems – improvement of service quality and employee satisfaction, reduced wastage, improved operating procedures. Some of these teams are permanent features of the unit's organization, and in other cases the teams are set up to deal with specific issues.

This chapter has also discussed different arrangements for consulting with or involving team members in making decisions. In all cases, as the team leader you need to clearly understand the stages that a team goes through in its development, and the factors likely to inhibit team development.

Stages in team development • • •

As the team is established and begins to develop, it goes through a number of phases that need to be understood by managers. An experienced team leader aids the team through the various phases, and recognizes the danger of inaction and cynicism that can occur if team members feel their efforts are not valued.

Searching stage

Often team members in new teams feel a thrill of enthusiasm as the team is first created. Particularly where team members are unused to being consulted, the team may experience a high level of commitment to the team and its goals. As the team leader, you need to recognize the benefits of this enthusiasm, but ensure that team members do not develop an over-optimistic expectation of outcomes.

Team members are also searching for a shared definition of the objectives during this phase. Clearly, an effective team leader provides the team with clear objectives, or facilitates the team in developing the shared objectives necessary for effective performance. Most effective team leaders avoid 'telling' team members what they must do; 'asking' is much more effective. The tendency to underestimate the degree of disagreement cannot be overstressed. The enthusiasm felt by members often leads them to assume they all share the same objectives, but they do not want to argue them out.

Exploring stage

Once the team has agreed on the broad objectives, they have to spend some time raising questions, making suggestions, evaluating alternatives and deciding on the appropriate course(s) of action. This stage will involve conflict as different team members suggest different courses of action; disagreements will occur and team members may form into sub-groups as team members come together round different suggested courses of action.

Team leaders need to be aware that this is a necessary phase through which the group must travel. You need to help the team to establish mutual understanding and a healthy respect for the creative tension that is necessary for the group to be most effective. Clearly, negative conflict can be harmful because it can prevent innovation and the working out of agreed paths; however, too much conformity or conflict avoidance can be equally damaging, because disagreements are never resolved. The team never formulates a consensus of action plans and priorities.

Alliance stage

The team eventually reaches a point where the members share an understanding of the objectives and what needs to be done. Each member understands not only his or her role, but also the role of other group members. There is also a shared understanding of the strengths and weaknesses of all team members. The team has a uniformity of purpose, members are committed to the outcomes, but respect the diversity within the group, recognizing that different views and interests are essential for the team to work effectively.

The team leader needs to help and enable the team to keep working towards the goals and outcomes identified. You need to encourage the team constantly to review objectives and action plans. There is a great danger of the team developing 'frozen thinking' at this stage – that is, the team, having decided on a course of action, continues to support the action, even when circumstances change and the action is no longer relevant.

Any disruption to the dynamics of the team – the loss of a member, a new team leader, new members or changes in the focus of the problem or purpose of the team – may cause the team to slip out of the alliance phase and back into the earlier stages.

Threats to team development • • •

Effective teams develop as the product of group bonds set up between specific individuals. In these circumstances, individual behaviour is influenced by a combination of individual and group motivations. Key causes of team failure include:

- high levels of instability due to staff turnover or movement around the organization
- limited opportunities for the team to meet and work through the stages needed
- limited support from more senior organization members
- restrictions placed on the team's ability to resolve the problem
- poor morale or inter-group conflict.

Benefits of working in teams

Clearly the reasons why teams have been set up differ, and the benefits that team working can generate will also vary, but there are some general benefits to be gained by the individuals involved, the management and the unit.

Benefits of teams to individual members include:

- increased job satisfaction
- personal development and growth
- career planning
- reduced fear of risk taking
- more involvement in decision-making
- increased recognition of his or her contribution.

Benefits to unit management include:

- decisions being made by the people most closely involved
- managers sharing the work load with others
- all are focused on the same objectives
- improved commitment and support for decisions
- more flexibility amongst team members.

Benefits to the licensed retail unit include:

- improved quality of products and services
- a culture of continuous improvement is created
- improved trust and openness
- better communications reduce misunderstandings
- reduced duplication
- improved working relationships
- improved customer satisfaction
- increased opportunities to achieve or beat performance targets
- improved employee satisfaction
- reduced staff turnover
- improved sales and profit performance.

Different types of teams will deliver different clusters of benefits, and thus team briefing sessions prior to a shift, or occasional briefings to the staff, will deliver different benefits to team structures based on autonomous work teams. In each of these examples the relationship between yourself as the team leader and team members is different. The amount of discretion allowed in the team is different and the extent to which they can make decisions is also different. In some cases team members merely receive information, whilst in others they are actively managing their own work situation. Clearly, the impact that these different arrangements have on your team members is also influenced by the nature of the team members. Chapter 4 explores some of these differences between individuals more fully.

Conclusion

The title of this chapter comes from F. W. Marriott's well-known quotation drawing the link between the management of employees and customer satisfaction. These views are widely shared in many licensed retail organizations that pay increasing attention to employee attitudes and 'internal customer satisfaction'. Although influences outside the immediate unit cannot be dismissed, the key to employee satisfaction is the immediate unit management in its role of team leader. There is very clear evidence that the relationships created by you as the unit manager can either enthuse and inspire team members, or confuse and de-motivate them.

Often the ideas that the manager holds about employees as team members are crucial to shaping the approach to team leadership. In some cases managers adopt a 'critical parent ego state' and are 'psychologically distant' from team members. In addition, these managers give key priority to managing output through their 'high concern for production and low concern for people'. Compound this with a 'directive' decision-making style and assumptions that employees are all 'just here for the money' (extrinsically motivated), and many employees will react negatively to working in the unit. Poor morale, absenteeism, low job satisfaction, high staff turnover and dissatisfied customers are likely consequences.

Effective team leaders are more likely to be 'psychologically close' to team members and adopt an appropriate array of ego states with a high proportion of the 'adult' ego state. They will have priorities that give equally 'high concern for people and high concern for production'. They adopt an approach to managing employees through team membership – even in situations where highly standardized production and service systems limit employee discretion. Even in these circumstances the manager's personal decision-making style is prone to be consultative and participative, wherever possible. In addition, effective managers understand that employees have an array of needs and priorities from work, and that employee satisfaction will depend on rewards that both make the person feel better and provide material benefits. Effective team leaders also understand the many benefits that team working can bring, and have a thorough grasp of how team effectiveness can be enhanced and developed.

Reflective practice

1 Using the case study in Chapter 15, identify the causes of staff turnover.
2 What steps would you take to reduce it?
3 What priorities would you make for action over the next three months?
4 Make a case for costing the value of employees into an assessment of unit performance.
5 What measure might you use?
6 Some managers argue that high staff turnover is a price worth paying for low labour costs and increased profits. Prepare arguments in support of this view.

Further reading

Argyle, M. (1989). *The Social Psychology of Work*. Penguin.

Biddle, D. and Evenden, R. (1993). *Human Aspects of Management*. Institute of Personnel Management, London.

Boella, M. (2000). *Human Resource Management in the Hospitality Industry*. Stanley Thornes.

Goss-Turner, S. (1989). *Managing People in the Hotel and Catering Industry*. Croner.

Maghurn, J. P. (1989). *A Manual of Staff Management in the Hotel and Catering Industry*. Heinemann.

Mullins, L. J. (1995) *Hospitality Management: A Human Resource Approach*. Pitman.

Roberts, J. (1995). *Human Resource Practices in the Hospitality Industry*. Hodder & Stoughton.

Rothwell, S. (1980). *Labour Turnover: its Costs, Causes and Control*. Gower.

It's people, people, people

After working through this chapter, you should be able to:

- identify ways of analysing differences between individuals

- evaluate critically the management of groups and behaviour of individuals as group members

- apply principles of assertion and deal with conflict

- devise plans for motivating team members.

Working with people

Bars and pubs are often described as 'people' businesses. As we have seen in the earlier chapters, frontline staff are the means by which an organization delivers its service to customers, and the management of employees needs to tap employee commitment and enthusiasm to 'delight customers'. The service interaction in most licensed retail organizations is inseparable, in that the customer is present when the service is delivered.

Customer reactions and involvement in the service are also important features of the service. Customer expectations and moods will form a vital basis for judging the success or failure of the service encounter. Pub customers are the receivers of the service provided by staff, and they also contribute the social dimension to other customers. Customer relationships and managing the relationships between customers is a particularly important aspect of bar and pub management.

Chapter 3 showed the contribution that effective team leadership makes towards creating the best circumstances for quality service delivery. This chapter aims to develop further your understanding as a manager of people, both as employees and as customers. The chapter explores some features of how individuals differ and may react in their own different ways to similar circumstances. Secondly, the chapter considers the behaviour of individuals as group members. Chapter 3 dealt with the benefits of managing individuals in formal work teams; this chapter considers some of the influences of group memberships that merely arise out of the work relationships. Thirdly, this chapter considers techniques that will assist unit managers in their relations with both customers and staff in assertiveness and in dealing with resolution of conflict. Finally, it explores some of the actions you can take to develop the motivation of your employees and their satisfaction at work.

Individual differences

There are many different ways of explaining people's behaviour and motives. The following section provides a basic introduction to some ideas that might help you as a manager better to understand customer and employee behaviour. At the very least, they lay down a model for analysing different people – obviously crucial when attempting to build a loyal customer base in the pub or bar.

Personality

There are a number of explanations as to why people do what they do. The trait theory of personality suggests that people's actions and personalities can be understood through an analysis of their personality traits. These traits are reasonably consistent characteristics, which are probably developed through a combination of inheritance and the social and physical environment. The 'nature vs nurture' debates amongst various psychologists reach different conclusions regarding the relative importance of each, but for our purposes it is probably true to say that a combination of each produces these personality traits.

One simple technique for understanding individual differences involves mapping people against two axes – extroversion/introversion and stability/instability. Extrovert people are most interested in the outside world of people and things, whereas introverts are more interested in their own thoughts and feelings. A stable

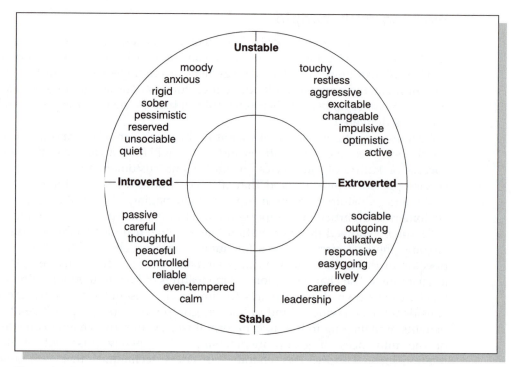

Figure 4.1 Personality profiles

	Average	
Extrovert		**Introvert**
Active		Inactive
30 29 28 27 26 25 24 23 22 21 20 19 18 17 16		15 14 13 12 11 10 9 8 7 6 5 4 3 2 1
Sociability		Unsociability
30 29 28 27 26 25 24 23 22 21 20 19 18 17 16		15 14 13 12 11 10 9 8 7 6 5 4 3 2 1
Risk-taking		Carefulness
30 29 28 27 26 25 24 23 22 21 20 19 18 17 16		15 14 13 12 11 10 9 8 7 6 5 4 3 2 1
Impulsiveness		Control
30 29 28 27 26 25 24 23 22 21 20 19 18 17 16		15 14 13 12 11 10 9 8 7 6 5 4 3 2 1
Expressiveness		Inhibition
30 29 28 27 26 25 24 23 22 21 20 19 18 17 16		15 14 13 12 11 10 9 8 7 6 5 4 3 2 1
Practicability		Reflectiveness
30 29 28 27 26 25 24 23 22 21 20 19 18 17 16		15 14 13 12 11 10 9 8 7 6 5 4 3 2 1
Irresponsibility		Responsibility
30 29 28 27 26 25 24 23 22 21 20 19 18 17 16		15 14 13 12 11 10 9 8 7 6 5 4 3 2 1

Figure 4.2 Dimensions of extroversion/introversion

	Average	
Emotional instability		**Emotional stability**
Inferiority feelings		Self-esteem
30 29 28 27 26 25 24 23 22 21 20 19 18 17 16		15 14 13 12 11 10 9 8 7 6 5 4 3 2 1
Depressiveness		Happiness
30 29 28 27 26 25 24 23 22 21 20 19 18 17 16		15 14 13 12 11 10 9 8 7 6 5 4 3 2 1
Anxiety		Calm
30 29 28 27 26 25 24 23 22 21 20 19 18 17 16		15 14 13 12 11 10 9 8 7 6 5 4 3 2 1
Obsessiveness		Casualness
30 29 28 27 26 25 24 23 22 21 20 19 18 17 16		15 14 13 12 11 10 9 8 7 6 5 4 3 2 1
Dependence		Autonomy
30 29 28 27 26 25 24 23 22 21 20 19 18 17 16		15 14 13 12 11 10 9 8 7 6 5 4 3 2 1
Hypochondriasis		Sense of health
30 29 28 27 26 25 24 23 22 21 20 19 18 17 16		15 14 13 12 11 10 9 8 7 6 5 4 3 2 1
Guilt		Freedom from guilt
30 29 28 27 26 25 24 23 22 21 20 19 18 17 16		15 14 13 12 11 10 9 8 7 6 5 4 3 2 1

Figure 4.3 Dimensions of stability/instability

person tends be calm and even tempered, whereas the unstable personality is changeable and touchy. Figure 4.1 shows how variations on the continua (Figures 4.2, 4.3) might result in different personality types depending on their location in one of the four quadrants produced.

The scales included against each dimension of extroversion/introversion build a model of personality traits in which the extreme extrovert is active, sociable, a risk taker, impulsive, expressive, practical and irresponsible. The classically introverted personality, on the other hand, is inactive, unsociable, careful, controlled, inhibited, reflective and responsible. In reality, few people are purely extrovert or purely introvert, or purely stable or purely unstable. Personality testing shows that people usually possess a combination or traits that are more or less extrovert, and more or less stable. Table 4.1 describes the four extremes.

Whilst this trait theory approach is attractive because it is easy to understand and seems to reflect 'common sense' – the ancient Greeks identified four similar types of personality – there are several problems with 'typing' personalities in this way:

- it leads to the tendency to assume too much about a person and that people will always react in the predicted way
- it leads to the tendency to assume that these types are unchanging over time
- it takes little account of cultural or other environmental influences on temperament.

That said, the traits identified can be useful in building a more detailed picture of individual behaviour, or the type of person needed for a particular role or job.

The stable extrovert	Tends to be warm hearted and outward going, demonstrates a temperament that is sociable, outgoing, talkative, responsive, easy-going, lively and carefree, with leadership qualities
The stable introvert	Tends to be listless and slow, demonstrates a temperament that is calm, even tempered, reliable, controlled, peaceful, thoughtful, careful and passive
The unstable introvert	Tends to be more depressed and sad, demonstrates a temperament that is quiet, unsociable, reserved, pessimistic, sober, rigid, anxious and moody
The unstable extrovert	Tends to be easily angered and quick to react, demonstrates a temperament that is touchy, restless, aggressive, excitable, changeable, impulsive, optimistic and active

Table 4.1 Four extreme personality profiles

Active learning point

Using the seven dimensions of extroversion/introversion and the seven dimensions of stability/instability given in Figures 4.2 and 4.3, map the ideal personality traits of one *front of house* job (bar person or waiter) and one *back of house* job (cook or cellar worker).

Selecting traits for licensed retail jobs • • •

People drawn to work in the licensed retail industry tend to have more extrovert personalities. However, it would be a mistake for you to employ people who are extremely extrovert, as people registering a high extrovert score on all seven dimensions can cause problems. For all the obvious benefits to licensed retail businesses of people who are active, sociable, expressive and practical, individuals who are risk takers, impulsive and irresponsible may create problems.

Research on managers and trainee managers for the licensed retail business show that the overwhelming majority have learning style preferences that are Activist. That is, they enjoy learning best through a combination of experience and learning by doing. They like to learn from concrete situations, and do not find reflection and theorizing comes easily. This type of manager:

- puts a lot of energy into doing things, tries out new ideas, likes to get things completed, enjoys activity, likes the present and expresses feelings readily
- often acts without thinking, makes mistakes because of a lack of planning, may repeat mistakes, and can operate unpredictably and spread confusion.

It is essential that effective managers are reflective practitioners, and management development programmes both in industry and at university or college need to understand that the learning style preferences of licensed retail managers are based on their personality profiles. People with extrovert personalities who do things because they feel right are attracted to management careers in the licensed retail industry. Management development must work from these preferences by developing skills in reflection and theorizing.

Beliefs

Beliefs reflect what people 'know' about the world. Knowledge in this sense is not just a reflection of factual knowledge, although factual knowledge is a belief system. Beliefs may include:

- factual knowledge (e.g. water is made up of two atoms of hydrogen and one atom of oxygen)
- what a person desires to be true (e.g. my favourite football team will win the cup)
- how a person identifies him or herself in relation to others (political and religious beliefs play this role)
- knowledge that cannot be proved, but individuals accept as a matter of faith.

Beliefs and perceptions often interact. Perceptions are in part shaped by beliefs – people perceive things in line with their beliefs. Beliefs are also reinforced perceptions – individuals perceive things that they notice because of their beliefs.

An understanding that individuals, managers, employees and customers may have different beliefs is important to you as the unit manager because:

- the manager must be aware that differences in beliefs can be a source of tension and conflict
- differences in beliefs about dress, language and conduct etc. can cause offence
- managers must be sensitive to the beliefs of others and be aware that humour or ill-considered remarks can be offensive
- the manager must aim to establish a shared belief in the success of the unit and the standards needed, and that effective performance will be recognized.

Values

Values are what people want to be true, both in the long run and about themselves as individuals. There are two types of values:

1 End values – how things should be in the long run, e.g. a comfortable life, a sense of accomplishment, a world at peace, equality, wisdom, self-respect etc.
2 Instrumental values – people should conduct themselves, e.g. be broadminded, cheerful, helpful, obedient, polite, self-controlled.

Tests show that different individuals will rank these differently. Values tend to be bundled. People frequently express a view of what they consider to be important through their values. Some people give priorities to the state of the world, whilst others give priority to values about their relationships with others or how they themselves should be. In some aspects, values reflect tendencies towards extroversion and introversion.

In addition to these general values held by individuals, there are several different sets of assumptions that people make about the values and priorities of others.

Active learning point

Complete Exercise 4.1, which will help you to evaluate how you think about the values that people apply at work.

Exercise 4.1: Values at work • • •

From each of the pairs of statements listed below, select the statement that you most support.

1.1 People are mainly interested in money at work
1.2 The most important thing at work is money

2.1 People work best if there is a good team spirit
2.2 The best motivation is self-motivation

3.1 People like to be left alone to get on with the job
3.2 Feelings get in the way of doing a good job

4.1 People will value their self-interest above all else at work
4.2 People need a boss who is easy to get on with

5.1 The most important thing at work is your colleagues
5.2 What people most want from work is a chance to use their skills and abilities

6.1 The best motivation is self-motivation
6.2 People have to be controlled if they are to work well

7.1 Feelings get in the way of doing a good job
7.2 People are more influenced by their colleagues than their boss

8.1 People need a boss who is easy to get on with
8.2 An interesting job is the best guarantee of good work

9.1 What people most want from work is a chance to use their skills and abilities
9.2 People are mainly interested in money at work

10.1 People have to be controlled if they are to work well
10.2 People work best if there is a good team spirit

11.1 People are more influenced by their colleagues than their boss
11.2 People like to be left alone to get on with their job

12.1 An interesting job is the best guarantee of good work
12.2 People calculate their self-interest above all else at work.

The exercise consists of statements reflecting common stereotypes at work:

1 The rational economic stereotype
2 The social stereotype
3 The self-fulfilment stereotype.

Each statement is paired with a statement from one of the other stereotypes, and the key given later shows how to work out the score.

As a manager, you may have developed fixed ways of thinking about people and the things they value at work. These stereotypes can cause difficulties when dealing with employees, because you see what you expect to see rather than what is actually there. Chapter 3 identified a widespread tendency for those in higher positions to consider the motives of people in lower positions as being more concerned with material benefits than their own. Using this model, they tend to apply the rational economic stereotype when thinking about the values and priorities of subordinates. The stereotype favoured by an individual manager reflects much about the manager's own values, and less about the values of employees. To understand people at work it is necessary to:

- accept that people are different to ourselves
- treat people as individuals and expect the unexpected, and
- use frameworks and theories as a guide, not as blinkers.

The rational economic stereotype views people as chiefly motivated by economic incentives and material rewards. The assumption is that people's values prioritize material and personal benefits. Dominant values prioritize ambition, achieving a comfortable life and obedience for example. Managers holding this view believe that people will act to maximize these material rewards in preference to any other benefits from work. Frequently this set of manager values prioritizes output efficiency, monetary incentives, competition between individuals and the close supervision of employees, together with a directive style of management.

The social stereotype views people as being motivated by social needs and being part of a group. It is assumed that values focusing on the relationships with others are most important to individuals at work. It is assumed that group membership gives individuals a sense of identity and support. Dominant values will prioritize true friendship, social recognition and helpfulness. Managers holding this view place emphasis on the human relationships at work, and provide opportunities for individuals to identify with group needs through team membership, department and organization identity.

The self-fulfilment stereotype views people as being motivated by a sense of accomplishment, and the need to develop abilities and skills. It is assumed that dominant values give priority to the quality of working life and opportunities for personal growth and development. Dominant values will prioritize a sense of accomplishment, self-respect and self-control. Managers holding this view place emphasis on job design, employee satisfaction, and autonomy. The focus is on delegation and participative management, training and employee development.

The scoring key for Exercise 4.1

The twelve sets of paired questions match a statement of one stereotype with another. By working through your preferences, it is possible to detect your ways of generalizing about people. In Table 4.2, put a circle round each statement you have selected for each of the twelve pairs – it will fall under one of the three columns that identify the stereotype. For example, if you have indicated a preference for statement 2 in the first pair, put a circle round 2 opposite pair 1. This will be in the social column.

Hospitality, Leisure & Tourism Series

Statement pair	Rational economic	Social	Self-fulfilment
1	1	2	
2		1	2
3	2		1
4	1	2	
5		1	2
6	2		1
7	1	2	
8		1	2
9	2		1
10	1	2	
11		1	2
12	2		1
Totals			

Table 4.2 Scoring key for Exercise 4.1

When you have indicated all the preferred statements, count the circled numbers in each column. There are twelve pairs of statements reflecting three stereotypes, so the maximum score for any one column is eight. A score of more than four indicates that you use this stereotype as a way of generalizing about people.

If your scores are fairly even on all three stereotypes, it may mean that you do not hold any of these stereotypes. If you score six or more on one and two or less on the others, you may think about people stereotypically.

The key problem with stereotypes is that they are restrictive and assume that people are 'all the same'. Managers who hold stereotypes believe them and act as though they are true, but they may not apply to some people and only partially apply to others. To be an effective manager and host to customers you should recognize:

- that people are complex and highly variable, and change as a result of experiences
- that it is a mistake to oversimplify people's actions and motives.

Attitudes

Attitudes are expressions of what people feel about things that they believe exist. These are usually expressed as statements of like or dislike and agreement or disagreement with statements. Attitudes are frequently expressions of inner emotional states of fear or envy, as well as expressions of values and beliefs. Although people do not always act in line with their attitudes, many organizations use surveys to gauge both employee and customer satisfaction.

Active learning point

Exercise 4.2 is an employee satisfaction survey, which explores employee attitudes regarding a number of dimensions including the employment terms, relations with management, the nature of the job and relations with co-workers. It will help you to evaluate employee satisfaction. Either complete the tasks yourself, of give it to a colleague or to your subordinates.

Exercise 4.2: Employee attitudes • • •

The questions in this employer survey aim to measure employee satisfaction. Please answer the following questions as frankly as possible. You may tick *one* of seven answers to each question:

- I'm extremely dissatisfied (Ex dis)
- I'm very dissatisfied (V dis)
- I'm moderately dissatisfied (Mod dis)
- I'm not sure (Not sure)
- I'm moderately satisfied (Mod sat)
- I'm very satisfied (V sat)
- I'm extremely satisfied (Ex sat).

	Ex dis	V dis	Mod dis	Not sure	Mod sat	V sat	Ex sat
1 The physical working conditions	☐	☐	☐	☐	☐	☐	☐
2 The freedom to choose your own working method	☐	☐	☐	☐	☐	☐	☐
3 Your fellow workers	☐	☐	☐	☐	☐	☐	☐
4 The recognition you get for good work	☐	☐	☐	☐	☐	☐	☐
5 Your immediate boss	☐	☐	☐	☐	☐	☐	☐
6 The amount of responsibility you are given	☐	☐	☐	☐	☐	☐	☐
7 Your rate of pay	☐	☐	☐	☐	☐	☐	☐
8 Your chances to use your abilities	☐	☐	☐	☐	☐	☐	☐
9 Industrial relations between management and workers	☐	☐	☐	☐	☐	☐	☐
10 Your chance for promotion	☐	☐	☐	☐	☐	☐	☐
11 The way the unit is managed	☐	☐	☐	☐	☐	☐	☐
12 The attention paid to suggestions you make	☐	☐	☐	☐	☐	☐	☐
13 Your hours of work	☐	☐	☐	☐	☐	☐	☐
14 The amount of variety in your job	☐	☐	☐	☐	☐	☐	☐
15 Your job security	☐	☐	☐	☐	☐	☐	☐

Are you a full-time employee, part-time employee or casual employee?
Are you male or female?
What is your job title?

Reading the survey

As stated earlier, the link between attitudes and behaviour is not absolute, but the employee satisfaction survey makes an attempt to identify what employees feel about work so that sources of dissatisfaction can be understood and acted upon. In addition, there is assumed to be a link between employee satisfaction and:

- customer satisfaction
- service quality
- productivity and up-selling
- staff turnover and retention.

In Exercise 4.2, what (if any) were the common causes of satisfaction and dissatisfaction? What actions might you, as the manager responsible, take to overcome dissatisfaction?

Perceptions

Active learning point

Look at the pictures in Exercise 4.3 and write down what you see, then complete the exercise.

Exercise 4.3: Perceptions ● ● ●

Interpreting information

Look at Figure 4.4 and say what you see. Try it with a colleague or group of colleagues.

Can you see the partial face of the bearded man? If not, look at the upper edge of the picture and imagine the picture of a bearded man with long hair, where the photograph cuts off the top of the head above the eyebrows. If you still can't see it, ask a colleague who can see it to explain it to you.

Figure 4.4 Interpreting information

Different perceptions

Look at Figure 4.5 with a colleague or group of colleagues, and say what you see. Do you all see the same image?

Figure 4.5 Differing perceptions

Do you see the picture of an old woman? Do you see the picture of the young woman? Do you see both? Keep looking at the picture until you can see both a young woman and an old woman. If you have difficulty, pair up with a colleague who can see the image that you cannot see.

Seeing things in context

Look at Figure 4.6.

Figure 4.6 Seeing things in context

Which is the largest of the three figures – is it the one on the right, the one on the left or the one in the centre? They are in fact all the same size. Take a ruler and measure them. The narrowing lines make it look as though the figure on the right is larger than the figure on the left. The context in which the image is set influences how people see the image.

Say what you see

Look at Figure 4.7 for ten seconds, then cover the book with a piece of paper and write down what you can remember.

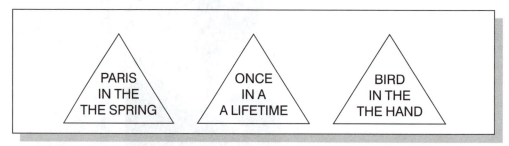

Figure 4.7 Say what you see

Did you write down: PARIS IN THE SPRING, ONCE IN A LIFETIME, BIRD IN THE HAND? If so, look again. What you should have written is: PARIS IN THE THE SPRING, ONCE IN A A LIFETIME, BIRD IN THE THE HAND. Most people look at these three triangles and see what they expect to see. They do not see the extra 'THE' or 'A'.

Observations • • •

Consideration of Exercise 4.3 establishes some useful points about human perception:

1 People interpret information and give it meaning
2 Different people may perceive the same things differently
3 The context influences the way people perceive things
4 Prior knowledge and experience influence perceptions
5 In some cases, perceptions are distorted by expectations.

Although the examples used are all based on visual perception, these general observations may be applied to the way people perceive through all the senses. In fact, a high proportion of human perception is shaped via the visual sense.

As a bar, pub or restaurant manager you need to understand these influences of perception, because customers, staff and even managers are all subject to their influences, and conflicts of perception are at the heart of many business problems.

Customers have different perceptions of service quality than managers and staff. Similarly, employees may perceive their relationship with managers differently, and there may even be differences amongst the employees.

As we have already seen, stereotyping is a common problem in human interactions. People expect people to act in a predetermined manner, and interpretation of their actions more often than not distorts perceptions to confirm the prejudgement. Managers need to understand their own predispositions that might end in a self-fulfilling outcome. For example, a number of the activities in this and earlier chapters show that some managers have a view that employees cannot be trusted. Often they set up control systems that over-control them and produce situations that fulfil their non-trusting prediction.

Active learning point

Complete the table in Exercise 4.4, describing yourself to someone you have just met.

Exercise 4.4: The social individual ● ● ●

In the table below, write down fifteen words you might use to describe yourself to someone you have just met.

Descriptor	Type	
	Group	Other
1		
2		
3		
4		
5		
6		
7		
8		
9		
10		
11		
12		
13		
14		
15		

Typically, most people cannot describe themselves without making reference to some social groupings that give them a sense of identity – nationality, regional origin, religion, political party, social class, occupation, family relationships, soccer club supporter, etc. How many of these words have you used to describe yourself?

Individuals in groups

Group membership, even when people cannot know all the other members, helps individuals to define who they are and, also importantly, who they are not. These labels shape behaviour and expectations, helping to establish codes of expected actions and beliefs.

Individuals belong to two types of groups. Secondary groups are groups to which people belong, or to which people affiliate, where the members are not known to each other. In other words, a person may declare that he or she belongs to a national group, say English, without knowing all the other people who make up the nation – the English. Yet membership of this group can result in all sorts of positive and negative behaviour – supporting the football team, conflict with supporters of other teams etc.

Individuals also belong to primary groups. These are small groups, usually not much larger than ten members, where all the members are known to each other. Typically, families and work groups are primary groups. In a formal way, the use of team working and autonomous work groups recognizes these social dynamics, but even in situations where teams and group membership are not part of the management structure, group membership will influence behaviour at work. Group membership influences include:

- provision of a sense of identity
- development of a structure, including roles such as leader
- establishment of norms and expectations about how members behave, and pressure for individuals to conform to the norms
- provision of a sense of security
- improvement of collective output through mutual support
- provision of a means of communication and development of shared knowledge
- unification of the group.

Group influences on individual behaviour can also result in conflict with other groups, and members will defend others from threats outside the group.

The potential benefits of group membership in providing a self-disciplining, mutually supportive framework for guiding individual performance are at the root of the use of work teams, autonomous and semi-autonomous work groups. Yet the social psychology of group influences means that all the positive and negative influences on behaviour are to be found in the workplace, and as a manager you must be aware of their influence.

Group membership amongst customers also has all these features. The positive benefit is that being part of a group helps to support individuals, and gives a sense of belonging together with building loyalty to the pub. On the other hand, conflict between groups can be a negative aspect – say between 'regulars' in different bars. However, properly understood and managed group membership is a positive feature of customer relationships.

Individual employees are members of the formal group structure that the organization sets up:

- departments within the unit
- occupational and job role differences
- different unit membership
- bars, pubs and restaurants in different brands within the group
- bars, pubs and restaurants in other companies; etc.

Managers can use these group memberships within the formal structure to develop a sense of common purpose and shared expectations. Thus creating a sense of 'us and them' can assist you in giving bar, pub and restaurant staff a sense of common purpose to see the unit succeed in comparison to other units in the group, or competitors. At the same time the formal structure can create a climate in which people in different departments are in conflict with each other, and form a barrier to effective operation. The traditional conflicts between kitchen and restaurant are a good example of the negative effects excessive conflict can produce.

Individuals simultaneously belong to informal groupings that are a natural consequence of people working together. These too can have both positive and negative effects. Informal group membership can provide mechanisms for mutual support and shared purpose, which lead to high morale and commitment, but can also result in norms of behaviour that restrict production and have a conflicting stance with management. Informal leaders can perform an important role in challenging you, the unit manager, as the formal leader.

To manage the unit effectively, you have to recognize the influences of informal group membership on individual behaviour and attempt to work with informal leaders. As was stated in the earlier chapters, team working and autonomous work group membership provide techniques. At the very least you can:

- work with group members to reduce staff turnover
- use groups to assist in problem solving
- encourage a sense of common purpose and shared objectives
- recognize and incorporate unofficial leaders from their groups
- aim incentives at group performance
- provide opportunities for effective group working to be established.

Influencing others

Effective unit managers need to be able to exercise a range of skills, attitudes, energies and behaviours to persuade others to act in a desired way. This book has shown that well-motivated and committed employees are essential to high quality licensed retail business performance. Traditional techniques of command and control and authoritarian management styles are not compatible with the development of employee motivation and commitment. Managing more involved and participative employees requires persuasion rather than instruction.

You need to exercise personal power that goes beyond structural power and even expertise. Personal power is used to influence people and actions. It is used to work through other people. The positive use of power aims to empower others and allows you to work through them without diminishing their personal power.

By empowering others, more committed employees deliver better quality decisions in an environment of mutual trust. It produces a win–win situation in which all benefit.

Having personal power therefore involves the exercise of skills in influencing others. Exercising personal power is not about bullying or threatening others through displays of aggression and conflict. Influencing others is the process of modifying, affecting or changing another person's thoughts, attitudes or behaviour. There are a number of ways that this can be achieved, though this section deals with being assertive. Assertiveness training is about empowering people and making them more self-confident.

Assertiveness

Assertiveness involves standing up for yourself without damaging other people's rights. It is about being aware of the rights and dignity of others without giving up your own rights and dignity. The approach requires that individuals develop an appreciation of each other's views and feelings without being either aggressive or non-assertive – in other words, standing up for your rights but not at the expense of others, and not allowing other people's rights to be expressed at your expense.

Suppose a work colleague keeps giving you some of their work to do. You decide that you do not wish to do it any more. The person has just asked to you to take on some more. You make one of the following responses:

- 'No Joe, I'm not going to do any more of your work, I've decided that it's not right for either of us for me to do both my work and yours' (*assertive*).
- 'Forget it, it's about time that you did it; you treat me like your slave. You're an inconsiderate s.o.b.' (*aggressive*).
- 'I'm rather busy, but if you can't get it done I think I can help you' (*non-assertive*)

Active learning point

Complete the questionnaire in Exercise 4.5. Each question has three answers reflecting assertive, aggressive and non-assertive responses. Can you identify which is which?

Exercise 4.5: Recognizing assertive, aggressive and non-assertive behaviour ● ● ●

Identify the assertive, aggressive and non-assertive responses to each of the following situations.

1 You are working out the unit's weekly returns and a unit manager colleague telephones to talk to you about next week's unit managers' meeting. You would prefer to finish what you are doing:
  - 'I'm happy to talk about the meeting, but I'm busy right now. I'll ring you back this afternoon.'
  - 'Look, I'm busy. It's always the same; as soon as I start to work on the figures I can't get on because of pointless interruptions.'
  - 'Well I'm busy, but I guess I can find time if you want to speak to me right now.'
2 Your area manager has criticized one of your staff. You feel the criticism is unjustified:
  - 'I feel your criticism is unfair. He is not like that at all.'
  - 'I'm the manager and know this person best. You should allow me to deal with my own people in my own way.'
  - 'I hadn't thought about it but I suppose you are right.'

3 A customer arrives late for a table booking. You are concerned that customers who are booked in later may be delayed:
- 'We have been holding the table for you. I would have appreciated it if you had telephoned'.
- 'Shall I show you straight to the table?'
- 'There are other customers waiting. This is very inconsiderate.'

4 A colleague compliments you on your report to the unit managers' meetings:
- 'Thank you.'
- 'It's nothing really.'
- 'What do you expect from me, I only do excellent work.'

5 One of your staff deserves a low appraisal rating because of continued poor timekeeping – a matter that has been raised before:
- 'Look, the company expects you to be here on time. It's very difficult for me. What problems have you got that cause you to be late?'
- 'I'm disappointed that your timekeeping has not improved since the last appraisal. Let's try to get things sorted out once and for all this time, so you can do well.'
- 'You never learn, do you? It's time to get yourself sorted out. You are for the high jump this time.'

Key

1 Assertive, aggressive, non-assertive
2 Assertive, aggressive, non-assertive
3 Non-assertive, assertive, aggressive
4 Assertive, non-assertive, aggressive
5 Non-assertive, assertive, aggressive.

The assertive approach provides a very powerful way of developing influencing skills and avoiding others' over-aggressive behaviour, or being treated as a bit of a doormat.

A common manager error is to assume wrongly that the only way to get the best of staff is to treat them in an aggressive way. The assumption is based on the misguided notion that discipline can only be imposed. Adopting an assertive approach is assumed to be a sign of weakness. However, nothing could be further from the truth. Assertive approaches help to share understanding, develop mutual respect and build self-discipline.

Similarly, some individuals feel that non-assertive behaviour creates harmony, because displaying disagreement results in conflict and disharmony. Again this is a mistake, because avoiding conflict does not remove the differences in perceptions or interests. Conflict is frequently based on different perceptions and on mis-understandings. In many cases, conflicts reflect irreconcilable differences of interest. In these cases, recognizing and managing the differences in an atmosphere of mutual respect is essential.

Dealing with conflict

Conflict occurs when the concerns of two or more people are incompatible. Conflict is an inevitable feature of licensed retail service organization life. Fundamentally, the relationships between organization and employees, between employees and customers, and between customers and the organization are all bound to result in different parties having needs that are in conflict with others. Even though customers, employees and the organization's management may work together in harmony for much of the time, deep-seated conflicts of interest are always under the surface. For example:

- in the employee/company dimension, wages for employees are costs for the organization
- in the employee/customer dimension, the customer's service needs represent work and effort for employees
- in the customer/company dimension, customer service satisfaction is sales revenue for the organization.

Figure 4.8 shows the conflicts of control between the three key parties to the service encounter. On another level, personal conflicts also occur between employees, between managers, and between customers. These conflicts, although not a fundamental part of the relationship, are bound to be a natural part of licensed retail organizations as a consequence of differences in personalities, beliefs, values attitudes, and perceptions amongst the people in involved.

Much licensed retail organizational rhetoric can be unhelpful because it suggests a harmony of interests where none exists. Employees are not internal customers, they are employees who work for wages; and the organization will only want to delight external customers so long as there is a profit to be turned.

If conflict is a natural and consequential part of organization life, it is not always a bad thing. Conflict can produce creative tensions that add to the vigour of

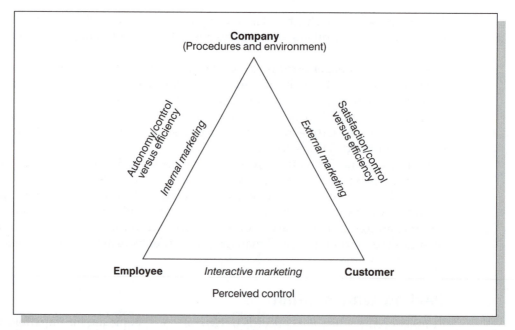

Figure 4.8 Control conflicts in the service encounter

decision-making and problem solving. By recognizing the natural tensions and conflicts that stem from the very nature of organizational life, as a manager you can use these conflicts to aid improved performance. At the very least, you can recognize the potential harmful effects and understand how conflict occurs. The following sections deal with conflict and how it can be managed (Figure 4.9).

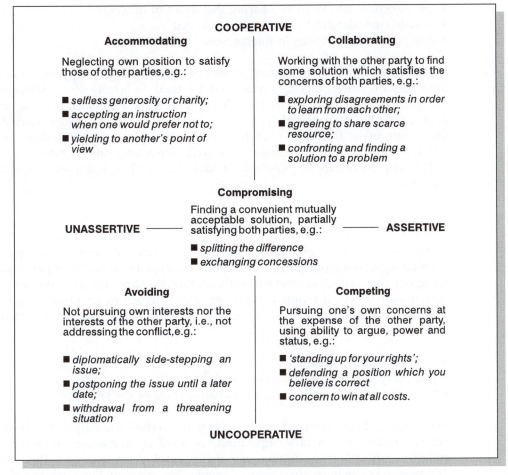

COOPERATIVE

Accommodating

Neglecting own position to satisfy those of other parties, e.g.:

- *selfless generosity or charity;*
- *accepting an instruction when one would prefer not to;*
- *yielding to another's point of view*

Collaborating

Working with the other party to find some solution which satisfies the concerns of both parties, e.g.:

- *exploring disagreements in order to learn from each other;*
- *agreeing to share scarce resource;*
- *confronting and finding a solution to a problem*

Compromising

UNASSERTIVE ———— Finding a convenient mutually acceptable solution, partially satisfying both parties, e.g.: ———— **ASSERTIVE**

- *splitting the difference*
- *exchanging concessions*

Avoiding

Not pursuing own interests nor the interests of the other party, i.e., not addressing the conflict, e.g.:

- *diplomatically side-stepping an issue;*
- *postponing the issue until a later date;*
- *withdrawal from a threatening situation*

Competing

Pursuing one's own concerns at the expense of the other party, using ability to argue, power and status, e.g.:

- *'standing up for your rights';*
- *defending a position which you believe is correct*
- *concern to win at all costs.*

UNCOOPERATIVE

Figure 4.9 Strategies for handling conflict

The means of managing the conflict can be mapped against two sets of issues – the extent that the manager is being assertive or non-assertive, and the extent that the manager is attempting to be cooperative or non-cooperative. The interplay of these two factors suggests that there are five potential approaches to dealing with conflict and conflictual situations. Without consideration and thought, the approach will be largely driven by the manager's personality, values, beliefs, attitudes and perceptions. In each case there may be situations where the approach is appropriate, and in all cases managers must be aware of the consequences of their approach – for example, in conflictual situations each party will react to the actions of the other party.

Collaborating ● ● ●

Collaborating is based on being assertive and cooperative. The approach recognizes the conflicts of interests, and considers an approach that is mutually acceptable to both parties by bringing together their diverse interests. Collaboration is used when:

- both sets of concerns are too important to be compromised
- the objective is to learn by sharing the views of others
- to gain commitment to the decision reached
- dealing with difficulties in interpersonal relationships.

Several techniques for managing employees in more a participative style provide examples of where this approach can be used to great effect. Managers who recognize the conflictual basis to the employment relationship know that this approach will not necessarily resolve the conflict, but it will ensure mutual respect and commitment to common goals. You should explore the possibilities of a win–win outcome. However, decisions may well take a long time to make.

The approach can be applied in dealings with employees, suppliers and customers.

Competing ● ● ●

Competing is based on being assertive and uncooperative. The approach is essentially pursuing one party's interests at the expense of the other party. Managers recognize the conflict of interests with employees, suppliers or customers, and are determined to get the upper hand. At root, the approach involves a win–lose outcome – one party wins at the expense of the other. Competing often occurs when:

- a quick decision is vital
- one party is convinced he or she is right
- the other party is attempting to take advantage of the situation.

Many pub and bar managers operate this way in relation to employees. In situations where employees have little opportunity to stand up to managerial power with the collective power of trade union membership, employee resistance to this managerial approach takes an individual form – absenteeism, poor quality work and high levels of staff turnover are consequences.

Avoiding ● ● ●

Avoiding is based on a non-assertive and uncooperative approach. Generally this approach has negative consequences because it avoids conflict and the problem remains unresolved. It is a lose–lose position. However, there may be times when this is appropriate when dealing with customers who are making complaints that are in your judgement unjustified. In other cases it might be appropriate:

- when other issues are more urgent
- in situations where there is a limited chance of a satisfactory outcome

- where the damage of conflict outweighs the benefits of its resolution
- to resolve an immediate tense situation
- if the conflict can be resolved later
- if the issue is a symptom of a bigger problem.

Giving customers the benefit of the doubt and avoiding conflict has the advantage of building customer satisfaction, but there is the risk that some customers may use the knowledge to make unjustified complaints as a way of getting discounts, etc. Similarly, avoiding conflicts with employees can have negative impacts when the problem remains unresolved, or where the employee gets the impression that 'anything goes'.

Accommodating • • •

Accommodating is based on an approach that is unassertive and cooperative. This approach recognizes that the other party has a justifiable point and that the individual should concede to it. It is a lose–win position. Dealing with a justified customer complaint and over-compensating for the problem caused is an example. This approach has particular relevance in the following circumstances:

- when one party realizes he or she is wrong
- when the issue is more important to the other party than to you
- when continued conflict would damage your cause
- to avoid disruption
- to develop subordinates by allowing them to learn from their mistakes.

This approach may also apply when dealing with employees, particularly where you recognize the justice of the employees' cause. The approach can, however, cause negative effects if you concede just to keep the operation running, and the problem remains unresolved, or if employees and customers gain the impression that the concession is a 'right' for all times.

Compromising • • •

Compromising involves moderate elements of assertion and cooperation. The approach accepts that the two parties have mutually powerful but different points of view, or that continued conflict is not worth the effort. It is a half-win–half-win position. It may involve negotiations with employees in industrial relations issues, or suppliers in disputes over supplies and payment. It is likely to be applied when:

- the cost of the potential disruption is greater than the point to be won
- there are two mutually powerful parties committed to mutually exclusive goals
- it is necessary to achieve temporary settlements of complex issues
- time pressures require an expedient solution to the problem
- a fall back position is needed when collaboration or competition fail.

Again the key danger is that conflicts may remain unresolved as the parties reach a settlement which they 'can both live with'. At heart, however, both feel they have conceded more than they wanted, and this stores up resentment for the future.

Key skills

The model described above gives a useful insight into conflict and how it can be handled. At the end of the day, there are only a limited number of outcomes from conflict between parties. These five positions highlight each possible outcome and the relationship of the parties. The key skills in resolving conflict are effective influencing through assertiveness and active listening. Being able to recognize the other person's point of view and ensuring that he or she understands your position is essential.

Motivating people at work

Unit managers in licensed retail businesses depend on employees to deliver the defined service standards that represent the brand. Working to procedures, not cutting corners, and working 'one best way' are common requirements of work in branded services. In addition, effective service is more than behaving like a pre-programmed robot. Customers expect to be treated like individuals; they want to feel the person serving them is genuinely concerned about their needs. Often it is said that employees have to supply emotional labour – to feel for the customer. Furthermore, licensed retail employees are frequently expected to 'up-sell' and persuade customers to buy more than they intended. Thus employees are expected to:

- work to a routine
- delight customers by treating them as individuals
- feel committed to customers
- accept the commercial objectives of the organization
- manage all these conflicting pressures.

Employee motivation and commitment are essential for the success of the pub, bar or restaurant, yet are often left to a haphazard process. The following suggests some ways of building your employees' motivation and commitment.

Understanding individuals

As we have seen, individuals differ in their personalities, beliefs, values, attitudes and perceptions at work. They are also different in their orientations to work. For some people work is a major aspect of their life that provides social benefits and a sense of identity. In other cases, work is a means to an end – they work because they have to, and they gain social benefits and a sense of identity through other aspects of their lives. Many licensed retail organizations structure their motivation strategies on the stereotypes introduced earlier:

- rational – economic
- social
- self-actualizing.

The more appropriate model is complex people – thus the same individual may well prioritize different rewards from work at different times, and may well want to satisfy all sets of needs at one time. The acceptance of the complex person model is important because it:

- prevents you from making wrong assumptions about people and their motives
- allows managers to be more responsive to employee needs
- recognizes that people may change over time.

Therefore, to understand people at work it is necessary to consider the individual and the total situation at work. Herzberg's dual factor theory is a useful model for understanding people and the factors likely to shape their motivations.

Satisfiers and dissatisfiers

Put simply, people experience an array of emotions at work. Some things make them feel happy and motivated and others make them disgruntled and de-motivated. There are expectations about work that employees take for granted as returns for their labour, and these include:

- physical working conditions
- company policy and administration
- security
- relations with supervisor
- salary and material rewards.

If these provisions are not appropriate, employees become dissatisfied. They may well constitute 'push factors' (Chapter 5) that cause employees to leave the firm. However, unexpectedly good provision will not cause motivation – thus an increase in pay may lead to increased effort, but this will only last for a short period.

It is possible for employees to experience an absence of dissatisfaction without being motivated.

Motivators are aspects of the work that make the individual feel better – the intrinsic factors discussed in Chapter 3. They arise from the way the job is designed and, most importantly, how they are treated as employees, and include:

- developing a sense of achievement
- recognition for work done
- the nature of the work itself
- developing a sense of responsibility
- the potential for advancement.

Employees who experience these outcomes from work are more likely to be motivated by their work experience. They make the extra effort, and actively engage with the job and the objectives set.

Motivators create good feelings and increase the will to work well.

Money as motivator

Using the rational-economic stereotype, many firms consider that financial incentives are a powerful inducement to work well. Tips from customers and commission on sales are used to stimulate workers in licensed retail organizations. In some cases, the reward package is made up of a low basic wage, commission on sales, and tips from customers. Clearly these reward schemes are intended to generate sales and customer satisfaction. In many ways, they can be effective because:

- financial rewards are linked to achievements
- they focus the employee on the desired objective
- they create an interest in the success of the business
- they encourage an entrepreneurial approach in staff
- they seem like a fairer reward for effort.

The problem is that they can generate negative effects as people focus more on doing whatever will maximize the financial reward, at the expense of other objectives. Tips, for example, put the employee in the position of having to work for two bosses – the organization and the customer. Sometimes the employee does things against company policy to maximize the tip. Commission based on sales can also have negative consequences if employees are overly pushy and offend customers. In both cases, competition for the highest tipping customers or the busiest stations in the restaurant can create harmful competition between employees.

Conclusion

This chapter has provided some tools for thinking about the people who are the employees and customers of licensed retail businesses. It is important in your role as manager to recognize that employees and customers are complex beings. These models are a useful starting point, and people are rarely consistently one thing or another.

Individuals differ in their personalities across an array of dimensions along degrees of extroversion/introversion and stability/instability. Even in these measures, individuals may be more prone to be on one dimension than others, but are rarely extreme extroverts or extreme introverts. Employee recruitment needs to take account of these factors. On another level, people are different in their beliefs, values and attitudes, as well as having different perceptions of similar things. Differences in employee, manager and customer perceptions can cause difficulties when expectations clash.

In addition to understanding employees as individuals, they also form informal groups in the workplace. The groups to which individuals belong influence individual behaviour. Earlier chapters have highlighted the use of group membership as a management device for influencing individual performance; however, informal group memberships are also important because of their impact on employee morale and behaviour.

As the unit manager, you have to be able to exercise personal power and influence others. Understanding assertiveness, aggression and non-assertiveness provides you with some valuable tools for reducing disagreement and for winning support. In particular, the impact on conflict resolution is valuable. Unit managers have to deal with conflicts on a number of levels and dimensions. Many of the relationships between customers, the organization and the employees are based on fundamental conflicts of interest. Coming up with approaches that minimize the negative effects of conflict is essential.

Finally, you need to motivate employees to work well. Understanding the motives and drives of the employees and their individual differences is an important starting point. In addition, employees have expectations about how they are to be treated that if not met will create dissatisfaction. More importantly, they have an array of needs that you can satisfy and which will lead to feelings of harmony and well-being.

Reflective practice

1 Using a bar, pub or restaurant known to you, devise a personality profile of a manager capable of running the unit.
2 How does an understanding of individual differences assist the licensed retail manager in dealings with employees and customers?
3 Show how an understanding of the influences of group membership on individual behaviour enables a bar, pub or restaurant manager to be more effective.
4 Using a manager known to you, discuss critically the main strategies for influencing people that are used.
5 Reflecting on a unit known to you, identify conflicts that occur in the work situation and show how you would resolve them.

Further reading

Biddle, D. and Evenden, R. (1993). *Human Aspects of Management*. Institute of Personnel and Development, London.
Mullins, L. J. (1995). *Hospitality Management: A Human Resource Approach*. Pitman.

CHAPTER 5

Now you see them, now you don't

After working through this chapter, you should be able to:

- identify the causes of staff turnover
- calculate staff turnover and retention using a range of techniques
- estimate the costs of staff turnover
- suggest ways of reducing labour turnover in given situations.

Staff retention and turnover in licensed retailing

Staff turnover continues to be a contentious issue in the licensed retail industry. Many managers see the process of staff leaving and being replaced as a natural and inevitable feature of industry employment. Providing they can continue to recruit people when needed, this is 'just the way things are'. It is not unusual, for example, for many organizations to keep no record of the number of staff who leave and are replaced, and it is rarer still for firms to cost staff turnover, or value the benefits of staff retention.

Some managers even consider staff turnover to be a good thing because it allows them to manipulate the size of their work force without resistance from employees and the need to make compulsory redundancies when trading conditions worsen. Increasingly, however, managers in large licensed retail organizations recognize labour turnover as both being costly and creating operational difficulties, particularly when trained or frontline staff leave the business. Consequently many now have detailed records of the levels of labour turnover, although few account for it when measuring unit performance. This chapter argues that staff turnover represents a considerable additional cost to the business. Unit managers can reduce the number of people who leave the organization, but fundamentally the organization needs to understand the levels, the causes and the costs of staff turnover, and the value of staff retention.

Causes and types of staff turnover

Staff turnover is best understood as the movement of labour out of and into a working organization. As indicated earlier, some practitioners and academics see positive benefits to *controlled* staff turnover:

- if poor performers are the ones to leave the organization
- if new employees bring new skills and ideas
- if the organization is refreshed by change brought in by new staff.

However, all too often it is the better staff that leave, and staff turnover is uncontrolled. In these circumstance staff turnover can:

- wreck planning
- have a disastrous effect on staff morale
- represent a considerable extra cost to the business
- reduce service quality
- cause customer dissatisfaction.

Active learning point

Using an organization known to you, list the benefits and problems caused by staff turnover.

Benefits of staff leaving	Problems caused by staff leaving
1	1
2	2
3	3
4	4
5	5
6	6
7	7
8	8
9	9
10	10

Frequently a vicious cycle is established where high staff turnover results in hurried recruitment and selection, poor induction, limited training, supervisory and management pressure and low morale, leading to further instability and labour turnover. Figure 5.1 shows this vicious cycle, and represents the experiences of many branded licensed organizations.

Some departures from the organization are unavoidable, because this is, in many ways, an inevitable aspect of organizational life. Reasons for *unavoidable* staff turnover include:

- retirement
- illness
- death
- marriage
- pregnancy
- leaving the area
- in the case of students, returning to college or home.

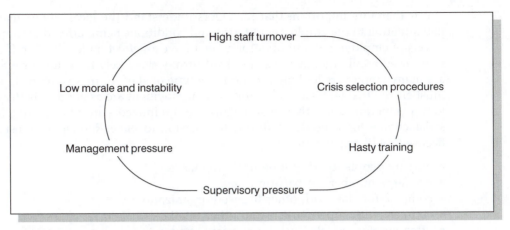

Figure 5.1 The vicious cycle of staff turnover

However, where labour turnover is high it is usually due to avoidable reasons that you, as a unit manager, can manage. Thus employee dissatisfaction with training and personal development, wage level, management styles and policies, colleagues, and overall job satisfaction are issues that you can attempt to match with employee expectations. Reasons for *avoidable* staff turnover include:

- dissatisfaction with wages
- the relationship with management
- lack of training
- work pace and stress
- relationships with other staff
- hours of work
- transport difficulties.

Frequently, no one single factor causes people voluntarily to leave an organization, and often their decision is shaped by both push and pull factors. Push factors are those issues that cause dissatisfaction with the current organization, and pull factors are the perceived benefits being offered by competing employers (Table 5.1).

Push factors	Pull factors
Discontent with leaders	More money
Poor image of the organization	Better hours
Poor terms and conditions	Permanent employment
Uneven work patterns	Alternative employment
Poor pay	Improved career prospects
Unsuitable hours of work	Improved training and development
Lack of autonomy	Empowerment

Table 5.1 Some push and pull factors in staff turnover

It is therefore important that managers understand the local labour market and pay attention to the employment terms and conditions being offered by other firms. Levels of employment and unemployment have an effect on levels of staff turnover in licensed retail organizations, and staff turnover is likely to be higher when there are many employers looking for the same type of staff. In these circumstances, you must ensure that terms and conditions of employment are as good or better than the local competitors, and that push factors are minimized – in other words, that staff satisfaction is high and the staff have few reasons to leave. Remember, most branded licensed retail organizations:

- employ people to do routine unskilled tasks
- use large numbers of part-time staff
- compete for staff with other licensed organizations
- compete with supermarkets and other retailers
- often employ people during unsociable hours
- recruit people from the local community.

Active learning point

Using a licensed retail unit known to you, identify the terms and conditions of employment that operate within the local labour market.

Terms and conditions	Unit	Local labour market	
		Minimum	Maximum
Hourly pay rates			
Average hours worked			
Full-time/part-time			
Other benefits			
Money/non-money			
Training given			
Part-time workers %			
Interesting/boring work			
Management/staff relations			
Employee satisfaction			
Levels of staff turnover			
Image of organization			
Travel arrangements			

Similarly, it is important to consider involuntary withdrawal from the firm as well as the voluntary cause suggested earlier (Table 5.2). Involuntary labour turnover

Voluntary	Involuntary
Another job	Conclusion of temporary employment
Return to college/school	Reduction in work force
Marriage	Poor performance
Medical reasons	Loss of licence
Relocation	Incapacity to do the job
Dissatisfaction with wages	Misconduct (absenteeism, lateness)
Dissatisfaction with work	Gross misconduct (dishonesty,
Dissatisfaction with conditions	disobedience, drinking, violence and
Resignation without notice	swearing)
Career advancement	
Personal development	

Table 5.2 Some voluntary and involuntary forms of staff turnover

occurs against the wishes of the individual employee. In some cases, perhaps where a fixed-term contract ends or due to a downturn in the business cycle, the turnover is understandable, but where misconduct, absenteeism or poor performance are concerned, you cannot absolve yourself of responsibility. Frequently, hurried and sloppy recruitment or poor training are important contributors to the cause of unacceptable employee behaviour.

As indicated earlier, many managers are unaware of the problem of staff turnover and adopt a fatalistic acceptance of people leaving the organization as a fact of licensed retail industry life. Providing it is possible to find enough people to fill vacant posts, managers frequently do not see high levels of labour turnover as a problem. In many cases they have no knowledge of whether the levels of turnover in their organization are high, low or average for the industry, and in some cases managers do not even keep records of how many staff leave and are replaced in any one trading year. This means that they have no means of monitoring trends or, most importantly of assessing the costs of staff turnover.

Counting the cost

Staff turnover represents both direct and indirect costs to the business (Table 5.3). In the case of direct costs, it is possible to calculate direct expenditure related to filling each vacancy. Advertising for replacements, recruitment agency fees, additional overtime payments, or payments to agency staff brought in to cover gaps, etc., are all examples of additional costs incurred when a job vacancy has to be filled. In addition, indirect costs can be identified; these are difficult to calculate physically, but nonetheless represent genuine costs to the business. Management time spent in all the stages of recruitment, selection, interviewing and induction could be spent in other ways. Similarly, lost training investment, the time taken for new recruits to match the job performance of the former employee, and lost business due to customer dissatisfaction all involve additional costs. In the pub and bar businesses in particular, regular customers like to be recognized and

Direct costs	Hidden costs
Advertising for replacements	Low investment in training
Management time spent recruiting, interviewing, selecting, inducting, training	Lost staff expertise
	Reduced service quality
Recruitment agency fees	Reduced productivity
Travel expenses for interviews	Increased wastage and costs
Postage and stationery	Customer dissatisfaction
Induction and orientation	Negative impact on remaining staff
Training	Opportunity cost of lost management time
Overtime cover	Uniforms
Agency staff cover	
Processing new recruit's documents	
Processing ex-employee's documents	

Table 5.3 Some direct and hidden costs of staff turnover

acknowledged by staff when they visit the establishment. This is difficult to deliver if there is a permanently high level of ever-changing staff.

The costs of staff departures can have very negative impacts on the business. However, there are different costs associated with replacement of different levels of staff. Figure 5.2 reproduces a graduated scale of different replacement costs through unskilled, craft and management positions. According to their calculations, the

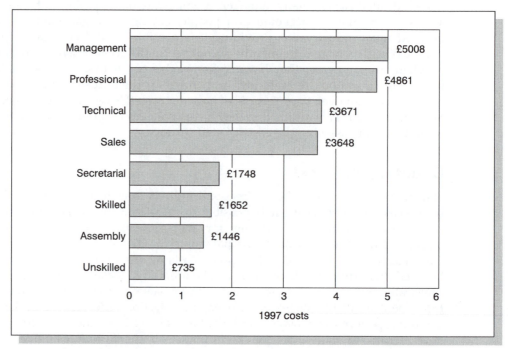

Figure 5.2 National estimates of staff turnover costs (£) (source: Institute of Personnel and Development, 2001)

Institute of Personnel and Development (1997) estimated that at the time of the study average replacement costs ranged from £735 per unskilled employee to £5008 for managerial and administrative posts.

These figures may appear to be high for licensed retail organizations, but recent research for the British Institute of Innkeeping showed that staff turnover in a major licensed retailer cost £500 per head in direct costs, and this did not take into account some of the impacts on customer satisfaction, service quality or employee satisfaction. Just taking these figures into account, staff turnover was costing the company in the region of £16 000 000 per year.

Whilst some costs will be incurred in replacing staff who have left the organization for unavoidable reasons, many of the costs of avoidable labour turnover represent, for most organizations, a hidden but real additional cost.

Box 5.1 provides an example.

Box 5.1   *The Bird in Hand*

The Bird in Hand is located in a popular attraction in Northern Britain. At the time of the study, the pub had been operated by Mr and Mrs Straw for six years. It contains nine double bedrooms, a public bar, a large lounge bar and a restaurant seating 100 people. The pub's most profitable business comes from the restaurant, which accounts for 50 per cent of revenue; accommodation represents 10 per cent, and wet sales account for the remainder.

The management of the pub is headed by the owners, who act as general manager (Mr Straw) and chief administrator (Mrs Straw). A pub manager and deputy manager, together with restaurant manager, bar manager and head chef, make up the remainder of the management team. Like many other pub businesses, the Bird in Hand uses numerical and functional flexibility in staff employment. With the exception of chefs, most staff are expected to work in different departments as business demands. There are twenty full-time staff, including the management team below the owners, and there are normally about forty part-time staff registered as being regularly employed by the pub. In some cases part-time staff work as many as thirty-five hours per week. Only the staff employed in cooking food are expected to be qualified in appropriate craft qualifications; all other staff receive fairly basic levels of training and most gain skills and job competence by actually doing the job.

Audited accounts for the period being studied showed the total sales revenue for the pub as just under £1 million per annum, and the profit and loss account registered a net profit of £295 000 (29.9 per cent). Salaries and wages accounted for £195 000 (20 per cent of sales revenue). On the face of it, the company was making a healthy operating profit, and Mr and Mrs Straw felt their management of the business was successful because they had 'turned the business round'.

Fifty-seven people left the employment of the pub during the twelve-month period of the study. With a nominal role of sixty employees, this represented a total labour turnover of 95 per cent. However, the rate for full-time employees was 130 per cent (twenty-six leavers) and for part-time employees was 77.5 per cent. Whilst a small minority of the leavers were voluntary, just under half of the terminations in employment were involuntary due to dismissal.

Typically for an organization experiencing high labour turnover, a large number leaving employment at the Bird in Hand had only been with the organization for a short period. Twenty-eight of the leavers left the organization within the first three months of their employment, and over 68 per cent of the employees leaving the pub did so within their first six months of employment. This pattern of labour turnover reveals a strong 'induction crisis', suggesting a problem in the recruitment, selection and induction of new recruits.

Overall estimates of the cost of replacement tend to underestimate rather than overestimate. The total cost of replacement of employees in the year of the study was £60 857, which represented an additional 31 per cent when compared to the total wages bill of £195 000. If this cost of £60 857 could be avoided, the net profit on the profit and loss account would be increased by 20 per cent. In addition, these figures take no account of the costs to the business of lost custom when ill-trained staff (or ever-changing staff) cause customer dissatisfaction, and nor do they account for extra wastage or theft when inappropriate recruitment takes place. These figures also fail to consider the opportunity cost to the managers' time – that is, what could the managers be achieving if they were not having to spend so much time recruiting new staff?

Measuring staff turnover

The measurement of staff turnover is an essential first step in both recognizing the nature of the problem and identifying the actions needed to reduce it. As with all other management information, the more detailed the information, the more you are able to understand the nature of the problem. There are a number of different measures that can be applied, and the following will provide a brief overview of some of the more widely used.

Staff turnover rate

This is the most commonly used statistic, and merely compares the number of leavers with the normal complement of staff. The rate is calculated as a percentage, so it is possible to express the rate using uneven bases. For example, it is possible to calculate the rate for:

- the national economy
- the industry
- different firms
- individual units in the brand
- departments
- different jobs
- full- and part-time staff.

The measure can be taken annually, quarterly or monthly. The staff turnover rate can be calculated to suit your need, but it is commonly calculated as a 'rolling twelve-month average'. The key to its attraction and wide use is that it is simple to calculate and it gives a broad indicator from which to compare time periods, jobs, departments, etc.

The formula is:

$$\frac{\text{Number of leavers}}{\text{Average number employed}} \times 100 = \text{Staff turnover rate (\%)}$$

For example, if forty staff have left and been replaced during the year, and the unit normally employs twenty-five staff, the calculation is:

$$(40/25) \times 100 = 160\%$$

As shown above, it is possible to build a more detailed picture by making the calculations for each job, for different departments, or different units in the firm. These calculations do help pinpoint some of the problems, but can produce a false impression. For example, the bald figure suggests that:

- all staff have left and been replaced and
- all jobs are equally affected.

It also gives no information about the time staff have stayed with the unit.

The staff retention rate

The staff retention rate allows you to calculate the number of jobs not affected by staff turnover. Thus it helps to feature the general extent, or limited nature, of the staff turnover occurring. The calculation is again concerned with a comparison with the normal establishment, but this time it takes account of the number of jobholders who can be described as long-term employees, typically those who have been with the firm for over one year.

To calculate the staff retention rate, the formula is;

$$\frac{\text{Number of long-term employees}}{\text{Average number employed}} \times 100 = \text{Staff retention rate (\%)}$$

In the above example, forty staff were replaced during the year, but fifteen of the twenty-five staff have been with the unit for over one year. The calculation is then:

$$(15/25) \times 100 = 60\%$$

In other words, although there is a general level of staff turnover in the unit of 160 per cent, the majority of staff are long-term employees – 60 per cent have been with the organization for over twelve months. The pattern appears to show that just ten jobs have accounted for forty staff leaving during the year. If this is evenly spread, the ten jobs each have four new members of staff who have joined and left over the year.

Clearly the staff retention rate can be calculated against any base. Usually, a long-term employee is defined as one who has been with the firm for over twelve months. This could be set against a two-year period, and it is possible to calculate length-of-service charts, which then plot the employment histories of employees who have been with the firm with two, three, four years and beyond. For most units this type of information is interesting but not essential.

The survival curve

The survival curve helps to develop a picture of new entrants and the organization's ability to retain new employees (Figure 5.3). As the name suggests, it concerns itself with the staff leaving the organization and then plots them against their length of service. The key statistics are gathered according to how long each leaver has been with the organization, and compared with the total number of leavers. The formula is:

$$\frac{\text{Number of leavers after 3 months}}{\text{Total leavers this year}} \times 100$$

$$\frac{\text{Number of leavers after 6 months}}{\text{Total leavers this year}} \times 100$$

$$\frac{\text{Number of leavers after 9 months}}{\text{Total leavers this year}} \times 100$$

$$\frac{\text{Number of leavers after 12 months}}{\text{Total leavers this year}} \times 100$$

$$\frac{\text{Number of leavers after 15 months}}{\text{Total leavers this year}} \times 100$$

$$\frac{\text{Number of leavers with over 18 months service}}{\text{Total leavers this year}} \times 100$$

The calculations can be extended to meet the specific needs of the organization. Typically, most turnover occurs within a short period of joining the organization, and in some cases the calculations for the first quarter need to be further broken down into monthly figures. The survival curve is valuable for identifying an induction crisis. That is a problem that occurs when the new recruit first enters the organization, and it may be caused by:

- poor recruitment and selection
- limited use of job description and person specification
- lack of a formal induction
- limited training
- poor staff morale amongst other staff
- team membership problems
- poor communication with the new recruit
- excessive job stress.

In the example above, forty staff left in a twelve-month period. Records reveal that the leavers had been with the organization for the following periods:

Leavers left after	3 months	6 months	9 months	12 months	15 months	18 months
Numbers	30	5	3	1	1	0
% of all leavers	75	12.5	7.5	2.5	2.5	0

In the example above, the majority of staff leaving the unit did so within three months of joining. This pattern is one that is typical for a business that is experiencing high labour turnover. Given the information from the staff retention rate there is an induction crisis, which may be a problem restricted to a particular type of job or a problem facing all new recruits, and may be caused by one of the reasons suggested above.

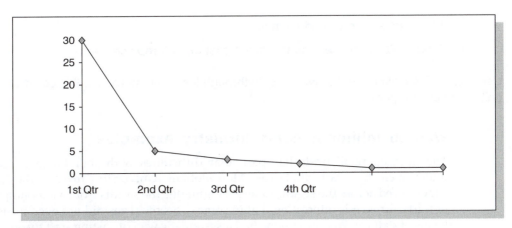

Figure 5.3 Example of a survival curve

Seasonal and temporary staff

Many licensed retail organizations use temporary or seasonal staff to meet the demand in predictably busy periods. In many cases, Christmas or summer trading represents a disproportionate additional sales volume and the unit manager needs to recruit extra staff to meet the peak in demand. Recruiting these individuals and releasing them after the period is finished does represent staff turnover, but it is planned and predicted. Calculations can, however, be distorted if no special account is taken of these employees.

In some cases, a student works in a unit during holiday periods, and then goes away to college or university and continues to work part time for the same organization during the term. It is possible to predict a student joining and rejoining units in the same organization six times in a year. The staff turnover could appear to be a problem if no special account is taken of this type of person. Many organizations now have a code for employees who are students so that they can be extracted from the calculation of staff turnover.

Active learning point

Using the information given to you in the case study in Chapter 15, prepare an analysis of the staff turnover. This should include using all the techniques outlined above, and an estimate of the costs of staff turnover to the organization. Use the formulae given above.

Whilst many licensed retail organizations are now calculating the rate of staff turnover, very few account for the total cost to the business of staff turnover. In part this can be explained because of the difficulties in accurately measuring the true impact of losing staff, who may have worked in the unit for varying times, and knowing the true cost of the impact of lost staff on customer satisfaction and service quality. Taking these points into account, all units should attempt to calculate both the level and the cost of turnover as part of the assessment of unit performance.

If a restaurant has sixty employees on the books at any one time, experiences staff turnover of 140 per cent and has estimated the direct cost of turnover as £450, the calculation will be as follows:

$60 \times 140 = 84$ staff replaced each year

$84 \times £450 = £37\,800$ spent on the direct cost of staff replacement.

Using the IPD's estimate of the wider costs through lost customers etc., this could be cost the unit over £65 000 per year.

Wasted millions: some industry examples

The licensed retail trade has particular difficulties with staff turnover. Research undertaken by staff at Leeds Metropolitan University reveals the problem experienced across the sector. Table 5.4 highlights the results from a telephone survey of thirty firms. It is interesting that in some cases the firms did not even measure the levels of staff turnover, and none had a systematic way of costing staff turnover to the firm. Researchers estimated the direct costs of staff turnover for unskilled staff in the licensed retail sector to be £500. As shown above, this is only part of the total costs, and the 'true' cost of staff turnover is probably nearer to the IPD (2001) estimate of £750 per person. Even so, the figures reveal some staggering results.

The results in Table 5.4 show that the level of staff turnover is high across all firms in the study. It ranges from 93 per cent in Case 8 to 305 per cent in Case 27, and the average across the thirty firms was over 180 per cent and the total cost to the industry was estimated to be £300 million.

Keeping your staff – it's not rocket science! Everyone can do it!

As yet, few organizations attempt to value the cost of staff turnover, although increasing numbers of the larger branded licensed retailers are now concerned with

Licensed retail organizations	Number of managed units	Number of staff employees	Staff turnover rate (%)	Cost of staff turnover @ £500 (£)
1	128	1169	160	935 200
2	96	1214	158	959 060
3	484	6841	203	6 943 615
4	162	2953	208	3 071 120
5	115	1631	123	1 003 065
6	53	1200	232	1 392 000
7	99	1631	193	1 573 915
8	68	280	93	130 200
9	64	855	188	803 700
10	87	940	163	766 100
11	50	623	235	732 025
12	300	3624	192	3 478 040
13	820	?	106	?
14	87	1325	175	1 159 375
15	103	1196	200	1 196 000
16	52	582	150	436 500
17	794	10 740	155	8 114 250
18	1910	22 923	180	20 030 700
19	34	467	220	513 700
20	32	?	150	?
21	32	412	236	486 160
22	40	463	200	463 000
23	37	?	200	?
24	55	486	90	218 700
25	31	412	280	576 800
26	42	531	155	411 525
27	115	1200	305	1 830 000
28	51	698	206	718 940
29	33	400	170	340 000
30	39	610	218	664 900

Table 5.4 Levels and costs of staff turnover in thirty licensed retail organizations

the impact of staff leavers on service quality and customer satisfaction. The link between employee satisfaction and customer satisfaction is well established. Increasingly managers are being asked to come up with strategies for reducing staff turnover and for managing internal customer satisfaction.

The following sections suggest some steps that you can take to keep staff and reduce the amount of unwanted and unplanned staff turnover.

Keeping records and costing staff turnover

To be able to manage staff turnover you must keep accurate records of staff leaving and joining the unit. There are a few suggestions to consider when you create a system within the unit:

1 When setting up the file, think carefully about the aims you have for the information. Resist the temptation to store too much information, as this will increase your workload.
2 Decide which key issues you are interested in:
   • the total volume of staff turnover
   • departmental or job title variations
   • evidence of staff retention and stability
   • the percentage leaving within a short period of joining the unit
   • potential variations by employee characteristics
   • differences between full-time, part-time and casual staff.
3 Decide whether to include all employees. You may need to make allowance for certain categories of staff leavers who are not a 'problem':
   • seasonal or temporary staff
   • students returning to college or home
   • staff leaving for 'unavoidable' reasons – retirement, death etc.
4 Try to create as accurate a picture as you can of the reasons for staff departures, and identify whether the reasons are:
   • due to push or pull factors
   • due to avoidable or unavoidable reasons
   • voluntary or involuntary.
5 Attempt to cost out staff turnover. Many organizations have some estimate of the costs involved in replacing members of staff. If not, the national survey figures given in Figure 5.2 can be used. Failing that, try to work out the direct costs of losing staff yourself. Table 5.3 suggests some of the factors that you might want to include.

Exit interviews

Many unit managers attempt to build up a picture of the reason for staff departures through the use of exit interviews. These are conducted after a person has given notice of their intention to quit, but prior to departure. At the very least they give the manager the opportunity to explore the experiences and motives of those who have decide to leave. The problem is that these interviews are notoriously inaccurate as sources of information. Employees, particularly dissatisfied employees, often find it difficult to express their views openly – a situation made more difficult if the unit management team is the key source of the employee's dissatisfaction. There are some tips that should help make the interview more effective:

1 The rules of good interviewing apply, so it is essential to have a quiet room without interruptions, and to prepare appropriately.
2 The interview is intended to discover the reason for the departure, not to persuade the person to stay on. The quality of information gathered will be a reflection of the trust and relationships between the manager and staff member. An open and trusting relationship will usually result in a more honest exchange of views.
3 Open-ended questions that allow individuals to explain in their own words means that their views are more likely to be helpful.
4 The style and tone of the interview needs to be friendly and open, rather than aggressive and argumentative.
5 Above all, recognize the difficulty that the employee faces and attempt to make the event as comfortable as possible so that you achieve an accurate view.

Monitor the local labour market

If you are to avoid some of the problems caused by competition in the local labour market, you need to be aware of current trends and the reward packages being offered by competitors. Pay rates and working hours are issues of particular concern to most employees. Many managers forget that although labour is a significant manageable cost to the business, it is a wage on which employees' live. Competitor firms offering regular hours and better rates of pay appear very attractive to employees who experience low wages and short hours of work.

Conduct a regular audit of local competitor pay rates, term and conditions, and the other factors suggested above. These are particularly important when trade is booming and there is competition for staff.

Employee satisfaction

When an employee makes a decision to leave the organization for a voluntary reason, the employee is, in one way or another, expressing dissatisfaction with the current employer. Employees in licensed retail organizations, in particular, have few courses of action open to them if they are unhappy with things. Few licensed retail organizations in the UK have any sizeable trade union membership, and there are few organizations that recognize and negotiate with trade unions. Grievances can be taken up, but these often set the individual in a difficult position with little power to change things that they do not like. For many members of staff, therefore, the only way of dealing with a situation that they don't like is to put up with it, or to withdraw from it.

Bearing in mind J. W. Marriott's famous statement:

> It takes happy workers to make happy customers

the level of employee satisfaction is an important issue for you as unit manager. Apart from the linkages with staff turnover, service quality and the concern to 'delight customers' requires service staff actively to deliver service that goes beyond predictable customer needs. Dissatisfied employees are unlikely to respond appropriately to customers.

Most branded licensed retail organizations have instruments for measuring employee satisfaction, but these can be both infrequent and long-winded. In some cases the questionnaires are too complex to fill out, and response rates from staff can be low.

An example of a questionnaire that is simple to use and to analyse is given in Chapter 3. This provides a seven-point scale against which the employee marks fifteen questions that have been selected to test out the employee attitudes to various employment factors.

Employees have a number of concerns that influence their motivation to work and, ultimately, their level of satisfaction and commitment to the organization. There are many theories about motivation, but you need to think carefully about the nature of your relationship with your employees and the different views they have of work, the reasons for working, and the rewards from working.

Like customers, your employees have expectations about work, and to manage them successfully you need to keep in touch with these expectations regarding:

Hospitality, Leisure & Tourism Series

- pay and rewards
- shifts and working time
- relationships with managers
- relationships with fellow workers
- the levels of interest in the job
- what is a fair amount of effort
- the amount of commitment to the job.

Some organizations go so far as to call employees 'internal customers'. The intention is to make the Marriott link, but this should not be overplayed. Employees are not customers. Their relationship with the organization is not that of a customer. They come to work to earn money to live, and for a cluster of other material, social and psychological benefits.

There is a natural conflict of interests between employees and employers, which has particular impact in service industries because:

- wages make a significant part of total service costs
- the labour element is often the most easy cost element to cut, and therefore the operating profits can be expanded at the expense of employee incomes.

If you expect employees to be loyal, that loyalty has to be earned, and it has to be seen as a two-sided arrangement. You need to be loyal to your employees and respect their needs.

Good communications

Developing a strong mutual understanding helps you as a unit manager to understand employees and their needs, and also helps employees to understand what they are doing and why. Clearly the employee surveys identified above help in this process, but they tend to be a one-way form of communication that can be limited by response rates and by their ability to reflect the issues that really concern employees. The following are some suggestions for improving communications:

1 *Team meetings*, as outlined in Chapter 2, can be before or after service, or on a regular basis, preferably weekly. The more frequent the meetings, the better the levels of communication. At their most effective, they include everyone and employees are paid to attend.
2 *Quality circles* or some form of representative group through which the staff can make suggestions is another way of getting staff involved in the business and of overcoming problems. Chapter 2 gives a more detailed outline of these arrangements. Whilst they do not involve all employees, quality circles can help communicate issues to the staff as a whole through the representatives.
3 *Appraisal interviews* with individual members of staff need to be a regular feature of unit management. These can give you a chance to share understandings with staff members.

The key point about these and other processes for improving communication is that a shared mutual understanding is one of the foundations for the development of trust and loyalty. You must understand the need to keep employees informed and to build these mutually trusting relationships.

Pay and rewards

Research with employees shows that this is one of the most important causes of employee dissatisfaction and one of the main reasons why people leave an organization. Clearly pay is not the only reward that employees get from work, but it is an important one that has to reflect their expectations if employees are to stay with an organization. It is one of the tangible elements of employment; a bit like comfortable beds or clean tables for customers, pay is a basic requirement on which other aspects of employee satisfaction have to be built.

1 *Hourly rates* have to be in line with the local labour market. Employees soon know if pay rates can be bettered in another restaurant or a supermarket.
2 *Take home pay* is made up of the hourly rate times the number of hours less any other stoppages or costs of employment that the employee has to contribute. The number of hours worked can be a particular problem for part-time or casual employees. If you cut back on the number of hours a part-time employee works, this will reduce the take home pay and may cause dissatisfaction. Whilst part-time employees allow you flexibility in employment, part-time staff who have constantly changing schedules have difficulties in planning their income and personal lives. Irregular hours are one of the most common reasons given for part-time staff leaving licensed firms.
3 *Incentive pay* is a feature of many licensed retail firms. The intention is that employees work harder to achieve better sales or profits if they have a financial benefit from the achievement. In some cases, the extra benefits are linked to training and performance standards. Whatever the objective, the incentive will be most effective when it is achievable and valuable to the employee.
4 *Tips* can be a source of considerable extra income for employees, although they can also create tension and conflict amongst the team. Some organizations now actively discourage tipping, because it confuses customers and creates an impression that employees only give good service in exchange for money. If you allow tipping, you need to consider the system by which tips are gained and shared amongst staff.

In addition to these financially based rewards, it is possible to reward staff with goods in kind – say by getting them to act as 'mystery customers' in other units in the brand. A free meal, a drinks allowance or a free weekend in another unit can be a mutually beneficial way of rewarding staff. Apart from the immediate benefit to the individual, by acting as customers they develop a better understanding of the service they deliver.

Finally, praise and recognition of good work can be used to reward people for their effort. 'Thank you' costs nothing, but can be very welcome to the individual employee.

Recruitment and selection

Getting the right employees with a clear view of what the job entails is the key to reducing staff turnover. As we have seen, high labour turnover is often fuelled by an induction crisis that is in part caused by sloppy recruitment and selection.

Chapter 2 provides a more detailed outline of the approach, but the key elements for the reduction of staff turnover are as follows:

1 *Forward planning* of recruitment is more likely to result in better recruitment of people who are likely to stay longer. Hurried recruitment is a major cause of subsequent staff turnover.
2 *Job descriptions and staff specifications* should define clearly what the job entails and the sort of person needed to succeed in the job.
3 *Attracting the right sort of applicants* through advertising, agencies or 'word of mouth' from existing employees is important. There is no point in attracting lots of applications from people who are unsuitable. Often employee stability can be achieved through recruiting by 'word of mouth' from existing employees, thereby building a team of employees who know each other.
4 *Selection interviews* need to be carefully undertaken. Involving more than one manager or undertaking several interviews can help ensure that the right person is selected.
5 *Following up references* helps to ensure that the unit is recruiting people who will behave in a reasonable manner. The failure to follow up references is a frequent cause of staff problems, particularly where someone has a previous record of absenteeism or even theft.

Induction and orientation

Systematic recruitment and selection of new staff needs to be followed by a formal induction and orientation programme. As we have seen, the induction crisis is a common cause of staff turnover. Joining any new organization can be stressful enough by itself. Staff who are 'thrown-in at the deep end', and given minimal training, introduction to the organization or the work involved, face additional pressure, and many people avoid the pressure by running away from it – that is, leaving. Chapter 6 deals with these issues in more detail, but if staff turnover is to be minimized you need to consider the following points:

1 Plan the start day or time to avoid a busy service period
2 Consider pre-training before the first work period
3 Use a 'buddy' system to help ease the new employee into the team
4 Carefully plan the first shifts to avoid undue pressure
5 Check with the individual about experiences and problems
6 Encourage other team members to be welcoming and helpful.

Training and development

Training individuals to be effective in their job has an immediate benefit in that it removes the pressure that incompetence or inexperience can place on the individual. Pre-training in particular can give the individual skills that help new employees to deliver better customer service and productivity from the start. Research shows that people who are trained prior to their first shift are more productive more quickly than those who receive no formal training. For the employees, training represents an investment in them as an individual, and is likely to encourage staff to stay with the organization – particularly if a formal programme of training can be shown to link to promotion and career development.

Supervision and management style

Building up employees' sense of personal worth and self-effectiveness, they will add value and quality to the service provided to customers. Recognizing the benefits that employees can contribute will have the added impact of encouraging staff to stay in an environment where they feel valued, thereby reducing levels of staff turnover. Similarly, if you treat employees as though they are worthless and adopt an overly autocratic style of management it is likely to add to the pressure to leave. Effective unit supervision and management attempts to reduce the effects of push and pull factors.

Box 5.2 explains the staff turnover problems detailed in Box 5.1, The Bird in Hand, earlier in this chapter.

Box 5.2   *The Bird in Hand – causes of staff turnover*

Interviews with new recruits and management at The Bird in Hand confirmed that there was little by way of a formal induction programme, with staff frequently being set to work alongside whoever was the most experienced person on duty at the time. Consequently, the degree of coaching and assistance given to new employees varied considerably. Many individuals felt anxious about the pressure and responsibility, and were too frightened to ask questions. Interviews with former employees identified that these levels of anxiety pushed them to leave the pub during this initial period.

The number of dismissals from the organization also suggests a problem with recruitment and selection of staff. Twenty-five employees were dismissed from the pub's employment. In two cases the individuals were managers brought in to manage the pub during the owner's absence; they were not properly briefed about the limits to their authority, and were subsequently dismissed for making unauthorized changes to the business. In the other twenty-three cases, dismissal was due to a cluster of factors. In most cases, problems were associated with behaviour and orientation to work. In one case an employee was dismissed for theft, and it subsequently emerged that he had been dismissed by his former employer for a similar reason. This case was typical. Not one reference was requested for a new recruit during the whole period of the study.

The pub had neither job descriptions nor person specifications available to help in the recruitment process. Those undertaking the selection had no formal record from which to check potential recruits' skills and orientations to work. The lack of a formal definition of the duties and responsibilities for the job and the skills required by those undertaking the role had a number of consequences related to labour turnover at the pub. Apart from the problem associated with managerial judgements in selecting people with the appropriate qualities to do the job, new recruits themselves were not given enough information to understand what the job entailed. Several former employees confirmed that the job was not what they expected it to be. Flowing from this, the lack of job descriptions and job specifications also meant that management had no instrument to appraise individual employee performance, or method of devising an appropriate training plan where performance was found to be deficient.

Of the fifty-seven leavers during the period of the study, thirty-two left voluntarily. Not surprisingly, career advancement was the most common reason given. Research shows that many employees use this explanation as a screen for the real reason(s) for leaving. Interviews with former employees confirmed that pay and hours of work, together with a lack of training opportunities, represented the largest number of reasons for voluntary labour turnover.

A review of competing establishments revealed that full-time rates at The Bird in Hand were as much as £20 per week below local rates of pay in other pubs. Part-time rates were not so far out, but were at the low end of local rates. Many part-timers resented having to clock-off duty during break times. The pay and hours issue revealed different experiences for full- and part-time employees. According to full-timers, 'it's as though they are trying to squeeze every last drop of energy from you'. On average, full-time waiting staff worked fifty to fifty-five hours per week. The part-timers were sent home often even when there was work still to be completed. Some complained of being sent home after just one hour of a shift period, because the management felt they were 'no longer needed'. The tendency to reduce staffing levels was a general source of dissatisfaction for many employees. Perhaps not surprisingly in these circumstances, many employees sought alternative employment that would give them better pay and conditions of employment.

Interviews with both former and current employees registered concerns about training and promotion prospects at the pub. The last two senior appointments had been made from outside the organization, and several staff registered a sense that they were unlikely to be promoted in the organization. The only formal training being offered at the pub was for trainee chefs, who were enrolled on part-time courses at the local college. For the remaining staff, no opportunities were offered for qualifications, no NVQs were offered, and nor were there any other opportunities to develop themselves within the organization. If these employees reflected the findings that pub employees have strong positive ambitions, then the only opportunities for development appeared to be outside the Bird in Hand.

Interviews with management revealed a failure to draw the obvious conclusions from their own experience and difficulties. The longest serving employee had been employed by the pub for four years, and he had been sent on the chef training course at the local college. The pub management's investment in the individual's development had contributed to his loyalty to the pub. Similarly, interviews with managers revealed concern about the general lack of skilled personnel in the licensed industry. Recent appointments to the post of head chef and restaurant manager had been as a result of 'poaching' staff from competitor organizations, and consequently a high salary being paid to the individuals. When pressed, senior management did not recognize a responsibility to train their own employees. They felt that other employers would in turn poach their trained staff. There was no recognition that training and the offer of career opportunities to employees would contribute to a reduction in labour turnover.

Conclusion

In many ways The Bird in Hand represents an employment relationship typical of many firms in the licensed retail industry. Employers working in environments where demand is subject

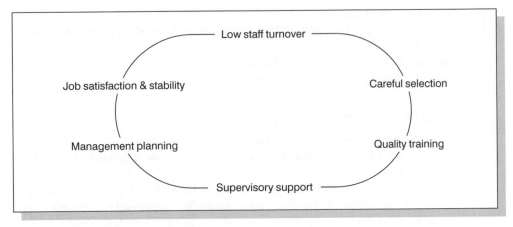

Figure 5.4 The virtuous cycle of staff turnover

to rapid fluctuation, and labour represents a significant proportion of total cost, manage the workforce in a way that maximizes direct managerial control. Labour costs in such businesses represent the cost element that is the most easily manipulated by managers, so the policy of reducing part-time hours and extracting as much effort from full-timers as possible appears to be rational. However, this takes little account of some fundamental industrial relations issues. As individuals, these employees have limited opportunities formally to challenge the power of the employer. That said, employees can resist their employer, although this takes a more individualized form. Absenteeism, lateness, poor performance, theft and ultimately withdrawal are all options that are typical of this kind of relationship. Thus the policy to maximize the exploitation of labour is short sighted and costly. The resulting employee frustration and subsequent labour turnover represent a considerable extra cost to the business. Managers are largely unaware of these extra costs because they have no system of recording or monitoring trends in labour turnover, or the costs this incurs.

Whilst there are inevitable tensions in the employment relationship – an income for one is a cost to the other – most progressive employers understand that loyalty is a 'two-way street'. Employers expecting loyal employee behaviour must in turn be loyal and fair to their employees. Providing people with fair incomes and with some justice in the way they are treated is not a major challenge to profits, and taking a longer view might even enhance them.

At its most basic level, as unit manager you must keep records that monitor performance and account for the costs of turnover in different sections of the business. You need to move to a virtuous cycle (Figure 5.4). That is, careful recruitment, selection and induction, leading to good quality training, increased supervisor support, improved management communication, increased job satisfaction and stability, and low labour turnover.

Reflective practice

1 Using the case study in Chapter 15, identify the causes of staff turnover in this situation.
2 What steps would you take to reduce it?
3 What priorities would you make for action over the next three months?
4 Make a case for costing the value of employees into an assessment of unit performance.

5 What measure might you use?
6 Some managers argue that high staff turnover is a price worth paying for low labour costs and increased profits:
  • prepare arguments in support of this view
  • prepare arguments opposing this view.

Further reading

Argyle, M. (1989). *The Social Psychology of Work*. Penguin.

Boella, M. (2000). *Human Resource Management in the Hospitality Industry*. Stanley Thornes.

Goss-Turner, S. (1989). *Managing People in the Pub and Catering Industry*. Croner.

Johnson, K. (1986). Labour turnover in pubs – an update. *Service Industries Journal*, **6(3),** 362–380.

Maghurn, J. P. (1989*). A Manual of Staff Management in the Pub and Catering Industry*. Heinemann.

Mullins, L. J. (1995). *Licensed Management: A Human Resource Approach*. Pitman.

Roberts, J. (1995). *Human Resource Practices in the Licensed Industry*. Hodder & Stoughton.

Rothwell, S. (1980). *Labour Turnover: Its Costs Causes and Control*. Gower.

Training improves business performance

After working through this chapter, you should be able to:

- identify the key benefits of training and development

- plan and organize staff training

- plan and organize training sessions to meet various needs

- evaluate training undertaken.

Employee training and development

Training and staff development are important aspects of your work as a bar, pub or restaurant manager. Many branded licensed retailers recognize that staff training is a key business technique that impacts on service quality delivery, customer satisfaction, sales growth and profitability. Even in organizations that do not have a formal training policy, it is important that *you* develop employees through formal training programmes. Most employees will learn merely by doing the job, but learning by experience is less effective than a formal training policy directed either at individual needs or at a collective need, undertaken by all staff. At its most minimal, training has to be provided to meet statutory obligations to employees and customers. All employers have an obligation to ensure that employees work in safe environments with co-workers who understand safe working practices. Similarly, employers are obliged to ensure that employees work in a way that is hygienic, handling food in a manner that reduces the risk to customers.

Training must go beyond these base-level legal obligations. Training *all* employees has direct impacts on business performance. Recent research for the Hospitality Training Foundation shows that training leads to:

- improvements in productivity
- improved sales per transaction
- reduced wastage
- lower levels of staff turnover
- lower levels of absenteeism
- improved service quality
- improved customer satisfaction
- improved employee satisfaction
- increased employee flexibility.

Apart from the benefits directly gained from training, it is also important to recognize that the failure to train employees is not cost-free. If you allow people to learn the job by trial and error, there are bound to be lots of errors. These will involve problems in service quality, employee dissatisfaction, higher levels of wastage, lower productivity, and reduced employee flexibility.

All training must start with a clear understanding of the aims and objectives of what you expect to achieve from the training activity. Adopt a systematic approach that focuses clearly on the needs of the person to be trained, the materials needed, and how the training will be evaluated.

The benefits of training

Estimating the benefits of training – particularly in the context of potential contributions to improved business performance – is clearly difficult to gauge. This is not surprising, given the variety of forms of training undertaken within the licensed industry, and because other variables impact upon training activity. For example, the quality of the training provided, the existing skills and capabilities of trainees, and the duration of training programmes all have an impact.

In addition, it is self-evident that a wide array of influences impact upon the business performance of an organization – for example, economic climate, level of investment, marketing, and promotional activities.

- Improved productivity
- Increased sales
- Reductions in labour turnover
- Reductions in absenteeism
- Reductions in waste
- Quality improvements
- Greater organizational commitment
- Reductions in accidents
- Greater flexibility

Table 6.1 Benefits of training

The main themes identified in the literature are included in Table 6.1. It is interesting that some people have called these the 'costs of not training' (Hall, 1975).

When considering the aims and objectives of employee training, it is important to remember that training:

- primarily changes individual behaviour
- provides, through changes in behaviour, direct benefits with regard to employee performance
- leads, by improved employee performance, to the desired financial benefits – reduced costs, increased sales and improved profitability.

Improved productivity

In this context, improving productivity is about improving the output of employees. Output is:

- the number of meals produced
- the number of customers served
- the number of rooms cleaned
- the number of sales made
- the cash value taken, etc.

measured against some indicator of the staff involved. Usually staff hours are used, because the time period is fixed. Where measures are set against shifts, or staff on duty, the precise time involved is likely to vary. To calculate the productivity rate:

$$\frac{\text{Output over the period}}{\text{Labour input}} = \text{Productivity rate in staff hours}$$

Thus if staff behind a bar serve 750 customers over a five-hour period, and there are five members of staff on duty (twenty-five staff hours in total), the calculation is:

$$\frac{750}{25} = 30 \text{ transactions per staff hour}$$

Hospitality, Leisure & Tourism Series

Table 6.2 shows how productivity can be compared using the numbers of customers served and the value of sales for employees who are untrained and those who are trained. The comparisons use both indicators because 'up-selling' (increasing the value of average sales) is an important additional source of revenue and profit.

	Trained transactions	Untrained transactions	Difference	Trained sales	Untrained sales	Difference
Shift	1434	1137	*297*	£4920	£3485	*£1435*
Hours	38	40	*–2*	38	40	*–2*
Rate per hour	37.73	28.4	*+33%*	£129.47	£87.12	*+48.6%*

Table 6.2 Comparison of trained and untrained employees in a bar

In Table 6.2, formally trained employees are more productive in transactions (number of sales is increased by an average of 33 per cent) and take more money by both serving more customers and selling more per transaction. Trained staff take on average £3.43 per transaction, whilst untrained (or informally trained) staff take £3.06 per transaction.

Clearly, different businesses may restrict the value of transactions because some businesses (or service periods) involve more single customer transactions, whereas in other cases each transaction involves more customers – parties, groups, or families. You need to keep a record of these matters, because they help you to track sales and will also help in evaluating the impact of various training initiatives.

A structured approach to training, rather than just allowing staff to learn by experience, helps new employees to become effective more quickly. Figure 6.1 shows that training new employees, either before work or as part of an induction programme, has two overall effects:

1 New, trained employees quickly reach their optimum output level
2 They have a higher optimum level output than staff who are not formally trained.

In this case we can see the effects of training on both the speed at which staff learn to become effective and the level of effectiveness reached. Some organizations see the benefit of training prior to the first shift as helping new recruits to develop basic skills before they are put in front of customers. They think that employee effectiveness and the impact of sales and customer satisfaction are too important to allow new staff to learn by trial and error.

Finally, before we move on from considerations of output, it is important to think about the effects of service quality. There is no point in serving many customers if a high proportion of them receive unsatisfactory service. Any calculation of productivity must therefore consider the impact of customer complaints and lost business. As we shall see later, employee training has an impact on service quality and levels of customer satisfaction.

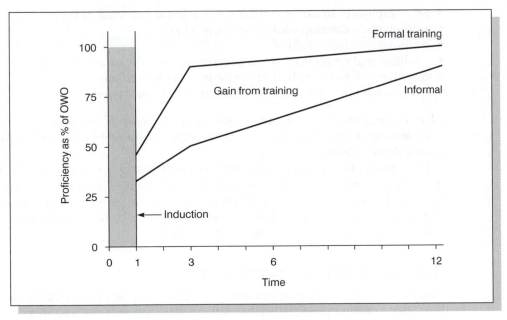

Figure 6.1 Proficiency and time taken to reach optimum work output (OWO)

In conclusion, training can have a dramatic impact on employee productivity. Trained employees:

- have higher levels of output than untrained employees
- reach their optimum level more quickly
- reach higher optimum levels than those who learn from experience
- produce better service quality at any given level of output.

Increased sales

As we saw in Table 6.2, experienced staff sell more product per head than employees who are untrained or inexperienced. The potential increase in sales per labour hour, or per transaction, is very important in many licensed retail units. The ability to 'up-sell' by persuading the customer to buy a larger drink, an extra portion, or a better quality room can increase the revenue per sale, and the profitability. An unpublished study undertaken by one major licensed retailer showed that 'trained employees' could increase the value of sales per transaction by between 25 and 30 per cent.

Staff turnover

As explained in Chapter 5, the causes of staff losses may be beyond the control of the unit manager. Sometimes local levels of employment and competition for staff create difficulties in staff retention. However, staff turnover is something you must attempt to manage, and providing staff with training is an important way of keeping them with you. Well-structured training helps:

- new employees to understand quickly what is expected of them
- employees to develop confidence in their job
- employees to feel effective
- establish that employees are important and worthy of investment
- employees to see a path of opportunities open to them
- create a learning environment committed to improvement.

All of these create reasons for the employee to stay with an employer. Conversely, an environment of low trust and low investment where employees feel undervalued causes them to leave.

The relationship between staff turnover and training is complicated because it is not a simple one-way process. As we have seen, training provides employees with reasons to stay with an organization; however, units with high levels of staff turnover are also likely to have lower numbers of trained employees, because employees don't stay long enough to be trained.

Reduced levels of absenteeism

Unscheduled days off are a problem for all licensed retail businesses. At the very least they put extra pressure on the staff who turn up for duty, and this can result in increased stress and dissatisfaction. More staff dissatisfaction leads in turn to added labour turnover and costs. In addition, they can result in increased direct costs when agency staff are brought in to cover for an absent employee.

As with the link to labour turnover, the precise nature of the linkage to training is uncertain. Do trained employees have a better sense of their duties and the skills needed to cope, and therefore feel less stressed and have less cause for absence? Or do employees who are absent just not get the training? Whatever the link, research shows that those firms who have an active training programme experience lower levels of staff absence. In many ways the link with staff turnover is strong, because absence is a mini-form of withdrawal from the job.

Reductions in waste and equipment damage

In many licensed businesses, food costs range from 25 per cent to 40 per cent of revenue. Similarly, alcoholic beverages frequently account for a significant proportion of costs. Other variable costs include:

- loss or damage
- accidental handling
- making up the wrong order
- the replacement of items that customers find unsatisfactory.

These costs are increased if the problems are made worse by ill-trained staff. Trained workers make fewer errors, and thereby minimize waste.

Training can have a positive impact on theft, pilfering and 'give-aways' to friends. Poor training or lack of training impacts on the 'professional' behaviour of employees. A value often present in employee training programmes stresses the need for honest practice. In licensed retail operations, many of the items that employees handle are highly consumable – food, drink and money – and levels of training impact on the amount of these stolen by staff.

Quality improvements

It is now widely recognized that the management of quality is a vital challenge if licensed retailers are to strengthen their competitiveness. Employee performance is a direct influence on employee experiences and service quality. Service employee training can be directed at employee delivery of the service, ensuring that they 'get it right first time'. Training employees in what to do if errors do occur is also important. Most research shows that when complaints and faults are dealt with immediately, customers are more likely to stay loyal to the organization. Chapter 7 highlights some of the ways in which employees can deal with customer complaints. Training employees how best to respond is an essential feature of effective complaint management.

Reducing customer complaints and increasing customer satisfaction are essential elements in retaining customers. Most licensed retail organizations are well aware that it is much more expensive to attract new customers to the business than it is to retain existing customers. Training results in improved levels of retained customers.

Organizational commitment

Most licensed retailers now conduct regular surveys of employee satisfaction, because they recognize that 'internal customers' have to be committed to the organization's service values to external customers. All things being equal, training has an impact on employee satisfaction and commitment. Whilst employee commitment can be measured it cannot be given a financial value, but it is nonetheless a benefit of training that can be measured through changes in employee satisfaction scores.

Greater flexibility

Greater employee flexibility brings benefits to an organization because managers are able to schedule the same individuals to undertake a variety of tasks. In part, additional training means that employees are:

- able to undertake a variety of different jobs
- more flexible in doing other jobs
- cheaper, because they can be used as and where needed.

This functional flexibility also enables employees to take on more interesting jobs, and in some cases training empowers employees to make decisions that were formerly undertaken by managers. Several licensed retailers now train for functional flexibility so that a proportion of the workforce can be used in the bar, restaurant and kitchen. For some employees, the variety makes the job more interesting. In other cases it is seen as part of an employee's development into management positions.

Improved ability to accept change

Overlapping (but distinct from) functional flexibility, investment in training can produce benefits regarding the extent to which employees are willing to accept change. Investment in training employees with a wide range of generic skills, or in the specific needs for change, are likely to reduce resistance to change and to aid transition from one form to another. For example, studies of empowerment initiatives show that the defining feature of the success of an initiative is the extent to which employees are prepared for new responsibilities and feel empowered.

In summary, training is undertaken to achieve business objectives, and it is important that you monitor the effectiveness of training to measure the extent that it has achieved the objectives set, whether this is to:

- improve performance
- increase productivity
- increase sales per transaction
- reduce staff turnover
- reduce staff absenteeism
- reduce wastage and equipment damage
- improve service quality
- improve customer satisfaction
- improve employee satisfaction
- increase staff flexibility
- improve the ability to accept change.

Box 6.1 provides an example.

Box 6.1 *J.D. Wetherspoons*

The approach to crew training by J.D. Wetherspoons has several features that exemplify best practice in the licensed retail sector:

- all staff are trained, including full- and part-time employees
- training is competence-based
- ultimately, training aims to develop a flexible work force capable of undertaking all jobs
- much training involves learning to do the job in 'the one best way'
- competencies are defined for each task
- completed training is rewarded through a pay increase.

Case study evidence from executives confirms that unit managers have a high impact on training levels. Despite a uniform approach and a strong cultural commitment to training at senior levels, some unit managers give training a lower priority, and as a result their units generally have:

- a lower proportion of fully trained staff
- a larger backlog of staff waiting to be trained
- below average responses to the training section on employee satisfaction surveys
- more critical employee comments about training in feedback session reports
- in turn, other managers seem to give employee training lower priority.

As a result, the lower trained units experienced:

- lower average transactions per annum per labour hour
- consistently higher staff turnover rate
- lower than average service quality grades
- lower than average employee satisfaction grades and ratings of employee attitudes
- a less flexible workforce to plan activities
- increased wastage.

Training your staff

As the immediate manager accountable for the business performance of the unit, you are responsible for ensuring that employees are adequately trained to meet the service needs of customers. Even in a situation where your line manager does not ask you to account for staff training undertaken, you must recognize that staff training is a key approach to ensuring effective unit performance. It is essential that you adopt a systematic approach:

1 Decide your training policy
2 Identify what training is needed
3 Plan the training to meet the needs identified
4 Prepare programmes to achieve training plans
5 Carry out the training programme
6 Evaluate the training undertaken.

As we have seen, planning and systematic organization of training in this way will yield many benefits, not the least of which is that it will communicate to employees their key role in service delivery and that you are prepared to invest time and effort in them.

Deciding the training policy

A declared policy about the aims and objectives of training is essential. In fact, many large branded licensed retail organizations have written policy statements that are included in staff handbooks. In these cases, you will not have to write the policy, but you will be expected to make the policy work on the ground. The J.D. Wetherspoons case study in Box 6.1 confirms that even in organizations with highly systematic and structured approaches to training, unit managers make a significant impact on the quality of training delivered at unit level.

If you do not have a brand or organization policy, you will need to write one yourself. A formal written statement assists both you and your staff to understand clearly the aims and objectives of your approach to training. There are a number of issues that the policy might consider:

1 Is the policy aimed at merely improving job competence, or at individual development?

2 Are all employees – full-time, part-time and temporary – included and covered by the policy?

3 How does this relate to your appraisal policy – do you follow through with plans for employee development?

4 Is the policy related to a wider commitment to being a learning organization?

5 What support will you make available for 'off-the-job' training and educational qualifications? How would you deal with requests for educational programmes not immediately related to job competence or workplace performance?

6 Who will be responsible for training management and delivery, and what resources are available in the form of people and cash?

Most importantly, you must ensure a degree of consistency and integrity in following through on the policy. A fine-sounding policy that is not followed through, or that is set aside when trading times are difficult, will soon be seen for what it is, and people will not take you or the policy seriously.

Identifying training needs

The identification of training needs usually flows from your staff appraisal process. Essentially, you are attempting to identify the knowledge, skills and social skills that employees need for both their present and future jobs. There are several broad areas that need to be considered:

- where individual performance of staff is not up to the standard you require
- where an identified business objective requires all staff to be trained to be more effective – say to improve productivity or to increase up-selling
- new staff induction training
- when planned changes require new skills or knowledge
- when individuals or teams will be changing jobs in the future and training builds their personal development.

It is a good idea to consider all the types of jobs in the unit. Make a list of these, and then think about the relationships between them. Where are there overlaps and relationships? Remember that you are thinking about job titles and not the current jobholders.

1 Consider flexibility; to what extent is it desirable to have people specialized in departments? For example, many staff specialize in one job or type of job (kitchen, bar, restaurant) because of a combination of personal preferences and effectiveness. Specialization frequently improves job skills and productivity, but at the expense of flexibility.

2 Does specialization lead to rigidities in the workforce? Is it desirable to train staff to be functionally flexible, so they can then be employed in different roles?

Once you have listed the job types, make a list of the duties to be undertaken in each job. This process of drawing up job descriptions helps you think carefully about the range of tasks to be undertaken and, flowing from this, the expertise, knowledge and social skills needed to undertake them.

1 Next, compare the performance of individual jobholders against the requirements of the job – both as needed now, and for the future.
2 Consider changes that may be needed because of expansion, new equipment, new products or new services.
3 Think about the personal development of existing employees, and the implications for training and development and further education.

Bring together all the training needs you have identified and arrange these in order of priority, bearing in mind their importance to your overall unit objectives and the ease with which they can be achieved. In some cases, short training activities during a quiet period may help you to address problems and can be of great benefit.

Contrast and compare the training and resources needed against the resources available to you. Obviously there may be extra resources you can call on, and a prior investment in building a base of staff or managers who are 'trained to train' will help because this gives you a better resource base. Like J.D. Wetherspoons (Box 6.1), an investment in 'training skill' helps to establish the resources needed for an ongoing commitment to training and the establishment of a training culture. Most importantly, the more people trained to train others, the fewer constraints there are on you delivering training.

The training plan

The plan of action flows from the identification of training needs and priorities. You have to make judgements about the extent to which an identified need has to be met immediately and, bearing in mind the comments about the costs of not training mentioned earlier, you need to consider the implications of delaying the delivery of an identified training need.

Again a written plan may seem overly formal, but it is an investment in time that is well worth making:

1 Decide the timescale of the plan. You may have a broad plan covering twelve months, but there may well be shorter-term objectives – say, to increase average sales per transaction. A realistic target helps you to evaluate the training.
2 Plan the resources needed and available to help you achieve your plan and budget for them – remember, you need to make the policy and plans work.
3 There is no point in being over-ambitious; even if you have identified more training activities than you can resource, be realistic and do not try to do everything – start with what you can and must achieve.
4 Set down the numbers to be trained and the various targets to be achieved.
5 Remember to include induction training, and the training needs of new staff. Where staff turnover is high, or where you are recruiting new employees for an anticipated busy period, you must allow time for new employee training.
6 Against each item on the training plan, identify where, when, how and by whom the training will be carried out.
7 Where appropriate, fix dates against the training events.
8 Build in the processes of monitoring and evaluation – has the training been effective?

Carry out the training programme

It is likely that there will be a number of different training needs identified in your unit. Some will be aimed at all or a significant group of your staff; in other cases you may want to train individuals.

The sessions might be short sessions taking no more than 20 minutes, or the training may require a series of different sessions building an integrated set of skills. In some cases you may want to train the individual how to complete a task, and in others you may want to train the person in knowledge and social skills.

It is essential that you plan these sessions very carefully and remember that you are intending to achieve specific outcomes.

1 What do you expect the trainees to be able to do after the session? Remember this is likely to be expressed in active verbs – make a Manhattan; wash down the counter; change the till roll etc.
2 Decide where and when the training will take place – in the workplace before service; during service but in a quiet period; during normal service. Remember that it is easier to learn knowledge, say recipes or legal issues, away from the pressures of service. Learning a skill requires practice, so this may be best done in service, although you may need to work alongside the trainee, and issues about planning the time period and choosing the right sessions may be relevant.
3 Draw up a list of the training events and stages needed, and the time each will typically take.
4 Specify the subjects to be covered.
5 Decide on the learning and teaching methods to be used – will the training involve materials (for example, when you are training a person to make a cocktail)? Highlight and list the materials you will require. Will you be using a video or online service?
6 Identify who will carry out the training.
7 Identify the means by which you will assess the trainee's achievement of the objective set. Will this be via demonstration, or observation whilst doing the job? Will it involve tests? Remember that the means by which you assess the trainee will be a by-product of the objectives set.

Some training tips

Training is ultimately about changing behaviour, so make sure that you are clearly focused on the behaviours that you wish to develop.

1 Learning and training are likely to be most effective when the trainee wants to learn and can see the benefit of the training.
2 People will learn most effectively when they are told what they going to learn.
3 People learn at different rates, and staff will have different knowledge and experiences on which the training will be built – make allowance for this.
4 Learning is made difficult when the trainee is frightened or anxious. Similarly, hurried or interrupted sessions can also create learning difficulties.
5 People have different learning styles, but in the main people attracted to licensed retail occupations are activist learners, and learn best by doing. In other words, practical involvement and completing tasks is most effective.

6 People cannot remember long strings of information or actions. You may need to break the training into steps during which time you provide short sets of inputs.

7 Learning is most effective when the training sessions are entertaining and use varied techniques.

8 Trainees need targets and they like to be able to monitor their own progress. The more the trainee has a sense of ownership of the training, the more effective it will be.

9 Build up the trainee's confidence by focusing on achievements. Reprimands for faults will create a climate of fear or reduced confidence that can present a barrier to learning.

10 Trainees will make mistakes, it is almost impossible to learn any new skill or technique without doing so, so expect these and treat them as positive learning opportunities.

11 All skill learning goes through a 'learning curve' during which trainees progress quickly, slow up or slip back and make progress again. It is essential that you understand that this is part of the normal learning process.

Remember that training someone is most effective when they have a chance to practise what they have learnt soon after the training session. So make sure that this is part of your planning process.

Finally, keep a record of the training that has been undertaken, and continue to monitor performance on a regular basis. It is very easy for people to slip back into old ways of doing things, particularly under pressure of service.

Evaluating the training undertaken

When the training programme has been completed, you need to evaluate its impact on the objectives that you set.

1 Were you able to carry out all the plan? Were there difficulties and problems? How might these be overcome in future?

2 Consider the elements of the training programme that worked best and worst. What can you learn from this?

3 Consider the training undertaken in detail; were some techniques more successful than others?

4 What are the priorities for the next period? Can you now concentrate on things that you identified, but weren't able to achieve in the earlier period?

5 Finally, using the objectives set out earlier, what business benefits have been achieved through the training activities?

Box 6.2 provides an example.

Box 6.2 *TGI Friday Restaurants*

Employee performance, particularly of frontline staff, has a crucial role to play. The success of the service depends 'on the worker's ability to construct particular kinds of interactions'. 'Dub-dubs', as the waiting staff are called, have to advise customers on the menu and how best to structure their meal. They also have to identify the customer's service requirements and deliver what is needed. In some cases, 'having a good laugh with the customers' is needed, in others, they need to leave the guests to their own devices, or create the necessary celebratory atmosphere to match a birthday or other party occasion. At other times they have to entertain restive children. Employee performance therefore requires more than the traditional acts of greeting, seating and serving customers. Employees have to be able to provide both the behaviours and the emotional displays to match customer wants and feelings. Similarly, bar staff provide both the showmanship needed to command a premium price, and the personalized service needed to 'connect with others'.

The organizational structure within restaurants is somewhat traditional and typical of this kind of business. Each unit has a restaurant manager responsible for the overall running and performance of the unit. A junior manager then heads up each of the two key elements of the operation: the senior service manager is responsible for the front of house operations (restaurant and bars), and the quality manager is responsible for the back of house operations (kitchen and stores).

Individuals are trained for specific jobs: bar, restaurant and kitchen. There is some evidence of staff moving from one department to another, but this is not a formal feature of the training, nor is it a widespread experience. Some employees play a supervisory role as shift leader and are given some extra pay, in the form of extra hours when they take on the role. The other positions of note are: hosts (responsible for receiving guests) and the expediter (responsible for ensuring the speedy production of meals from the kitchen, and appropriate garnish of dishes prior to service to customers).

The training starts before the new recruit is put to work. A one-week course 'front-loads' training for every new employee. The course focuses on the nature of the brand and service offer to customers as well as specific product knowledge – recipes for the 100 food and cocktail menu items. This programme ends with a test on the content of the course. Those who pass the induction programme exam move to specific job training in the bar, restaurant and kitchen. In the kitchen, a recruit is trained to a specific 'corner' and supported by a training manual and a more experienced employee. The new bar recruit also works alongside an experienced employee, who takes the recruit through various cocktail recipes and drinks service. In the restaurant, the new recruit is put to work in a quiet section of the restaurant and given just two tables to serve. As the recruit becomes more experienced, this is increased until he or she is able to take on a full station of four tables in a busy part of the restaurant.

Staff appraisals of each employee's job performance are undertaken by the restaurant management every three months. Future training and development needs are then identified and plans put in place to action them.

The ABC of training

The following section provides you with a simple step-by-step set of practical tips for undertaking a training session. Remember, the training session may be either a short session undertaken during a quiet period, or a more detailed session prior to the shift. In all cases the following steps will help both you and the trainees gain the most benefit from the session.

Preparation

Although training might be undertaken during periods of any service shift, it should never be unplanned. You must ensure that:

- there will be no interruptions during the session – it is difficult to concentrate on the training when there are interruptions
- you are prepared and have all the materials and knowledge needed to conduct the session effectively – a lack of preparation or knowledge makes it difficult for the trainees to learn
- all the materials and equipment you need are also working – nothing can be more off-putting than a training session where the things needed are not available or not working.

Effective training is totally dependent on effective preparation and planning.

Attention

You need to gain the trainee's attention before starting. Effective training will be dependent on the trainee wanting to learn and being attentive and responsive to the trainer. Here are some steps that you might go through when setting up the trainees and gaining their attention.

1 *What*. You must state clearly and simply what the trainees are going to learn. Try to avoid jargon, or explain it in terms that trainees will understand. Work from the principle that 'if they can get it wrong, they will get it wrong'. Clear explanation is the key.

2 *Interest*. The second aspect of gaining trainees' attention is to create interest in what is to be learnt. Being motivated to learn is dependent on the trainees feeling that they will be learning something that they are interested in and a task they want to be able to do. To gain the trainees' interest:
  - show the finished product
  - give a brief background of the product or task
  - recount a positive personal story about the task
  - relate the task to the trainee's own interests
  - ask a question.
  Avoid long, complicated explanations, because the trainees will become bored. Your purpose is to develop trainees' interest in learning.

3 *Need*. The third aspect of building the trainees' attention and motive to learn is to establish the benefits to them. In other words, you are trying to answer the 'What's

in it for me?' question. Trainees who see the benefit to themselves are more likely to learn quickly and effectively. The benefits may be:

- safer, easier working
- respect from other staff members
- better relationships with customers
- pride in doing a good job
- any material rewards paid to trained employees.

Breakdown

Training is communicated through demonstration of the task in question. This should be planned and undertaken in stages. This is where the planning and preparation stages are important, because poorly considered training programmes often result in trainees being given only part of the story. It is very easy for the experienced trainer, who does the task automatically, to miss out some key fact or judgement.

The task needs to be broken down into its key steps. Complicated tasks may be learnt in a series of stages, whereas in other cases the whole task is demonstrated in one sequence.

Explain each step as you go, picking out key points or areas where things can go wrong. Asking and inviting questions are important parts of this stage. You are trying to make it as clear as possible.

Again, remember that ' if they can get it wrong, they will get it wrong'. This is not a comment on the skills of the trainees; it is a fact of training life.

Check

This stage is concerned with ensuring both that the trainer has trained the trainee to the required standard, and that the trainee is capable of undertaking the task to the required standard. There are two aspects to the check stage:

1 The verbal check
2 The practical check.

In the *verbal check*, the trainer uses testing questions to ensure that all the information has been understood and all the new information can be recalled. Factual questions might be asked about specific knowledge about the task or service being taught, e.g. 'What temperature should raw meat be stored at?' More open-ended questions are relevant to understanding the general reasons why some things are done, e.g. 'Why is correct food storage an important aspect of safe food handing?'

The *practical check* is the most important part of the training. The trainee works though the task and shows that he or she can complete the task to the required standard:

1 The trainee completes the task uninterrupted. Frequent interruptions and comments from you can cause loss of concentration and confidence.
2 When evaluating the trainee's performance, focus on the strengths and positive aspects, and go through those aspects that were not done correctly in an unthreatening and non-blaming manner.

3 Remember, everyone makes mistakes when learning something for the first time. Often they go through a learning curve that includes downs as well as ups, so expect people to need to practise a new task several times, and be aware that they will make errors even about things they seemed to have mastered at an earlier stage.

4 When the appropriate standard has been reached, give praise and leave the trainee to get on with it. He or she will need to work on the task for a while before output and performance reach their best.

5 Go back and check with the trainee, every now and again.

Some process of performance review and appraisal is essential. It is not good enough just to train staff and leave it there; if you want to sustain high levels of performance you must continue to monitor and evaluate performance. Sometimes you will have to go back and re-train staff, if their performance slips away from the standard expected.

Conclusions

Employee training is one of the key elements in successful unit management in licensed retail operations. Through training production and service staff, you are able to deliver consistent performance to customers. In most licensed retail brands there will be some element of training employees in the 'one best way' to perform tasks. This is in many cases the means by which the brand consistency is achieved. Obviously this aspect of training takes on added significance in uniformity-dependent brands like J.D. Wetherspoons. However, even in these brands there is an aspect of customer service training that has to go beyond the 'one best way'; some customer service needs are difficult to predict and script. Service staff should be trained in how to respond to unusual requests, and this aspect of training takes on more significance in choice-dependent and relationship-dependent services. In these services, staff training is likely to involve more role modelling, critical incident acting and values learning rather than learning to do things in a set way.

An investment in training will help you achieve wider business benefits. It is important to remember that training is aimed at changing employee behaviour, and financial benefits flow from these changes. So improving employee productivity, increasing sales revenue, reducing staff turnover, and reducing wastage and equipment damage have an impact on sales revenue and costs. This in turn impacts on operating profits. Staff training improves service quality, increases customer satisfaction, and leads to the increased likelihood of customers returning to the unit. Similarly, staff training impacts on employee satisfaction, with increased flexibility and willingness to accept change, and these produce more intangible, but nonetheless real, benefits.

Finally, your approach to training needs to be systematic, planned and ongoing. It should be part of a general commitment to being a learning organization – that is, a complete commitment to developing both managers and employees. In these circumstances, training and development needs flow from staff appraisals and performance review processes. Employees' future development needs and their current work performance enable you to come up with a plan of what needs to be achieved and the priorities for action needed. Benchmark training organizations like J.D. Wetherspoons set standards of excellence that many licensed retailers could follow. In this company, not only is the training provision made available; it is made an important business performance indicator, and managers are made accountable for the training taking place.

Hospitality, Leisure & Tourism Series

Reflective practice

Answer the following questions to check your understanding of this chapter.

1 Discuss critically the business benefits of training in licensed retail operations. Make the case for and against an investment in training.
2 Describe the steps you will take in identifying training needs in a licensed retail operation.
3 Contrast and compare different approaches to training, and show how you might evaluate training effectiveness.
4 Using a licensed retail operation known to you, devise a training plan for both production and service staff. Explain your answer.
5 Discuss critically the different approaches to training and employee development in licensed retail operations. To what extent can there be 'one best way' of training staff?

Further reading

Beardwell, I. and Holden, L. (1994). *Human Resource Management: A Contemporary Perspective*. Pitman.

British Hospitality Association (1998). *Creating Hospitality's Virtuous Circle of Employment*. British Licensed Association.

Maghurn, J. P. (1989). *A Manual of Staff Management in the Hotel and Catering Industry*. Heinemann.

Mullins, L. J. (1998). *Licensed Management: A Human Resource Approach*. Pitman.

CHAPTER 7

Serve hot food hot, and cold drinks cold, and everybody smiles

Learning objectives

After working through this chapter, you should be able to:

- identify the key problems in managing service quality in licensed retail operations

- discuss critically the different approaches to service quality management

- operate a suitable service quality management system

- evaluate service quality and create correction strategies.

Managing service quality

The major underlying theme of this book is that service quality is an important business strategy that is fundamental to success in competitive licensed retail operations. Customer retention and the attraction of new customers depends on ensuring that customers have a clear idea about what to expect from the licensed retailer, and making sure that they get it. This theme is developed more fully later, but this chapter title from the *My Kinda Town* training manual sums up the key issues for licensed retail operators – that is, you deliver what you say you will deliver; you will be supplying both products and services; and employee performance is a fundamental element of successful service delivery.

Although managing successful licensed service quality is not 'rocket science', there are some important difficulties and tensions for you to manage. As we have seen in Chapter 1, licensed retail services differ and require different forms of standardization and control. The varying combinations of products and services and the importance of employee performance, together with different customer expectations of successful service encounters, make for complexity in managing service organizations. This combination is rarely found in the management of manufacturing organizations.

Several systems of service quality management and performance monitoring have been introduced. Total Quality Management, ISO9000, Investors in People and other systems are all devised to ensure that internal management processes make sure that quality is delivered 'right first time'. In addition, these systems certify individual businesses and units as a message to external customers and clients. This matter should not be dismissed lightly, because:

- customers are often uncertain about the quality of experience they will receive
- benchmark labels help customers feel more secure about the service they will get
- when applied properly, these systems can help deliver real benefits in the management of service quality.

Different systems deliver different benefits, so you need to select the system most closely suited to your needs. The following chapter explores some of the problems associated with defining and managing licensed retail service quality. It briefly outlines some of the more widely applied approaches to quality management, and details some steps that you can take to ensure that your unit achieves high levels of customer satisfaction.

Licensed retail service quality

As indicated in Chapter 1, the core features of services are intangibility, inseparability, variability and perishability, leaving licensed retail organizations with some difficulties and dilemmas to manage in their delivery.

The *intangible* elements of services make it difficult for customers to establish the benefits to be gained from a service prior to the purchase. This can only be done as a result of receiving the service. For intangible services:

- it is difficult to measure and define the expectations of customers, service employees, and managers regarding what the intangible benefits should be

- successful service delivery frequently depends on customers developing feelings of comfort or belonging, which are difficult to generate.

The *heterogeneity* of services is also a feature that distinguishes them from typical manufacturing production. Service delivery is frequently variable and difficult to standardize because of the personal nature of the contact between the customer and the service deliverer (the staff member). Thus:

- individuals may well vary in their interpretation of customer needs
- elements of human 'chemistry' may interfere with performance – some individuals may be more personally committed to successful service encounters
- customer expectations of satisfactory service may well vary and be difficult to predict.

Hence it is difficult to say the service delivery is homogeneous, even where the service is relatively simple.

The third important feature of services is that the production and consumption of the service is *inseparable*. This creates a number of differences with typical manufacturing firms in that consumers:

- are themselves participants in the service delivery, say as customers in a bar, café or restaurant
- interact with the service deliverer, the environment and other consumers
- are party to the service interaction and will partially shape it; they will have their perceptions of the service encounter shaped through their perceptions of the service environment and the perceptions of fellow customers.

Finally, services are typically subject to *perishability* because they are temporal. Bed spaces in hotels or seats in restaurants represent capacity for a given period only. Thus:

- it is not possible to store up sales and satisfy them at another time
- loss of service output cannot be made up at a later date – in many cases the service is time-specific, and once lost is gone forever
- the empty hotel bed or unsold restaurant meal represents revenue never to be regained
- licensed retailer service deliverers are not able to stockpile services, make up lost service production through overtime working, or multi-source services to allow for fluctuations in the demand and supply of services
- service quality faults cannot easily be reworked and given back to the customer, as might happen with a manufactured product
- service demand has to be satisfied as and when it is required, making it difficult to plan service delivery to meet service demand.

Finally, most licensed retail services are supplied to customers who do not 'own' the service as supplied; they cannot take it away or return it if unsatisfactory. Because of the intangibility and perishability features, customers are frequently buying the right to a service or an experience. This creates problems of loyalty and memory. Unlike the possessors of a tangible product that is taken home, licensed retail consumers rarely have permanent reminders of the product's features or benefits. Repeat purchases will be based on a bundle of memories, experiences and expectations, so individual perceptions and differences become important issues.

Licensed retail products and services

Licensed retailers supply a combination of products and services and, as we saw in Chapter 1, there are differences between different types of offers made to customers. The service offer may be:

1 *Uniformity-dependent*: customers expect that the product and services delivered will be uniform and standardized. Customer evaluations of service quality in these cases will be largely concerned with the consistent delivery of standardized products and services delivering 'good value' for money.
2 *Relationship-dependent*: customers experience more contact with service personnel and evaluate service quality in terms of the intangible aspects of the service encounter. The relationship with service personnel in particular produces appropriate feelings in the customer.
3 *Choice-dependent*: customers want security of the branded product but also want wide choice so they can make the occasion suit their mood and needs. The product range in both food and drink items is usually extensive. In addition, the service personnel have to be flexible enough and capable of giving the performance to match the customer occasion.

In each of these types of licensed retail operations customer evaluations of the quality of the experience will be different, because customers are seeking different sorts of experiences and using the outlets for different occasions and with different expectations of a successful service encounter. In all cases, however, licensed retailers are supplying a bundle of products and services that include tangible (and therefore measurable) benefits as well as intangible benefits, which are more difficult

| | Characteristics of the experience | |
	Tangible	Intangible
Nature of product	The food and drink product Serving goods – plates, glasses, cutlery, linen etc. Information – menu Process – e.g. credit cards	Atmosphere Décor and furnishings Feelings Comfort
The service contact	Actions Process Speed Script Corrective action	Warmth Friendliness Care Service Hospitality

Table 7.1 The quality characteristics matrix (adapted from Lockwood *et al.*, 1996)

to evaluate. Table 7.1 provides some examples of the tangible and intangible aspects of products and services.

Table 7.1 does not include an exhaustive list of product and service tangibles and intangibles; Figure 1.2 provided a more in-depth list. However, it does show that some aspects of licensed retail operations are more measurable and capable of being monitored than others on the list. Given the variations in service types given above, the significance of different features will vary between different types of licensed retail operations, and the nature of how the characteristics are defined will also vary. For example, speed is one of the tangible aspects of the service provided. In most licensed retail brands, operational standards lay down target times for greeting customers or serving their meals and drinks.

In McDonald's Restaurants, for example, the service standard states that customers should not be queuing for more than ninety seconds, and customer orders should take no more than three minutes to complete. Speed of service is one of the key elements of the company's offer to customers, and is very consistent with the customer occasion based on refuelling. For other customer occasions, customers would not value overly speedy service. When customers are having a special meal out, for example, more leisurely service times are required, and hurried service would be seen as a service fault.

Active learning point

In three brands known to you, describe the key characteristics of service quality in each brand. Contrast and compare the similarities and differences between them.

Characteristics	Brand A	Brand B	Brand C

As unit manager, your problem is in understanding what these expectations are and then sharing them with the employees on the front line so they can deliver the service in a way that matches with customer expectations.

With regard to service:

1 Consumer expectations of service quality become an important definitive feature of service quality when set against experiences of the service.
2 Customers have a base level of expectations of the service – the minimum they expect. They have a level of expectation about what the service should be like with regard to what they want.
3 Customers also predict what they expect the quality to be like.
4 Customers may vary in their expectations; customers with more experience of a service may well have higher expectations than those who have less experience of it.
5 Licensed retailers have a role in shaping expectations; advertising and other promotional activities may influence consumer expectations.
6 It is important that the service delivered in your unit matches these expectations.

The key aim is to meet customer expectations in such a way as to ensure that customers are not just satisfied that their expectations have been met, but also that their satisfaction is such that they will return. It is worth considering Herzberg's motivation model here. Herzberg suggested that there are two sets of factors that people potentially evaluate when considering positive and negative responses to service:

1 *Hygiene factors.* These are characteristics such as cleanliness of the toilets. Customers have an expectation of the required standards, and will be dissatisfied if these are not met. However, when these standards are met, this does not motivate customers to return.
2 *Motivators.* Motivators, on the other hand, are those characteristics of service that customers value highly – mostly intangibles, like being made to feel important and valued, and hospitality, and will motivate customer loyalty.

Herzberg's model is valuable because it suggests that there are some characteristics that, if they do not meet expectations, will cause customer dissatisfaction. On the other hand, meeting customer expectations in these characteristics is not a guarantee of customer loyalty – there is just an absence of dissatisfaction. Real customer motivators are those characteristics of the service that customers value most.

As unit manager, you have to ensure that you understand customer expectations – particularly the hygiene factors, which might cause dissatisfaction, and the motivators, which will motivate customers to return.

Some licensed retailers use SERVQUAL to compare customer's expectations with their experiences. SERVQUAL shows where service delivery has strengths and weaknesses. The performance of different competitors can be compared with the service organization's own performance. In particular, it reveals 'five service gaps' where there may be a mismatch between the expectation of the service level and the perception of the service delivered. Table 7.2 highlights the five dimensions that have been identified for the basis for the SERVQUAL system of quality evaluation.

Dimension	Definition
Reliability	The ability to perform the promised service dependably and accurately
Tangibles	The appearance of physical facilities, equipment, personnel and communication materials
Responsiveness	The willingness to help customers and provide prompt service
Assurance	The knowledge and courtesy of employees, and their ability to convey trust and confidence
Empathy	The caring, individualized attention paid to the customer

Table 7.2 The five dimensions of service

Any gaps will focus on the points at which expectations of service requirements by management, the standards set, the standards achieved, or the service standards communicated to customers produce a situation where customers' perceptions of the service delivered do not match with the expected service.

Responsiveness, assurance and empathy are elements of this model that underscore the importance of employee performance in the service encounter. Given the nature of services, it is often difficult to predict what employees have to say or do in given service encounters. Although some employee tasks can be predicted, standardized and trained for, frontline staff are often required to respond to unforeseen situations, even in classic uniformity-dependent operations like McDonald's. Some writers look to critical incidents in which employee responses can be shown either to save a situation and create customer satisfaction, or to create customer dissatisfaction. Their findings suggested three broad groups of incidents – employee responses to service delivery system failures, employee reactions to customer needs and requests, and unprompted and unsolicited employee actions (Table 7.3). Each group represented a cluster of incidents in which employee behaviour could result in customer satisfaction or customer dissatisfaction.

Employee responses to service delivery system failures can be critical, because customers are more likely to excuse a service failure if the fault is acknowledged and quickly corrected. Any problem that is not corrected at the unit may result in complaints to head office and, more importantly, a lost customer. Taking into account the fact that each customer tells friends and relatives, the lost custom can cost far in excess of the price of a replaced meal or free bottle of wine.

Similarly, employee reactions to customer needs and requests are important in all service situations because there are bound to be occasions when customers want something that is not normally sold via the brand, or where they make a mistake and want some assistance in correcting their fault. Customers are much more likely to respond positively if they are treated with flexibility and the service employee makes every effort to meet their needs.

Unprompted and unsolicited employee actions incorporate actions that are outside the customer's expectations of the service encounter. Where employee performance is beyond the customer expectation of the service, the incident can produce satisfaction – exceeding customer expectations may involve the detail of

Critical incident	Customer satisfaction	Customer dissatisfaction
Employee responses to service delivery failure	Could be turned into incidents that employees use to advantage and to generate customer satisfaction – for example, if an employee reacts quickly to service failure by responding sensitively to customer experiences (perhaps by compensating the customer or upgrading the customer to a higher status service)	More frequently, however, staff responses were likely to be source of a dissatisfaction – where the employee fails to provide an apology or an adequate explanation, or argues with the customer
Employee responses to customer needs and requests	Employees' responsiveness, flexibility and confidence that they can match whatever is needed by the customer are important sources of a positive customer response	Similarly, employees' intransigence, inflexibility and perceived incompetence are all likely sources of customer dissatisfaction
Unprompted and unsolicited employee actions	This might involve employee behaviours that make the customer feel special, or where an act of unexpected generosity takes the customer by surprise	Customer dissatisfaction could be the result of a failure to give the customer the level of attention expected, or inadequate information, or might involve inappropriate behaviour such as the use of bad language, etc.

Table 7.3 Positive and negative responses to critical service incidents

employees' performance. Employees in TGI Fridays are encouraged to perform in a way that underpins the brand's offer to customers, which involves humour and a 'fun' atmosphere. Often this involves providing balloons or singing songs at a birthday celebration.

The issue of employee performance and customer satisfaction takes on added urgency when firms begin to consider the costs of lost business and the benefits of generating customer loyalty:

1 In a pub context, one firm estimates that every pub customer spends an average of £785 per annum in public houses. A customer lost due to an unresolved complaint means a direct loss to that business of that amount. In addition, it is estimated that a dissatisfied customer tells another thirteen people about their experience. The potential cost of one unresolved complaint is therefore, fourteen times this amount – £11 032.

2 In a restaurant context, it has been estimated that if an organization lost one customer per day for a year, the total cost to the business would be over £94 000 per annum even if customers only spent on average £5 per week with the organization.

3 Similarly, it was estimated that repeat custom only cost one-fifth of the amount needed to generate new customers. Within a hotel context, this was closer to one-seventh – in other words, attracting a new customer costs seven times what it costs to get an existing customer to repeat.

The financial implications of customer satisfaction, and the key role employees play in the service encounter, have brought about concern to ensure employees are equipped to maximize their effectiveness. It is essential that you 'invest in your staff'. Figure 7.1 shows the links that are made between customer satisfaction, customer turnover, employee satisfaction and employee turnover. In the upper part of the figure, a virtuous cycle results in a continuous improvement in all the elements. The lower portion of the diagram presents a vicious cycle in which declining customer satisfaction results in reduced customer retention, which results in employees having to work harder to recruit new customers, which reduces employee satisfaction and increases employee turnover, and in turn impacts on customer satisfaction.

This section has attempted to show that licensed retail unit managers have problems in the management of service quality. The very nature of the service encounter is difficult, because it involves subjective assessment of what is expected

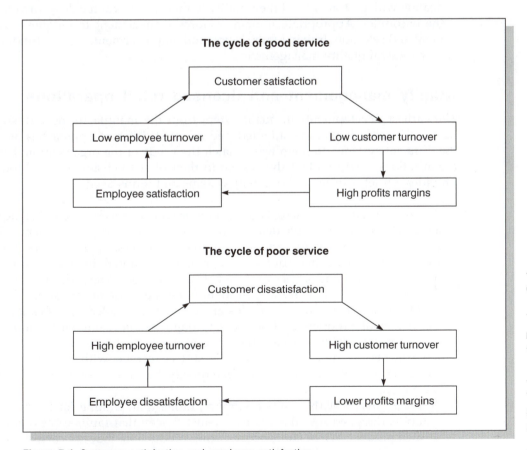

Figure 7.1 Customer satisfaction and employee satisfaction

on the behalf of customers, frontline staff, and management. Branded licensed retailers have attempted to simplify some of the problems by sending clear messages to customers as to what to expect, and then adopting systematic approaches to service delivery so that these expectations are met. This section suggests several key concepts in managing service quality:

1 Licensed retail operations supply both products and services to customers, that result in tangible and intangible benefits. It is easier to manage the tangible aspects of the offer, but both are important and need careful monitoring.
2 As a unit manager, you need to understand that customers use the same restaurant and bar on different occasions with different expectations and motives. You need to understand these different needs and expectations so that you are able to focus on what customers consider important.
3 Customers have different expectations of the service characteristics supplied and rank these differently. For some aspects expectations are that the service will be up to a basic standard, although over-provision of these things will not always motivate customers to return. You need to understand the motivators – those aspects of service that will build real customer loyalty.
4 Employee performance in the service encounter is seen to be key to much of the customers' experience. Their responsiveness, assurance and empathy when dealing with customers and their ability to manage critical incidents are crucial to the encounter. Appropriate human resource management techniques – recruitment and selection, training, motivation and empowerment – are all fundamental to successful quality management.

Quality management and licensed retail operations

The earliest developments in quality stem from the manufacturing industry, and licensed organizations have adopted and adapted different approaches, although the different systems do not always match the needs of the organization. Different organizations need to adapt the system to their offer to customers. The following provides a brief overview of different systems and terms used:

1 *Quality inspection.* Here, actual output of a product or service is checked against a standard specification and defects are then reworked or sent for scrap. Whilst quality inspection is undertaken via line managers, quality inspectors and mystery customers, the approach is frequently limited by the nature of the licensed products and services. It is not always possible to rework a faulty product or service. Also, there is no way of identifying the cause of the fault.
2 *Quality control.* Here, quality is designed into the detailed specification in the production of products and services through detailed standards, and quality checks are introduced through the various stages of the process – say between departments. At root, the approach is still concerned with the detecting and correcting of faults. It will not improve quality, but it does show when quality is not present.
3 *Quality assurance.* With quality assurance, rather than waiting for faults to occur, quality is designed into the process in such a way that faults can't occur in the finished product. When faults occur during production, they are corrected as they happen. The approach involves developing a documented and planned quality

system. Quality assurance requires total organizational commitment and involvement of all employees in the process. A key problem is that although quality assurance may deliver consistently faultless products and services, it may not be what customers want.

4 *Total quality management*. Here, the focus is on customers and the satisfaction of customer needs. The system is totally directed at customer satisfaction and the removal of any barriers to achieving this. People in the organization are key to achieving customer satisfaction – employee training, motivation and empowerment are important. Again, successful implementation needs total cultural commitment, and this can be difficult because it is often hard to change the organization's culture.

The approaches listed above are not of themselves mutually exclusive; one approach builds on another and, as we'll see later, effective quality programmes often incorporate aspects of all these approaches. So systems based on total quality management still need to involve quality inspection and quality control, whilst the number of faults and problems should be greatly reduced.

Although licensed retail organizations can develop their own quality systems, many find that nationally and internationally recognized systems are helpful as a way of providing a framework in which to work. As stated earlier, many of these systems are also recognized by customers and clients, and help to reassure them about the quality of service they will receive. In addition, in some markets – workplace retailing, for example – many firms will only deal with companies who are themselves recognized quality suppliers.

Total quality unit management

As a unit manager in a retail unit, you may be involved in managing service quality in compliance with an award scheme operated by the company. However, you may also be managing a unit where there is no imposed system. In these cases, the philosophy of total quality management (TQM) will be very helpful to you.

Licensed retail organizations require quality systems that are holistic enough to allow for the characteristics of services and the varied perceptions of customers. TQM appears to offer service organizations the system needed.

Even though there are several forms of total quality management, Table 7.4 lists several broad features of TQM that are found in most descriptions of the initiative.

Remember:

1 At heart, the TQM initiative locates a commitment to quality services as a core organizational concern. The commitment of senior management is crucial, and the approach has to permeate every aspect of the organization.
2 The approach has been particularly attractive to licensed retail organizations because it aims to create a cultural environment in which employees, operating independently, are guided by a commitment to delighting customers because they have internalized the organization's objectives and values.
3 These internalized values, beliefs and objectives ensure that employees aspire to customer satisfaction and quality improvement, without extrinsic controls or inducements.

1	Highest priority is given to quality throughout the organization
2	Quality is defined in terms of customer satisfaction
3	Customers are defined as those who have both internal and external relationships with the organization – including employees, shareholders, the wider community
4	Customer satisfaction and the building of long-term relationships are at the nub of the organization
5	The organization's aims will be clearly stated and accessible to all
6	The principles, beliefs, values and quality are communicated throughout the organization
7	Total quality management creates an ethos that pervades all aspects of the organization's activities
8	Core values of honesty, integrity, trust and openness are essential ingredients of TQM
9	The total quality organization is intended to be mutually beneficial to all concerned, and operates in a climate of mutual respect for all stakeholders
10	The health and safety of all organization members and customers are prioritized
11	Total quality offers individuals the chance to participate and feel ownership for the success of the enterprise
12	Commitment is generated in individuals and teams through leadership from senior management
13	TQM results in an organization-wide commitment to continuous improvement
14	Performance measurement, assessment and auditing of the organization's activities is a common feature of TQM
15	TQM aims to use resources more effectively, and members are encouraged to consider ways of using resources more effectively
16	TQM requires appropriate investment to ensure that planned activity can occur

Table 7.4 Principles of total quality management

The similarities between TQM and empowerment are not accidental, because many of those writing about the benefits of TQM as an approach for managing service organizations also advocate the need to empower with the authority to correct defects and respond to service failures as they occur. Furthermore, employee empowerment is important so employees can respond to unusual customer requests, or use their experience and creativity to look for ways of delighting the customer. These aspirations for TQM and empowerment are relevant to the three critical incidents that could create or damage customer satisfaction:

1 Dealing with service failures
2 Responding to requests for unusual service
3 Providing extraordinary interactions.

All are occasions when employee behaviour impacts either positively or negatively on customer satisfaction and perceptions of service quality. TQM provides an organizational setting in which empowered employees, through a heightened sense of their own personal efficacy, will respond in the desired way.

Forms of total quality management

All the companies that have been quoted in this text have their own ways of dealing with the management of service quality. They incorporate many of the concepts of total quality management, even though they do not all call it by that name. The following three forms of TQM provide you with some options, although there is unlikely to be an ideal match to the three licensed retail types that we identified earlier.

The 'hard' version of TQM

This definition places emphasis on the production aspects, such as systematic measurement and control of work, setting standards of performance, and using statistical procedures to assess quality. This is the hard production/operations management type of view, which arguably leads to less discretion for employees. This approach has compatibility with uniformity-dependent licensed retail services. Applying the terms used in Table 7.1, the service offer depends on products and services that are largely tangible and thereby measurable. We use McDonald's as a good example of the 'hard' approach, because it provides a useful insight into how this could be applied in some licensed retail operations (see Box 7.1).

Box 7.1 *McDonald's Restaurants Limited*

McDonald's Restaurants use **quality**, **service**, **cleanliness** and **value** (QSCV) as core organizational aspirations. All the company's service quality-monitoring processes assess QSCV; recognizing that value is a psychological concept, this is assessed using different techniques from the other three. Quality measures consider the physical food and drink products against standard specifications and appropriate temperature checks. Service includes waiting and queuing times as well as the time taken to process orders, and correct delivery of items. Cleanliness relates to the appearance of staff and premises, including front and back areas as well as external approaches – car parks and surrounding pavement areas.

All restaurants are assessed on a regular basis using 'mystery diners'; these represent a form of quality inspection, again using all the key QS&C measures. Area supervisor audits and manager-conducted assessments perform quality control checks. Customer comment cards ask all customers to comment on immediate service experience, and these are further supported by customer surveys that are given out to customers and entitle the customer to a discounted meal when they are returned. Customer complaints or praise received at head office also detract from or add to the quality score. All the sources of assessment are brought together in a series of grades that are used to evaluate unit performance. These quality assessments are used as points of entry for manager bonus schemes. Thus if a restaurant is increasing turnover and profits but failing to match quality targets, the manager will not be eligible for bonus payments. Only when service quality markers have been met will bonuses be paid.

Standardization and the accompanying psychological benefits are important features of the offer made by the company to its customers, and this shapes much of its management of human resources. Its brand values are tightly drawn and closely managed. Even franchise businesses are bound by the disciplines of the brand. The service dimension is largely shaped by concepts and practices developed in manufacturing industry. The approach draws on principles and

---

techniques such as the standard procedure manuals, division of labour, scientific management, and the use of technology to minimize the need for much employee discretion. Employees are trained to perform the various production processes in the 'one best way', and their performance is monitored through Observation Checklists. The McDonald's approach has much in common with the hard form of TQM and empowerment that is largely associated with winning commitment and developing the sense of personal efficacy; there is little in the way of decision-making authority passed to employees.

The 'soft' approach to TQM

The soft approach incorporates the characteristics identified by Peters – 'customer orientation, culture of excellence, removal of performance barriers, team working, training, employee participation, competitive edge'. From this perspective, TQM is seen as consistent with open management styles, delegated responsibility and increased autonomy of staff. Quality auditing is done by employees or management, and through consideration of customer feedback. The approach to employee empowerment is through participation, particularly through the working of autonomous work teams or individual targets for the service encounter, as in Marriott Hotels. Teams play an important role in both controlling individual performance and delivering employee commitment to organizational quality service targets.

The offer to customers, though still incorporating tangible benefits via products and services, relies more on intangible benefits from the service element. The approach is consistent with relationship-dependent licensed retail services. Box 7.2 provides an example.

Box 7.2 *Harvester Restaurants*

The Harvester Restaurants brand has some features that depend on tangible aspects of product and service. Standard recipes and operational manuals, standard décor and service processes provide measurable aspects of the offer to customers; however, the approach relies heavily on service relationships. The service values expressed in the phrase 'treating customers as though they were guests in your own home' provides a core value of homeliness, hospitality, tradition and naturalness.

Employees work in autonomous work teams that self-manage the service quality to customers. Each team is empowered to deal with customer complaints and whatever it takes to ensure customer satisfaction. This includes replacing meals, and providing free bottles of wine and other 'give-aways' to customers. Frontline teams in the restaurant and bar area are actively encouraged to deal with complaints without recourse to a manager. Complaints and difficulties are recorded after service through the use of representative meetings. All team members who act as 'shift co-ordinator' at some point in the week attend a weekly co-ordinating meeting, at which customer comments and experiences are discussed. A record of these meetings is made available to staff through a record book, which is freely accessible to all full- and part-time staff.

Recurring problems or difficulties are discussed with the immediate teams prior to each service occasion, and employees are able to make suggestions or immediate tactical decisions that positively impact on service quality. In the case of customer complaints to head office, employees and the 'team manager' thoroughly investigate the problem together. Where the system works properly, complaints are dealt with in the unit and many restaurants report no formal complaints to head office over the whole year.

The combined approach

A third approach to TQM is defined as a mixture of 'hard' and 'soft'. It is comprised of three features:

1 An obsession with quality
2 The need for a scientific approach
3 The view that all employees are part of one team.

Empowerment is through employee involvement, in that employees are encouraged to engage in the performance and identify with the performance of the unit.

Hard measures are used on the tangible aspects of the product and service. Standard procedures manuals specify dish and drink recipes and presentation, and service times and procedures are also specified. Staff are engaged in the activities through teamwork, careful recruitment and training. Team briefings and appropriate motivation and rewards are also an important aspect of the approach.

This approach is consistent with service styles that are choice-dependent. Services that rely on a highly standardized tangible offering in products and services but also require employees to deliver a quality experience will match with this approach to quality management. Box 7.3 provides an example.

Box 7.3 *TGI Friday Restaurants*

In many ways, TGI Fridays incorporates elements of both hard and soft approaches. Standard procedures manuals laid down production and presentation specifications, and service times are much more prescriptive than at Harvester Restaurants. Employee performance is not quite as prescribed as at McDonald's, although tests on product knowledge are used to ensure that frontline employees have the requisite technical knowledge to be able to advise customers. Employee performance is judged against time and against behavioural service requirements, such as checking customers are happy with the dish served. On the other hand, employee performance and the ability to identify customer service needs is evaluated at a more evaluative level. Ultimately, the company aims to create a cultural environment through which employees can provide a performance to which customers will respond favourably. A mixture of both personal material rewards (sales-related bonuses and tips) and appeals to team working are elements through which individuals are encouraged to deliver the quality experience. Careful staff selection and pre-work training are also key elements to the approach.

Prior to all service periods, employees attend a team briefing session that is formally organized by a senior member of the team. These sessions encourage staff to make suggestions and promote ideas for good service. They are also encouraged to tell jokes and even perform tricks and contribute to a 'fun' atmosphere.

Service quality management includes formal monitoring of service times through a computer program that manages the delivery time for starters and main courses, and through formal quality checkers ('expeditors') who stand at the service hatch and check that dishes are presented correctly before being served to customers. Employees are required to contribute to the customer's celebration or party atmosphere, so their performance is therefore key to the success of the brand. Their performance is monitored by managers on a quarterly basis, and 'best' staff are given a choice of shifts and restaurant service areas.

A manager usually deals with customer complaints. Managers monitor difficulties and problems. Where there are general difficulties, these are raised at the briefing sessions.

The naming of initiatives that prioritize customer service quality vary; *total quality management*, *customer service organization* and *total quality organization* are all variations of an approach that all have similar intentions, conceptual origins and ideological roots:

1 All basically suggest that service organizations can benefit from an organization-wide commitment to quality, the development of a customer quality dominated culture, employee empowerment, etc.
2 Many of these approaches recognize that competitive advantage can be gained from delivering consistent service quality and ensuring customer satisfaction.
3 Each identifies employee performance as playing a crucial role in identifying potential faults and thereby continuously improving performance, and as interacting with customers in ways that can either deliver customer satisfaction or dissatisfaction.

Conclusion

This chapter has shown that customer service quality management is an important, if not vital, aspect of your role as unit manager. The retention of existing customers and the attraction of new customers to the business are essential for sales growth. Certainly, the loss of regular customers has a real material impact on income and sales. In addition, dissatisfied customers rarely keep their experiences to themselves, and if they tell their friends and acquaintances the lost business can run into thousands of pounds.

Service quality management is difficult because customer satisfaction is associated with customer expectations. Not all customers use the unit for the same occasions, and their expectations and assessment of incidents critical to service success vary. In addition, employee assessments of customer needs may not match the customer expectation. Moreover, the nature of the service encounter itself is difficult because of the intangible aspects of service and the difficulties caused by the perishable nature of services. You cannot rework a smile or a false greeting.

Given these difficulties, many licensed retail organizations have explored a number of national and international award schemes that both provide a framework for designing and delivering quality and also provide a 'kite-mark' for customers and clients. Even in situations where there is no award system, total quality management provides a useful model for you to apply in your unit. Different types of service offer will require different TQM approaches, but all depend on a cultural commitment to delivering high quality service, and in all cases employee skills and performance are essential to meeting customer expectations successfully.

Reflective practice

Answer the following questions to check your understanding of this chapter.

1 For a licensed retail unit known to you, describe the key elements of the product and service offer to customers. What is the significance of the tangible and intangible aspects of the goods and services?
2 In the same business, consider the main customer occasions served by the unit. Describe different customer expectations of successful experiences. Do they use different critical success factors?
3 Would one of the quality award schemes benefit this unit? What do you see as the key benefits and limitations of the award schemes?
4 Highlight the steps needed to introduce a total quality management programme in your unit.
5 Discuss critically the various approaches to total quality management, and identify the approach that best matches the needs of the business unit you have in mind. Explain your answer.

Further reading

Lockwood, A., Baker, M. and Ghillyer, A. (1996). *Quality Management in Hospitality*. Cassell.

Teare, R., Atkinson, C. and Westwood, C. (1994). *Achieving Quality Performance: Lessons from British Industry*. Cassell.

CHAPTER 8

Get it hot to the table on time

After working through this chapter, you should be able to:

- explain the nature and benefits of a systematic and preventive approach to managing food operations

- define food operations outputs required to meet business goals

- analyse any food operation and its systems and processes to identify possible failure points and the nature of controls needed

- identify, plan, implement and evaluate effective and efficient management controls for any food operation.

Managing food operations

Food operations profitability

Throughout, the text has clearly focused on two key strategies for improving profitability in pubs, bars and restaurants; generating sales and/or controlling costs. Growing sales can improve profits, but usually managers who also understand that cost control is at the heart of profitability run the most successful units. The management of the food operations in your unit has clear and direct implications for each of these. Obviously, the greater the percentage of food in your sales mix, the greater will be the potential for the management of food operations to influence the unit's profitability. Using a fairly simple breakdown, it is easy to see how the food operations influence both sales generation and cost control:

1 *Sales generation*. The quality of products and service delivered to customers is a direct result of the management of the food operations, and is one of the key determinants of the level of sales generated. The *effectiveness* of food operations describes how well they deliver the consistent quality required – correct items at the correct time, in the correct place, to the specified standard.
2 *Cost control*. The cost of food is a high proportion of the unit's variable costs. Control of variable costs, in particular, has a dramatic effect on profitability because these represent the largest proportion of total costs, and in many ways are difficult to control. The *efficiency* of food operations describes how well they control costs. An efficient food system operates within the cost constraints set (at minimum cost).

The issues of cost and quality control are closely integrated within the processes and systems used to produce and deliver food to customers. As such, they are not dealt with as separate entities here. This chapter will focus on the general principles of controlling the processes and systems as applied to both costs and quality. Where appropriate, it will highlight specific implications for either costs or quality.

Food operations in licensed retailing

This chapter focuses on managing food. It is a legitimate question to ask why this is so, rather than considering food and drink operations together. The answer is, because the processes and systems for drink are simpler, as drink generally requires much less processing within the unit. However, many of the same principles apply to drink as to food, so a great deal of the chapter is transferable. The industry is a relative newcomer to the production and delivery of food, whereas it has over 200 years' experience in the provision of drink. The systems for control of the drink element are therefore reasonably well established and effective! The food systems are much less well developed, and clearly present potential areas for improvement. Where specific issues or controls are appropriate, reference will be made to drink.

In recent times, perhaps most noticeably in the last three to five years, the provision of food in pubs has been a dynamic and rapidly changing market. There has been enormous growth in the market. Demand has increased as customers have moved from other sectors of catering, and supply has increased in terms of numbers, variety of product and quality of provision. It is difficult to determine the cause and effect involved here. Has demand increased as a result of the improved and increased offer, or has the offer developed in response to the increased levels of demand? Ultimately, for the purposes of this text at least, the answer to this question is of academic interest only. What does matter is that provision of food in pubs has become increasingly important. As this realization has become more widespread throughout the industry, the nature of food operations has changed; they have become less and less craft-based, and more systematic in approach.

Systematic approaches

It is useful here to explain briefly what we mean by 'systematic' in this context. Systematized catering is essentially the same as any other approach to food production and service, in that it goes through the same process and involves largely the same activities. What differentiates it from more traditional approaches is the way in which the process and its associated activities are managed. This management is characterized by a number of key elements:

- pre-processed ingredients
- greater use of technology at the expense of labour
- mass production
- standard operating procedures – little or no discretion for operators
- simplified, deskilled procedures
- limited activity at the point of purchase
- standardized products – limited variety or added value
- higher volumes and lower margins.

The management of food operations in licensed retailing usually incorporates some or all of these elements. The balance of these and their specific nature will depend on the brand and the customers it is attempting to appeal to. The very latest developments in food provision reflect an attempt to recognize and appeal to the more sophisticated and food-aware elements of the market. This has seen a number of attempts to develop brands that can offer greater variety and added value for customers – brands such as Vintage Inns, and Chef & Brewer. These brands seek to offer a product that is presented as unique and more individual – one that is less standardized and perceived as being of higher quality and greater value than other pub, bar and restaurant food offers. However, from an operations point of view the issues and requirements remain, consistency of quality and control of costs. The strategy used to ensure these in other brands – systematization – is still valid here, albeit given the added need to offer variety and higher levels of quality. The challenges may be greater, but the principles of the approach remain the same.

Food operation systems

In all licensed retailing operations, the potential variations in quality, product perishability, vulnerability to mishandling, and errors during production and service, as well the possibilities for theft, present particular difficulties for managing food operations. Branded licensed retail operations have attempted to overcome these difficulties by introducing brand standards and standard operating procedures. As a unit manager, you have to work within the specified systems in order to achieve the standards set. It is therefore important to understand the controls already in place and to be able to recognize potential gaps in the control of the process used in the production and service of food and drink to customers.

Before looking in detail at the control of the processes, we need to explore the nature of food operations in licensed retailing operations in more detail. A simple way of understanding the nature of the food operation is to view it in systems terms, as a systems model. The basic elements of any system are the inputs, process and outputs:

1 *The inputs* are all the elements that are brought in to the system in order for it to operate. In the case of food operations, this means raw materials, staff, equipment, information (customer orders, material prices etc.) and money, for example.
2 *The processes* are all the activities and tasks undertaken in order to convert inputs to the form required. These include the storage, preparation, cooking and service tasks, together with associated activities such as stocktaking, cleaning and maintenance.
3 *The outputs* are all the products produced by the action of the processes on the inputs. This includes the outputs we are trying to achieve – satisfactory food products, satisfied customers, information and financial performance – and conversely, those that are unavoidable by products of the system – e.g. food waste and energy.

If we take our earlier list of the characteristic elements of systematized food operations, we can see that these fit well with the systems model (Table 8.1).

Although we have suggested that all food operations in licensed retailing brands tend to be systematized, this does not mean that they are the same or that they operate in the same way. There are varying degrees of systematization. A simple classification of systems, based on the menu and food products offered, could include *simple*, *routine* and *complex* menus.

Systems component	Characteristic element of systematized food operations
Input	Pre-processed ingredients Greater use of technology at the expense of labour
Process	Mass production Standard operating procedures – little or no discretion for operators Simplified, deskilled procedures Limited activity at point of purchase
Output	Standardized products – limited variety or added value Higher volumes and lower margins

Table 8.1 Systems model

Simple menus • • •

Simple menus are very basic standardized menus, requiring limited handling of raw product and largely involving the reconstitution and appropriate presentation of products. These operations are most often reliant on the supplies of pre-portioned, pre-prepared, packaged products that require little processing on site. Processes are usually restricted to simple cooking operations and re-heating pre-cooked products; as a result, skill requirements are limited to assembly and presentation. Menu items usually have low material costs and failures involve minimal cost to the business, however failures can be more costly if multi-portion packs are used. Simple menus are often used in high-volume, low-margin businesses.

Routine menus • • •

As well as pre-prepared products, routine menus involve basic one-stage cooking of raw products. Price is a less sensitive issue in customer choice, and material costs are higher than those involved with the simple menus. Here, the skills are largely focused on cooking raw product using simple cooking techniques, the reconstitution of some foods, and the presentation of dishes prior to service.

Food is usually bought in pre-portioned packs and there is minimal processing in the unit. Some simple preparation of raw ingredients is required (e.g. salad), but most items are supplied in a form that minimizes the handling on site. Some bought-in products, pre-prepared, may add to menu choice.

Complex menus • • •

Complex menus include some dishes that are prepared and cooked from raw ingredients, and may therefore involve more elaborate stages in the process and/or more expensive materials. Failures with these products can be extremely costly if not detected early in the process. Customers are less price-sensitive and menus are designed for the discerning diner. Although menus are still centrally designed by brand managers, there is less use of reconstituted foods, and local managers may be encouraged to develop their own 'specials' or to search out local suppliers.

The operation requires more processing of products and some dishes that have more complex processes. The operation may depend on some dishes being produced from items bought locally, depending on price and availability. In most cases, however, dishes are based on pre-designed menus in which standard recipes and operating procedures aim to produce dishes that are consistent and common to the brand.

The service element is a more important part of this offer, although most operations still use plated dishes. There are higher service standards in relation to staffing numbers and the quality of products served. Examples of this operation are found at Chef & Brewer, Vintage Inns, and De Alto properties.

Box 8.1 provides an example.

Box 8.1 *Scottish and Newcastle menus*

Scottish and Newcastle (S&N) provide an excellent example of how the classification of menus is used to organize food delivery in a managed pub estate. They developed a programme called 'Targeting Bigger Food Sales' to provide a range of menus for their blueprinted managed estate. The goal for this, as described by their then managing director in his briefing note, is to:

... focus the right offer to the right groups of customers to ensure we maximize the opportunities available ... because ... a focused offer not only generates additional sales in its own right, but delivers increases in drink sales as well.

The evidence for this is claimed to be an increase in food sales at twice the rate of growth of the market as a whole, and this in a period of high market growth.

A programme revision, to broaden and develop the offers, was driven by the view that:

... pubs that are known for a dish or special range of dishes, consistently outperform those simply offering 'pub food'.

In the S&N programme, managers have the choice of a variety of menus, based on the blueprint for their venue and the current level of food sales. The estate is split into two groups of pub blueprints; 'mainstream' or 'sophisticated', and each has a food strategy and offers to go with it:

1 'Mainstream' pubs are community pubs of all descriptions, the venues being hybrid and night-time. Their menus are based on 'Value and Calories'.
2 'Sophisticated pubs' are quality venues and town pubs. Their menus are based on 'Care and Variety'.

The offers (menus plus systems) available are split into two elements:

1 Background menus – menus of standard dishes, accompaniments etc. Five of these are available, with varying degrees of complexity and variety.
2 Concept menus – the dish or range of dishes that a pub becomes known for.

At the basic end these stand alone; as the outlet becomes more sophisticated, a 'concept menu' is added to the 'background menu' to make the full offer.

This can be summarized in a simple diagram:

Sophisticated blueprints	Menu/offer		Menu/offer	Mainstream blueprints
Increasing level of pub sophistication and volume of sales	Background menus (BM)	Simple menus	Snack Express Red hot value RHV plus Lite bite All-day breakfast Background menus	Increasing level of pub sophistication and volume of sales
	BM1			
	BM2			
	BM3	Routine menus		
	BM4		Whole hog Steak and ale Background menus Steak selection British Pies	
	BM5			
	Made to measure	Complex menus		

> The background menus are the same for mainstream and sophisticated blueprints.
>
> As can be seen, the offers available range from the most basic fully pre-prepared, standardized and deskilled menus to fairly complex value-added menus. In the sophisticated category, value is added by building concepts onto background menus to add to variety without greatly increasing complexity.
>
> The 'made to measure' offer involves a process by which pubs are supported in the development of individualized menus and systems. A detailed programme involving area managers and catering executives is used to prepare the offer. It includes hygiene and service quality audits, head office design and marketing support, together with a series of planning meetings.

The nature of the offer and the degree of simplicity or complexity of the processes involved has clear implications for the control of food operations. In simple terms:

- simple menus involving minimal processing have fewer operations that require judgement and thereby have less room for human error
- more complex menus involve more processes and more expensive dishes, so if errors do occur they cost more.

The basic steps involved in controlling food operations are likely to be similar across all pubs, bars and restaurants. However, the levels of simplicity and complexity involved in an operation will have an impact on the details of the control systems introduced. These details are therefore derived from a full understanding of each individual system, and we can begin to develop this detailed understanding by mapping the system.

Mapping the food operation

The specific details of the approach you take to managing food operations in your unit will be dependent to a large extent on the systems and processes laid out by the brand. Even though a number of these important decisions will have been made elsewhere, it is still important for you to know how the systems are designed in order to control and minimize the risks of failure. There are two reasons for this:

1 It will allow you to implement the controls effectively and efficiently, as the system was designed, and ensure that you are not tempted to cut any corners!
2 It will allow you to evaluate whether the current system achieves its objectives. This is part of your role in contributing to the continuous improvement of the brand, but it also enables you to control your own unit better.

Accepting that control of food operations will involve application of the brand's set guidelines, there are still a number of decisions you will have to make regarding how to implement the set control procedures. There may well also be areas that need control for which no set procedures exist. In both of these cases you must be able to recognize these specific areas and understand what is needed for effective control.

Guidance for control of food operations often focuses on the traditional control process (Figure 8.1).

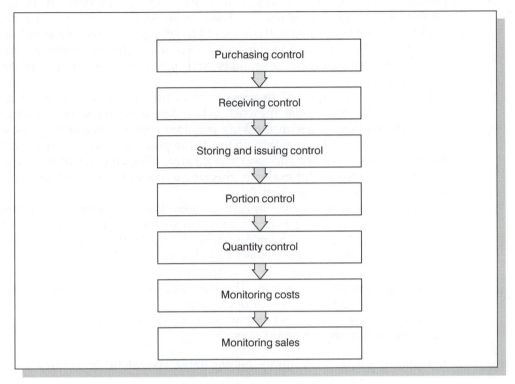

Figure 8.1 Stages in the control process for food and drink

The difficulties with this in licensed retailing brands are two-fold:

1 The control process was designed for traditional, craft-oriented systems, and as such does not necessarily represent the priorities of systematized pub, bar and restaurant food operations.
2 It is a generic system that encourages equal effort and resources to control all the aspects it covers. This blanket coverage may well be necessary for effective control; however, it may not. It does not help you to identify the critical areas for control in your business, and may mean that you waste time and resources controlling things of limited importance at the expense of more important aspects.

Preventive control

As discussed, a key principle of managing food operations is to do so in a way that is right for your business and not use an approach that assumes the priorities for control based on some generic system. Another key principle for food operations management is to identify and manage potential failures before they occur.

The accurate identification of potential points of system failure before they occur is one of the key benefits of the systematized approach to food operations. This is so because of the structured nature of the processes and the standardized nature of all the activities. Identifying potential system failures is known as a preventive or proactive approach to management. This kind of approach is most usually associated with quality assurance. There is no reason, however, why preventive thinking cannot be applied to the issue of identifying potential failure points for cost control as well, and hence in this text we are using the preventive approach as a framework for managing operations and not simply as a quality assurance methodology.

The alternative approach to preventive control is the retrospective approach, which is still the most usual approach in branded licensed retailing. A retrospective approach to quality relies on checking prepared products before they are served to customers. This most commonly occurs at the point of service – often the hotplate interface between kitchen and food service area. Checking may also occur at points earlier in the process – for example, checking a batch of pre-mixed sauce before it is added to any main course items.

In the basic systematic food operations often found in licensed retail brands, the opportunities for checking during the process are limited, as once actual preparation of the food has begun there are few or no breaks in the process until the food is served to the customer. This means that failures are not detected until the product is completed, and these failures are usually 'fatal' – i.e. they cannot be rectified without producing a completely new item. This makes the retrospective approach potentially more expensive in these kinds of operations.

There are other clear and important benefits to the preventive approach to managing and controlling food operations:

1 It allows you to concentrate on the most critical likely failures and thereby prioritize your effort.
2 It saves you time once it is in place.
3 It prevents waste.
4 There is less chance of failures getting through to customers and thereby causing dissatisfaction.

While the benefits of managing food operations proactively are clear and of real value, it would be remiss of us not to mention the downside:

1 It does take time to set up, and the initial analysis can require a lot of thought.
2 There may well be contradictions with the established procedures of the brand. This is a difficult one to deal with, as it is not appropriate for you to go against the brand systems; equally, it is difficult to follow procedures that you think are not as effective or efficient as they could be.
3 It needs constant monitoring to take account of changes in materials, products, staff etc. Potential failure points may change over time, and the approach must keep up with these changes.

A preventive approach to managing food operations requires you to carry out the following steps:

1 Define clearly the outputs required
2 Map the food operation's processes in the unit
3 Identify and prioritize possible failure points.

Step 1   Define clearly the outputs required • • •

In pub, bar and restaurant food operations, the outputs we are primarily concerned with are the food products served to customers and the costs associated with producing these. You will probably have clear output standards already set for both of these – food specifications for the products, and budgetary targets for the costs.

Step 2   Map the food operation's processes in the unit • • •

To do this, you must identify the stages that must be gone through to produce the food items, and all the activities that take place at each stage. This is potentially the most time-consuming part of the process, but you have a head start on other operations here. The brand standards and operating procedures that exist already are likely to cover the majority of what should happen in the food operation.

Figure 8.2 is a general diagram that can represent any possible food operation in a licensed retail unit, and covers all the possible stages in the process. From this you can model the system as operated by your unit, and begin to add in the necessary detail required for effective and efficient control.

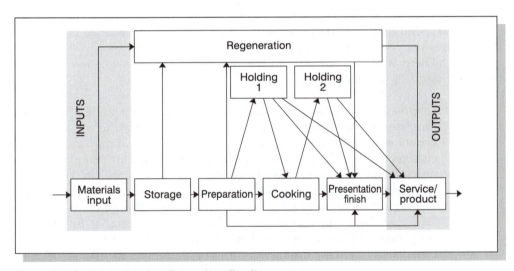

Figure 8.2 Food operation in a licensed retail unit

It is largely because of the systematic nature of the operations in licensed retailing brands that it is possible to represent the food operations in this way. The complexity and unpredictability of more craft-oriented or less structured systems make this approach more difficult. One of the main benefits of being able to model the operation in this way is that it encourages and enables you to begin your consideration of control with the desired outputs, rather than with materials and/or methods, which would traditionally be the initial focus. This means that:

• you know exactly what the food product should be like and how it should be presented to the customer

- you know how much each item should cost and how long it should take to produce
- the identification of potential failure points and priorities is simplified.

Step 3   Identify and prioritize possible failure points ● ● ●

With the desired outputs as the focus, it is possible to consider each element of the inputs and the processes and how they should combine to deliver the outputs as required. If the output is not delivered as required, this is considered to be a failure.

As an example, take poor quality raw material inputs – salad items in particular. This is likely to have an impact on the cost of menu items containing these ingredients (output) due to increased waste and hence more being needed to prepare the prawn cocktail garnish, for example. Also, poor quality inputs may increase the time taken to prepare these items – increased trimming and checking (process). It is also likely to have a detrimental impact on the quality of the output, if it is not possible to trim and present it to the standards specified. A full understanding of the relationship between the inputs, processes and the outputs is therefore necessary if the operation is to be controlled effectively. With this understanding, you can begin to identify where failures are most likely to occur in the system.

There are numerous possible failure points in every system – usually far too many to spend time and effort preventing every one. What is needed is a way to prioritize the key points for control.

There are three elements to the risk that determine whether a potential failure point is a key one or not:

1 *Severity.* How critical is the failure if it occurs? Leaving a hot main course on the hotplate for a minute too long may well begin to dry the edges of the meal. This is not too severe as long as it does not wait too long – it may mildly disappoint the customer rather than cause catastrophic dissatisfaction. Similarly, preparing too much bread may cause waste but the costs of this are unlikely to be massive. However, a customer who receives a piece of broken glass in their soup is unlikely to return, no matter how hard we try to retrieve the situation.
2 *Likelihood.* How likely is the failure to occur? A customer finding glass in their soup may well be an outcome of critical severity, but it would take a chain of increasingly unlikely mishaps for it to occur, and so the likelihood is low. On the other hand, meals waiting longer than they should to be collected may not be a critical failure, but this failure is much more likely to occur for any number of reasons.
3 *Difficulty of control.* How difficult is it to control or prevent the potential failure? A failure may not be critical if it is simple enough to prevent or remedy. Take the hotplate example. A meal that has been waiting too long may quite easily be remedied by smartening up the plate before it is served – depending, of course, on the type of meal.

To determine if a potential failure is a key point of control or not, you can calculate the criticality number and index as follows:

1 For each of the three elements of risk give the potential failure a score out of 5 (where 5 is the worst case and 1 is the least risk).

2 Multiply the three numbers together to give you the criticality number.
3 Compare this number with your criticality index (see below). If it is greater than the index, then it is a key point that must be proactively managed.

Each potential failure has a maximum criticality number of 125 ($5 \times 5 \times 5$). You must decide above what score a risk becomes a key control point – the criticality index. This could be when it is above forty (33 per cent critical), for example. Also, you may decide any risk that scores five out of five for one or more of the elements is critical, irrespective of its overall score. These decisions will be taken on the basis of your experience and the priorities of the business and the brand.

If we were to score the above examples, the result may well be something like this:

Failure point	Severity	Likelihood	Control	Criticality number	Key point of control
Food waiting too long	2	4	3	24	No
Glass in food	5	1	3	15	Yes
Too much bread	2	3	3	18	No

(Criticality index = 40; any failure point scoring 5 for any element to be deemed critical.)

You can see from this that only the glass is considered a key point for control, by virtue of its severity, even though it actually scores a lower criticality number than the other two failures.

Managing key points of control

Once you have identified the key points of control, it is necessary to decide how each of them will be managed. Given that you will be operating to a number of set standards and specifications, a lot of these decisions will have been taken already. As we have pointed out, however, you still have to make these standards work, and you must also be able to put together coherent criticisms and suggestions for improvement where appropriate. It is likely that your management of the key points of control will involve the following:

1 Identifying and communicating the correct standards for the outputs. This includes deciding how you will know if they are being achieved and how you will go about monitoring this, together with any materials needed to do this.
2 Ensuring that the correct equipment is available and that the correct actions and tasks etc. are performed.
3 Deciding and communicating who has responsibility for each key control point.

One of the options when managing key control points is to design out a potential failure risk – in other words, change the operations so that a risky procedure no longer happens and the outputs are produced in another way. For example, you could decide to change the materials for the fajitas from steaks and chicken breasts to pre-cut meat to avoid the preparation needed and the failure of portion control and waste at this point. This is a change in the process rather than control or management of the existing process. We have not considered this option in detail, as your authority to change the system, in the short term at least, is likely to be limited. If it *is* possible in your situation, it can be an effective tool in the management of food operations.

Implement, monitor and feedback

Even with preventive management and control, checking and monitoring is still necessary. In this case, however, monitoring is about making sure that controls have taken place as required, and not about checking the state of prepared goods or services. Again, the monitoring you undertake will no doubt include a number of set procedures from the brand. As with other brand standards and processes, they should be incorporated into your own food operations management and you should constantly be evaluating them to make sure they perform the task required.

It is possible that you will require other monitoring procedures, in addition to those put in place by the brand. These would most likely focus on the key control points identified for which there are no effective controls or checking mechanism. The monitoring undertaken has to be specific to the circumstances, and there is therefore little value in discussing it in general here. As we go on to look at the food operations process in detail and to highlight possible key points of control, we will bring out the monitoring needs and processes as appropriate. Any monitoring must possess certain characteristics for it to be fully effective, and you must bear these in mind when considering your systems. Monitoring must be:

1 *Unobtrusive.* You must be able to monitor without disturbing the operation of the people and systems being monitored.
2 *Accurate.* The data you get from any monitoring must provide a clear and precise picture of the situation being monitored, so there is a need to ensure that it is difficult to massage or otherwise interfere with the figures to present a more favourable appearance, for example.
3 *Timely.* Data from monitoring are only useful for management purposes if they represent the current situation as currently as possible. All data are historic to some extent, but there is a big difference between what happened yesterday, last week or last month.
4 *Easy to implement.* A more complex monitoring system may well appear to give more detailed or accurate information. This will only be true, however, if it is so simple to use that there is no temptation to cut corners or simplify the data gathering.

These then are the principles of any preventive management approach for food operations. We will now look at how these principles apply to the generic food operations process identified in Figure 8.2. When considering this discussion, it is important to bear in mind that we are still dealing in general principles and not the specifics required to make effective management happen. This means that the possible failures (key points of control) and the actions required to manage and monitor them will all be generic. It is your role to take the principles discussed and illustrated here and to apply them to the management and control of your own food operations. This involves:

- the effective implementation of brand standards and specifications as laid down already
- the development and implementation of appropriate controls that do not exist within the brand standards
- the critical review and evaluation of both existing standards and those developed by yourself.

We will take each component of the food operations system – outputs, inputs and process – in turn and follow the preventive approach to managing food operations identified above. For each key control point we will:

- identify the possible failures, what may cause them and what effect they could have
- explain the controls that could be put in place to minimize the risk of failure – this will include the management tasks and activities and the monitoring required.

Specific monitoring requirements have been identified. As a general principle, the monitoring of food operations should involve:

1 Observing performance
2 Recording observed performance
3 Analysing records for information about problems or successes.

Outputs • • •

Remember, we are talking about the food products served to customers and the costs generated in producing these as the outputs of the food operations system. Because producing the output as specified is the objective of the management and control of food operations, the product specifications and targets assume even greater importance than normal in these circumstances. We begin by examining the possibilities of failure in the product specification itself. Beyond this, all other key points for control are reviewed on the assumption that the product specifications are correct.

Key point 1: Product specification

Failure effect	Specification not followed as focus for operations, outputs not produced as required
Failure causes	Lack of awareness of specifications Lack of understanding of specifications Lack of belief in specifications

Control activities	Communication from management to raise awareness, understanding and belief in product specifications Constant management focus on correct specifications as desired objectives Specifications clearly presented, easy to follow and understand Specifications readily available to all staff Recognition and reward for conspicuous devotion to standards from staff Corrective coaching with staff as required
Monitoring	Record all communications with staff about specifications Check availability of specifications and record their use by staff Spot checks, tests etc. with staff – recognize success 'Mystery customer' evaluation of finished products Formal staff involvement in monitoring finished products Wastage – production and plate

Key point 2: Service/production interface

Failure effect	Food quality not as required before service to customer Meals not as ordered Leads to waste and/or customer dissatisfaction
Failure causes	Food not presented as per specification Food held too long at the hotplate interface Meals not prepared as per order – wrong meals presented or items not presented together
Control activities	Efficient and accurate order-taking procedures Process for communication of orders to kitchen Storage and scheduling of orders in the kitchen Facilitate communication between kitchen and service about readiness of food and of customer. (These are controls that relate only to this stage of the process. There may be other controls, effective for these issues, which will be considered in the inputs and process stages)
Monitoring	EPOS and IT systems now automate a great deal of this process and provide records of all transactions for monitoring purposes. These do not control the interface, however; manual monitoring is still required Spot checks during service on production schedules Customer feedback – formal and informal

Most problems that occur at the output stage of the process are caused by difficulties with the inputs or process elements of the food operation. In some ways, applying controls at this stage can be seen as too late. It is like reverting back to the retrospective approach. This is especially so for food quality issues. Management of this stage is, then, about the coordination of production and service, which is often not specified in the brand standards. The key elements are:

1 Accurate and timely orders from the customers to production
2 Scheduling:
  • taking each order in the order in which it was received
  • preparing, finishing and presenting food for when customers are ready.

Inputs • • •

Key point 3: Materials

Placing orders:

Failure effect	Inaccurate orders placed No orders placed These can lead to wastage, overstocking or item shortages
Failure causes	Poor records of stock usage and holding Poor forecasting of materials requirements – can be linked to inflexibility of automated order systems Basic human error – being forgetful!
Control activities	Establish order routines (purchasing plan) – frequency, of orders and deliveries Standards for goods ordered – quality, quantity (total and pack size) and price Regular and structured calculation of material needs Development of par and buffer stock levels for at least key, if not all, products Wide training and awareness of standard order requirements and procedures
Monitoring	Clearly visible records of all orders placed – time, amount, person responsible etc. Analysis of sales against forecasts and orders to check for accuracy of materials requirement forecasting

Hospitality, Leisure & Tourism Series

Receiving goods:

Failure effect	Poor quality of goods received (against order) Wrong quantity of goods received (against order) Wrong timing of deliveries Leads to production efficiency and quality problems
Failure causes	Errors from suppliers Poor/inaccurate checking on receipt
Control acivities	Establish standard receiving procedures: • responsibility – who does it? • when and where it should be done? – must be free from distractions • quantity checks – counts and weights • quality checks – against standards for each product • price checks – against agreed prices Ensure required equipment is available and operative Full training for those responsible in all procedures and awareness throughout staff
Monitoring	Record all checks – verify with stamp/signature; copy for all parties involved (including timing of deliveries) Special note of all problems identified Record receipts in appropriate IT system

Key point 4: Equipment

Failure effect	Failure of equipment to perform as required
Failure causes	Incorrect function/capacity of equipment Too complex or difficult to operate Insufficient knowledge of function
Control activities	Full training from suppliers and tests of competence Availability of manuals and operating procedures for reference Make sure all management are competent on all equipment Ensure awareness and implementation of maintenance procedures
Monitoring	Record of all staff competent on equipment Record of all problems associated with each piece of equipment – regular analysis for trends or common issues Record of all maintenance – planned and irregular – for each piece of equipment

Key point 5: Staffing – numbers and capability

Failure effect	Insufficient staff to operate food system as required Staff present not capable of operating food system as required
Failure causes	Incorrect scheduling of staff Staff failure to report for work as required Wrong grade/level of staff present Too many new or inexperienced operatives present
Control activities	Establish staffing standards for numbers and grades required for particular business levels. This needs to be more sophisticated than a percentage of sales (see Chapter 11) Accurate and timely forecasting of sales and therefore labour requirements – regular standards and special occasions Clear and visible scheduling procedure Effective communication of rotas
Monitoring	Accuracy of sales forecast as before Record of staff non-attendance Keep records of rotas and allocations against which to compare levels of business and staff performance

Process • • •

Key point 6: Storage and issuing

Failure effect	Deterioration in quality of materials Wastage Theft
Failure causes	Incorrect storage conditions: • equipment • containers • temperatures Incorrect storage procedures: • length of time • combinations of goods – cross-contamination Wrong goods issued – number or type Poor security of goods issued

Control activities	Temperature standards for storage of all items Awareness of standards through training staff and marking items Designated equipment for specific items or groups of items: • raw meats • fresh fish • dairy, fruit and vegetables, and other grocery items • cooked meats (in separate fridges or fridge compartments, for example) Designated and clearly marked containers for specific food items. Sturdy, washable and sealable containers Arrangement of stock – not crowding items, correct shelving and easy access Regular cleaning schedules for all storage areas and equipment Rotation of stock based on FIFO (first in first out) – clearly marked delivery and use-by dates (links to goods issues) Accurate calculation of stock in use needed (including buffer stocks) Clear policy, responsibility and authority for issuing goods (empowerment versus central control) – includes the requisitioning process
Monitoring	Clear records of when all items are placed in stock Spot-checks on stores – dates of goods, temperatures, containers etc. (this should be a systematic process with proper records). Regularly review records for common difficulties or apparent trends Some of this monitoring should be on a regular basis – fridge temperatures every two hours, for example, with facilities to record the temperatures at the point of storage Records of cleaning schedules having taken place – random checks on cleanliness of storage areas Records covering what was requisitioned and issued, when, by whom and to whom Security monitoring is a difficult issue and is beyond the scope of this text; however, it is still a vital element of the management of food operations, and one that you must tackle

Key point 7: Preparation

Failure effect	Incorrect pre-preparation leading to: • over-production and wastage of food items • unavailability of food items • poor quality of finished product
Failure causes	Wrong quantities of items prepared Wrong mix of items prepared Items not prepared to specification Non-availability of materials Poor quality of materials used
Control activities	Detailed production schedules based on sales forecasts: • may be per day, per session, per hour or even per order; a choice based on batch or job production • batch size – how many items to be prepared at once Full staff knowledge and capability required to produce to specification – training and coaching Linked to other controls: • product specifications – under outputs • purchase, storage and issuing controls – under inputs
Monitoring	Checks again need to be carried out on product quality and size etc. as per the checks at receiving, storage and issuing Accuracy of production schedules – against actual sales and numbers wasted (from stock and after service) Monitoring as per other controls applied

Key point 8: Cooking/regeneration

This area of food operation management will perhaps have more direct specifications and controls developed by the brand than any other. This is the area that is most often the focus of food control at brand level. There are likely to be standards and specifications for the majority of these possible failures. With the growth of more complex branded food offers there are more and more opportunities for unit-specific dishes to be offered on standard menus, and this is likely to require the development as well as the application of the kind of controls identified below. The key objective for all these controls is consistency of output, through consistency of ingredients, methods and quantity.

Failure effect	Wastage of food – raw materials or finished products Food products not produced to specification Delays in production/service

Hospitality, Leisure & Tourism Series

Failure causes	Incorrect quantities produced – overall or batch size Timing wrong: • length of cooking time • items cooked too early or too late Specification not followed – can be avoidable or unavoidable Insufficient or poor-quality materials
Control activities	Adherence to prepared standards: • standard portion size • weight – raw material or finished product • volume • number – often based on pack size Standard recipe: • ingredients – type, quality and proportion • methods – timings, equipment and actions • measured/portion equipment • references (recipe cards, photographs/diagrams etc.) for all finished products at the point of production Training – key here is the operatives' awareness of what each stage of the process should look, feel and even taste like, so they can constantly check for potential problems Standard costs: • based on raw materials in each finished product • takes account of yield, cooking loss, accompaniments and additional ingredients Production schedules as discussed above (preparation) Linked to other controls from product specifications, restaurant/kitchen interface, purchasing, storage, and preparation
Monitoring	Stock usage by portion, unit, weight etc. Record items used in production, wasted in production and wasted in service Count and record opening and closing stocks per period (weekly or more often for management purposes) Reconcile sales and production of each item and in total – actual versus forecast usage of raw materials (see finance variance analysis) Measure cooking loss and yields on key items; evaluate against accepted levels Service times and delays Monitor staff compliance with operating standards, through observation – both formal and informal Customer and staff feedback (This is the main area of process monitoring. It is important to remember that it doesn't have to be you that conducts all the observation and recording in this area. There is a great deal of scope for the empowerment of staff and/or the use of external observation)

Key point 9: Holding

Failure effect	Spoilage of finished items giving poor quality of products delivered to customers Wastage of finished products Delays in service and efficiencies for service staff
Failure causes	Items waiting too long once prepared: • prepared too far in advance • not removed by service staff Wrong holding conditions: • temperatures and humidity • containers
Control activities	Adherence to production schedules Effective communication systems between production and service (see production/service interface, above) Application of standard recipes Staff training
Monitoring	Check and record hold times Service times and delays Customer and staff feedback Observation of staff performance

Key point 10: Finishing/presenting

Failure effect	Food not finished/presented to correct standards
Failure causes	Non-compliance with standard recipes and procedures Non-availability of materials or equipment Poor-quality raw materials
Control activities	Adherence to product specifications Staff training Material quality controls as discussed above
Monitoring	Check finished products against specification Observation of staff performance

It is clear from this review of potential key control points that a number of the controls necessary and the methods for monitoring performance are common to more than one key control point. This is important, as it means you don't need different controls for every possible failure in the food operation and you can develop an approach that is consistent across all activities in the process.

Conclusion

The food operation in pubs, bars and restaurants makes an important contribution to the profitability of most units nowadays, and the management of the food operation is key to maximizing this profitability. Effectively controlling the quality and costs of the food system outputs has therefore become a key task for unit managers. Whenever products (outputs) are produced that do not meet the required standard or wastage etc. occurs, this is deemed to be a failure of the system.

This chapter proposed a single approach to the management of food operations, which, if successfully implemented, will control both costs and quality. The approach proposed is a systematic and preventive one that logically and progressively analyses the system to determine what could go wrong and proposes appropriate actions to stop this from happening. The objective of this is to prevent costly failures from occurring rather than retrospectively trying to deal with failures that have already occurred. The approach is considered to be particularly appropriate for managers of branded operations owing to the simplified, planned and systematic nature of these food operations and the standardized nature of their product outputs.

Requirements for the application of this approach are considered to be a clear understanding of the system outputs – food and costs – and of the stages in the process leading to them. Evaluation of each stage to identify and prioritize possible failure points, together with an identification of the control and monitoring procedures for each one. These are discussed in the context of a generic food operations process that facilitates unit managers mapping their own operations and applying the preventive approach in their units.

Reflective practice

1 Explain the difference between systematic and preventive approaches to managing food operations and the more traditional craft-based approaches found in pubs, restaurants and bars.
2 What are the advantages of a systematic and preventive approach to managing food operations? Why is this particularly appropriate to food operations in branded units?
3 Identify all the stages in food operations processes. What are the possible failure points for each stage, and how may these be prioritized?
4 What is the process for systematic preventive management of food operations? What is the importance of each of these stages for management in branded pubs, bars and restaurants?
5 Evaluate the purpose and value of the key management controls used in the systematic preventive approach.
6 Why is monitoring necessary, and what methods of monitoring food operations are available to unit managers within the systematic preventive approach?

Further reading

Baker, K. (1999). *Internal Control and Fraud Prevention in Hospitality Operations.* Hospitality Press.

East, J. P. (1993). *Managing Quality in the Catering Industry.* Croner Publications.

Jones, P. and Merricks, P. (1994). *The Management of Foodservice Operations.* Cassell.

Lockwood, A., Baker, M. and Ghillyer, A. (eds) (1996). *Quality Management in Hospitality: Best Practice in Action.* Cassell.

Zaccarelli, H. (1990). *Food Service Management by Checklist: A Handbook of Control Techniques.* Wiley.

CHAPTER 9

On turning a profit

After working through this chapter, you should be able to:

- explain the nature of financial control and the key cost and sales concepts
- collect and record the data necessary to measure and control the performance of the business
- analyse and interpret the financial data collected or provided using cost–volume–profit techniques
- take decisions and implement courses of action on the basis of this analysis and interpretation.

Financial control in licensed retailing

The reason your outlet is in operation is commercial. The principal and overriding objectives of the unit concern making money – generating income and turning this income into profit through effective controls. You provide a range of goods and services to your customers in order to meet their needs and therefore satisfy them. These goods and services are only supplied to customers on the basis that they can generate value for the company – that is, they are worth more to the customer to buy than they cost you to make. If this is the case they will produce sales (revenue, income) that are more than the costs of production and service, and therefore generate a surplus (profit).

You may well think that this is such an obvious principle that it does not need saying again; however, it is the fundamental determinant of whether an outlet is successful or not. As such, it is the focus of your role as manager, which is to maximize the performance of your unit by:

- generating sufficient levels of sales and therefore revenue for the unit
- ensuring that the cost of operating the unit is low enough to generate a satisfactory surplus (profit) from the revenue earned.

Ensuring that maximum profit is derived from turnover is one of the ways in which a competitive advantage can be gained. If you can become the best-controlled business, then you will greatly increase the margin between costs and sales and may well achieve a position of cost leadership – a powerful position to hold, and one well worth aiming for.

Generating sales is considered at length elsewhere in the book. Chapters 9 and 10 consider the principles associated with ensuring that a satisfactory surplus is derived from the sales generated, and some of the tools needed to achieve this, under the heading *financial control*.

In order to control the finances of a bar, pub or restaurant effectively, the manager needs to achieve a number of objectives. The manager must be able to:

- understand the principles of control, and develop from this an appreciation of the role of targets and measures of performance
- understand the nature and importance of various targets and measures of performance and be able to apply these in practice.

These are seen as the key principles of financial control as practised by managers of pubs, bars and restaurants, and will thus form the basis of the content for Chapters 9 and 10. This chapter will introduce some general concepts about the control of costs and sales, and from these will develop a framework for understanding the different types and elements of costs and the relationship between costs and sales.

The principles of control

Traditionally, consideration of control in business terms has centred on two key themes:

1 Imposition – where there is a person or group of people 'in charge' with the authority to impose their requirements on whatever is being controlled

2 Regulation – where those with the authority identify variances between what is and what should be, and instigate appropriate corrective action.

This is a *negative* approach to control, as it focuses on those 'in charge' directing, regulating and constraining those responsible for carrying out the operations. Thus it fails to deliver the empowered approach to management as advocated by this book. Many hospitality retail organizations take this approach, assuming that employees cannot be trusted and control must be imposed. More enlightened, and often more effective, is an approach to control that involves communicating clear goals, developing and encouraging team members to ensure the correct capability is present, monitoring performance, and coaching and counselling for corrective action where necessary.

The control cycle

Control is an iterative process, following a simple cycle (Figure 9.1).

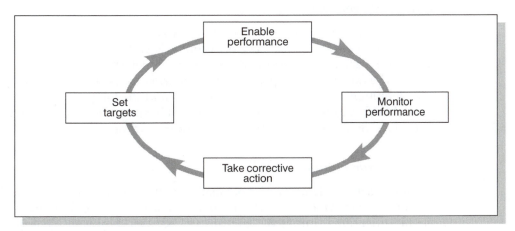

Figure 9.1 The control cycle

A number of targets have implications for financial control. Some are discussed in detail here, and some will be dealt with elsewhere in the book:

Set targets • • •

1 *Service standards*. These are developed to ensure the quality and reliability of service delivery to customers. They must cover both tangible and intangible elements, and they have direct implications for costs and the level of sales generated.
2 *Product quality standards*. These are used to identify the quality of raw materials and finished products for food and drink, as well as other materials put before customers.
3 *Quantity standards*. These are concerned with portion size, production levels and stock levels needed to meet expected demands. They are key to cost control, in

making the management of purchasing volumes, preparation and service quantities simpler.

4 *Standard costs*. These are derived from the purchase price and quality of supplies and the preparation standards used. They may be applied to a fixed unit of cost – a bottle of beer, for example, which can only be sold in a set quantity. They may also be concerned with items that have to be measured and are hence open to service in incorrect as well as correct measure – for example, draught beer.

Enable performance

There are two key control elements to enabling performance:

1 Standard procedures – these specify the correct methods and processes for all tasks that are carried out in the operation
2 Employee capability – these ensure that staff have the skills, knowledge and ability to perform all the tasks required of them.

Monitor performance

Simply enabling performance will not in itself ensure that performance meets the required targets on each and every occasion. It is still necessary to monitor actual performance against that required, in order to determine the standards being achieved. The timeliness of reporting for monitoring purposes is vital. These reports are, by definition, records of past performance, and the longer it takes to report on this and therefore to recognize areas of unacceptable performance, the longer it takes to put things right with the appropriate corrective action.

Take corrective action

All control actions taken are potentially ineffective if they do not lead to improvements in performance. This is not to assume that there will always be major difficulties identified during the control process. You may well have times when everything appears to be running smoothly. However, even in these times, it is dangerous to stand still. Good managers and good operations will always look to move forward, to improve performance so as to maintain and improve their competitive position. There will be times when the control process identifies major variances from the targets set, and at these times the immediate instigation of corrective action is vital to avoid serious damage to the health of the business.

Financial targets and business performance

We will now go on to look more closely at the control process and the tools and techniques that can be used by pub, bar and restaurant managers for the financial control of their businesses.

The focus of control in these chapters is aimed at ensuring that the financial targets of the business are achieved. Ultimately these financial goals are the key goals for the business, and their achievement (or otherwise) will be used as the main yardstick by which your performance and the performance of your operation is judged. However, there is a danger that this thinking may lead to a neglect of the other important goals that the business has. In the licensed retail sector, particularly in branded organizations, this thinking has been all too prevalent in recent times. There has been over-concentration on financial targets at the expense of 'softer' business goals such as ongoing customer satisfaction, staff satisfaction or labour turnover. The performance of a business should not be judged on financial measures alone; a full balanced scorecard of measures should be used.

This explanation is by way of warning. As we get into the discussion about the nature of financial control and how best to go about achieving it in your unit, there is a danger that we can forget about other aspects at the expense of turnover and profitability. We urge you not to let this happen. Over-emphasis on financial measures of performance is a short-term focus that can have detrimental impacts in the long term. Constantly looking for ways to reduce costs may well produce greater margins and profitability in the short term, but could also lead to a reduction in the quality of products and service offered to customers and a consequent reduction in business levels in the longer term. This highlights another important factor that you must bear in mind when applying controls; that all the activities you carry out and all the processes you implement in order to control the financial performance of your unit will have implications for other aspects of the business beyond the immediate focus of their attention. The obvious issue here is the potential for reductions in quality mentioned above. However, there are less obvious but equally important implications for, for example, staff morale, relationships with suppliers and the local community, the maintenance of resources etc.

All these key principles can be illustrated by an example from the very early days of bars, pubs and restaurant brands, in the dark ages of the 1980s (Box 9.1)!

Box 9.1 *Harvester Steak House*

Harvester Steak Houses was a reasonably new brand, having been developed by Imperial Inns and Taverns and recently taken over by Forte. One of the key service attributes of the brand was a greeter at the door of each restaurant, who met customers, made them feel welcome and found out their requirements. This was usually the person responsible for the soon to be infamous 'Have you ever been to a Harvester before?' enquiry. The principle of a greeter was something that made Harvester different and that customers remembered (along with the two-metre animated model of Worzel Gummidge in the entrance!). As the brand developed, increasingly the focus was on costs and controlling expenses wherever possible. One of the outcomes of this was a requirement to minimize the wage bill. A reduction in targeted wage percentage of 2 per cent put increasing pressure on the concept of a greeter – greeters were fine at busy periods when there was always a steady stream of customers entering the unit and being shown to tables, but at quieter times it became less financially viable to have greeters at the door and not actively engaged in productive work. The choice was clear; either maintain the service quality and brand standards of a dedicated greeter, or remove the greeter and get closer to the targeted labour cost percentage. Over a period of time these greeters gradually became extra members of waiting staff and lost their unique role, and with it the brand lost one of its unique propositions. This is a familiar conflict, and one that has been played out within this and other brands many times over the years. It does illustrate the principles discussed above well, though. This was a financial cost target imposed from outside the unit, and the controls necessary to achieve it did not necessarily provide the extra benefit desired, especially in the long term. In addition, the imposition of financial targets was done at the expense of other, equally important goals, in a clear display of short-term benefit leading to longer-term drawbacks.

Despite these potential conflicts, financial control is still a vital element of running your operation successfully, and without it you will not achieve the unit's full potential. If financial control is, as we have suggested, about achieving the targets set, then we must begin by understanding these targets. There are a number of financial goals that it is important for any business to achieve, and some of these are clearly focused on tactical level operational activities, such as the operation of a single unit.

Most conspicuously, we are concerned with revenue, costs and profitability and the relationships between these.

The most worthwhile way that you as the unit manager can contribute to the achievement of these objectives is by maximizing the performance of your individual unit in terms of revenue and profitability. The number of unit and area manager reward and bonus schemes based on one or a combination of revenue and profitability highlights the importance placed on these goals by operating companies.

The most usual expression of these financial goals is in the form of budgets. The preparation and use of budgets will be discussed later, in the financial control section.

Identify and understand cost and sales data

We have shown that profit depends on the costs of operating the unit being less than the revenue generated from customers. Therefore the information needed to control the unit comes from data about costs, sales and profitability. Although it may seem obvious, this is not always easy to achieve. All decisions made by unit managers have a potential impact on either costs or sales, and therefore profitability. An understanding of the concepts of costs and sales and the nature of their relationship will help to improve the quality of the decision-making within units.

Costs

Costs can be defined as the expenses incurred in producing and delivering goods and services to your customers. This is usually money, of course, but the cost may not solely be the money paid out in the production of the good or service. It might include the costs of other benefits forgone as a result of offering this product or service. For example, when calculating the cost associated with the greeters at Harvester (see Box 9.1), it is easy to forget the *opportunity cost* associated with not having them present on the door at all times. If there are periods of time with no one to greet customers when they arrive, there is an increased potential for lost customers who feel uncomfortable and therefore go elsewhere.

In this circumstance, the cost of a lost table for two may be the contribution to profit made by that table – say £20. If the cost of the greeter is £5 per hour, or £25 for a five-hour shift, we can see that if the greeter is not employed the cost saved is £25. However, there is an opportunity cost of £20 because of the revenue foregone. This means the savings are minimal without the greeter, and if more than two customers are lost costs will actually increase.

Some costs are incurred in the form of a one-off payment and do not change over time; other costs are incurred every time a product or service is sold, and these vary directly with the level of sales. These are called either fixed or variable costs, and this is the first key cost concept we need to consider.

Fixed or variable costs ● ● ●

This concept describes how cost items relate to revenue, and is illustrated in Figure 9.2.

Fixed costs

1 Fixed costs are unchanged over time – at least in the short term. They are not influenced by the levels of goods and services produced and delivered. In other words, they are not affected by operating levels. In reality all costs change to some extent over time, as this change is outside the accounting period concerned then it is safe to consider the costs as fixed.
2 Fixed costs generally accrue to the unit as a whole, rather than being directly attributable to individual items or even departments of the unit.
3 Fixed costs decrease as a proportion of sales as the level of sales rises – in other words, the greater the revenue we make, the lower the percentage of fixed costs.

In licensed retail brands it is usual for the unit manager to have little or no influence over the level of fixed costs accrued by his or her unit.

Variable costs

1 Variable costs are related to business volume, and are therefore directly affected by operating levels. A change in sales volume has a direct impact on the total costs.
2 Variable costs can usually be more closely apportioned directly to particular items or departments within the unit.
3 Variable costs remain largely constant as a proportion of sales.

Semi-variable costs

Very few costs are truly fixed or variable, even some of those usually classified into one or the other group. However, some costs are clearly and easily classified as semi-variable.

1 Semi-variable costs vary partly with the level of sales, or have an element that varies with sales.
2 Semi-variable costs have an element that is fixed no matter what the level of sales, or remain fixed between certain threshold sales levels, only increasing once the threshold level has been reached.

Labour can be taken as an example of semi-variable cost. A minimum number of staff, and therefore wage cost, is required to open the pub even if there are no customers whatsoever. This number of staff may well be able to cope with bar sales of up to £1500 on their own. Beyond this level of sales an additional member of staff will be required to maintain service quality and efficiency, and each additional member of staff can take £500 during the course of the session. As the bar gets busier more staff are needed and can be afforded, but this is not a straightforward linear relationship. Wage costs are fixed up to sales of £1500, and then between £1500 and £2000, but taken as a whole the cost of wages is variable dependent on the level of sales. In reality, this situation is further complicated by issues of productivity and the impact of incentives or technology, for example, but it serves to illustrate the concept of semi-variable costs simply enough.

Figure 9.2 illustrates how the different costs associated with operating a pub, bar or restaurant are related to changes in sales levels.

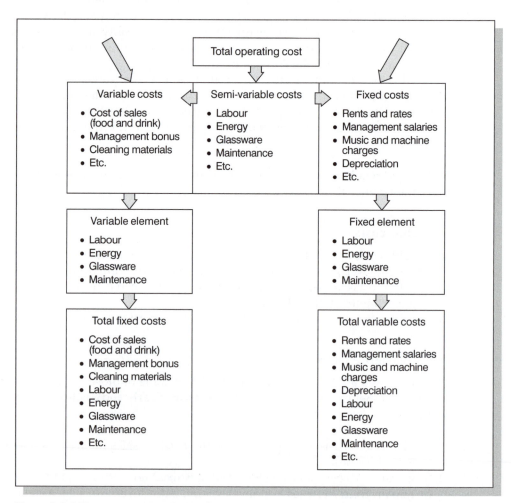

Figure 9.2 Different types of costs in licensed retailing

Controllable or uncontrollable costs • • •

We have already hinted at the idea that some costs are within the control of the unit managers while others are not. For the purposes of this text, we are concerned with those costs that are under the control of the unit manager. Take food, for example. The yields achieved from raw ingredients, the levels of waste and theft, and the portion size of meals produced, are all under the control of the unit manager. These factors will have a direct impact on the cost of food used. The type of ingredients used, production methods and the specification of the finished dishes also have an impact, but these items tend to be decided as part of the overall brand standards and management at unit level is therefore often expressly forbidden from changing them – in the short to medium term at the very least.

It is also usually the case that fixed costs are beyond the scope of authority of the unit manager. This is very much the case as far as direct influence is concerned; however, there may well be occasions when these costs can be influenced indirectly. Take, for example, the costs associated with maintenance, which are often defined as fixed costs – or as having a very large fixed element. Training in equipment use, given to employees at unit level, may well have goals of increasing efficiency or product quality. An improved use of equipment is very likely to reduce damage and therefore the costs of unplanned maintenance as well, even though this was not a direct goal of the training.

Which costs do and do not come under the remit of unit managers is a key area of debate, and goes to the heart of the empowerment issue. The importance this text places on empowering unit managers is clear, but you still have to manage in your own particular circumstances. So whether a cost is controllable or not, as a unit manager you need to be fully aware of its impact and indirect possibilities for control. The decisions you take should still take account of these issues, even if you have no direct influence on them.

Unit or total costs • • •

Understanding costs in any bar, pub or restaurant means you have to be able to break them down and apportion them to specific units of the business. In practical terms, a unit can be many things. It may be the smallest element to which it is realistically possible to apportion costs – such as separate items of food or measures of drink, full dishes or complete meals. A unit may also be larger, for example the whole bar or restaurant (if these are separate entities), or even just food or drink. Basically, a unit of cost can be anything that is discrete, can be identified separately, and to which costs can be accurately apportioned. For this to be worthwhile there obviously has to be benefit to knowing the specific costs associated with a particular unit or between units. The specific costs of the energy required to froth the milk for your cappuccinos may well be possible, if difficult, to calculate. However, it is debatable whether the effort associated with doing this is worthwhile for the contribution it would make to more effective control.

Sales

'Sales' is a financial concept; it is the income generated when customers exchange money for the goods and services provided by your business. Sales can be generated from a number of different goods and services. In licensed retailing, however, sales primarily come from two sources – food and drink. These are sometimes referred to as income streams. There are other income streams in many bars, pubs and restaurants. These include:

- gaming machines (AWP/SWP)
- tobacco
- telephones
- accommodation
- various exotic vending machines, such as single-use toothbrushes.

None of these usually reach anywhere near the importance of food or drink for the industry as a whole. In a few units accommodation is a key income stream, at least matching the food or drink streams, but these operations are still relatively rare although they are growing in numbers. The revenue gained from gaming machines is small, relative to food and drink. However, its importance in terms of profit generated is greater due to the large margins it provides.

The sales concepts discussed here can be applied equally to any of these income streams, but we will concentrate our attentions on the key ones of food and drink.

Having stated that sales is a financial concept, it is actually possible to express sales using both monetary and non-monetary terms. The choice of measure used for sales will depend on the purpose you have for considering them and the accuracy and currency of the information you have. For the purposes of financial control it is more likely that sales expressed in monetary terms is a more useful measure. This is because it is then easier to set sales against monetary costs and to calculate and understand the relationships between the two, which are so important for control.

However, these monetary measures may be distorted over time by changes in pricing policy or inflation. This is the main reason for employing these non-monetary measures, to see trends developing etc. without these distortions.

For the purposes of analysis, it is often useful to establish the relationships between monetary and non-monetary measures of sales. This enables decisions to be made with the objective of increased sales in mind, using either increased profitability or volume as the means to achieve this. The concept of menu engineering is useful for this, and is discussed in more detail in Chapter 10.

Table 9.1 lists the monetary and non-monetary measures that can usefully be applied to sales in licensed retailing units.

The concept of *barrelage* is unique to licensed retailing, and has been a widely used measure of sales within the industry for many years. However, we are not considering it as a measure for the purposes of this text, because we believe it to be an anachronism left over from days when beer was the be-all and end-all of pub sales. Given the growth in wine consumption and food sales, together with other income sources, barrelage as a measure of a complex sales mix does not tell us anything we need to know about managing our business better. Neither does it give us a simple or accurate picture of total sales by which we can judge overall performance. It may well continue to be used when making initial attempts to consider the value of particular premises, but for our purposes it holds no value.

Monetary measures	Non-monetary measures
Total sales Total monetary value for the whole business, over a certain period (from one hour to one year)	*Total sales volume* The number of each item of product sold over a given time; may be further broken down into numbers per bar in a multi-bar operation, for example
Average sales per customer Average spend – the average amount spent by each customer over the course of his or her visit; in bar situations this will often involve more than one transaction (see below)	*Total number of customers* Important, because not all of them may actually be spending money
Total category sales As total sales, but for just one group of products or services – i.e. from a single revenue source such as food or soft drinks	*Sales mix* The most widespread and well known of these non-monetary measures; measures the units sold of each different product, category of products or department
Sales per transaction Average bill – total sales divided by the number of transactions conducted (see above)	*Transactions* Total number of bills, checks and/or sales at the bar; provides information on the number of sales occasions
Sales per server The total amount taken by any individual server, again over a given period (shorter rather than longer); more sophisticated analysis may give sales per server per category	*Average transaction* Related to other measures (not money), such as per staff hour, lunchtime vs evening, or weekday vs weekend
Average sales per server Average amount taken by an individual member of staff, again over a given period (shorter rather than longer); can also consider sales against number of customers served	
Sales per seat/area Measures the amount taken per restaurant cover or square-foot space; measured in total or per time period etc.	

Table 9.1 The monetary and non-monetary measures of sales

Analysing the financial data

Understanding the basic sales and cost data

The data about sales and costs are presented using the profit and loss account for the unit, sometimes called the income statement. This is the financial statement that forms the basis of most of the cost and sales analysis and hence the financial control decision-making that you will undertake in your business. This statement represents a snapshot of the performance of the business over a certain period of time. The

Hospitality, Leisure & Tourism Series

period it covers can vary from as short as a week to a year or even longer, although it is rare for it to extend beyond a year. For the purposes of control, the shorter the time period, the more effective it is. This is because it reduces the lead time between something occurring that needs to be controlled, and management noticing this and being able to take the required action.

It is more than likely that the accounting for and preparation of the profit and loss reports will be done as part of a head office finance function. These reports will be prepared on the basis of data provided by you, direct from your unit. In the more sophisticated operations, a great deal of these data will be provided automatically via the electronic point-of-sale till system. To understand the profit and loss reports provided for you and to be able to use these effectively in controlling your unit, you need to understand the principles upon which the profit and loss account is based.

To make sure the information provided by the profit and loss report is as accurate and useful as possible for decision-making, we must understand the concept of *matching*. This means that the profit and loss statement is concerned with the revenues received during this period, and the costs associated with these revenues and only these revenues. In other words, all sales and costs covered in the profit and loss report must have occurred during the particular time period. For example, January's profit and loss report should not include the cheque you received in January as payment for the local firm's Christmas party in December, as you have already recorded this as revenue for December. Similarly, it should not include the money you paid out in advance for the party supplies for next month's Burns' night celebrations. Here, the profit and loss account is concerned only with the cost of sales for January.

In a number of hospitality operations the profit and loss report is broken down into different departments if there are readily identifiable and discrete revenue generating areas – the obvious breakdown being the accommodation, conference and banqueting, and food and beverage departments in a hotel. For our purposes, the only breakdown of revenue we are concerned with is the split between food and drink. It is usually possible to deal with these two aspects of the operation separately in reporting terms at least. This is the case even where there is no obvious tangible barrier between the two, such as in a restaurant or specific food area. There are other potential revenue streams in licensed retailing, such as cigarettes, door money, machine income (AWP, SWP, SWOP etc.) and room rental. The contributions these make and the ways they are dealt with by a company's financial systems can be very different. For the purposes of our text we have chosen to consider an operation that has a simple revenue profile, with just food, drinks and AWP/SWP machines.

Table 9.2 represents the detail of a week's trading in our unit. These figures are based on those of a real unit.

In Table 9.2, sales are derived from food and drink. These two areas have a different cost base and they are accounted for separately, with different costs of sales. This cost of sales figure relates to all the expenditure that comes about as a direct result of producing and delivering these sales. The relationship between sales and costs of sales is then expressed as the gross profit. The usual convention in licensed retailing is that this figure is concerned only with the costs directly incurred – mainly the stock items. It does not include any labour, not even that which is directly apportionable to production and delivery of sales. Whether to include the cost of labour directly involved when calculating GP is an area of debate, but in most cases it is not done this way so we have chosen to follow this convention here.

	Week 21	% cost of sales	Fixed cost element	Variable cost element
Sales				
Drink	14 724	63		
Food	7929	34		
(AWP/SWP)	820*	3		
Total	23 473	100		
Cost of sales				
Drink	7657	52		7657
Food	2774	35		2774
Total	10 431	46		10 431
Gross profit				
Drink	7067	48		
Food	5155	65		
(AWP/SWP)	820	100		
Total	13 042	56		
Labour	5483	23	3310	2173
Controllable costs				
Operating expenses	2908			
Other controllable costs	743			
Total	3651	15	2110	1541
Controllable profit	3908	17		
Non-controllable expenses	2292	10	2292	
Total net profit	1616	6.8		

* AWP/SWP sales represent the income accruing to the unit only.

Table 9.2 Example operating profit and loss statement for the Dog and Duck

Table 9.2 shows percentages so the performance can be understood better. This makes for more accurate comparison between this and other time periods, with other restaurants in the chain and with budgets. Hence, a lot of the analysis of these data that will aid your decision-making is done using percentages rather than absolute figures. As a guide to these percentages, remember the following:

1 The sales ratios for food and drink are calculated against total sales:

Drink sales as a percentage of total sales: $\frac{14\,724}{23\,473} \times 100 = 63\%$

Food sales as a percentage of total sales: $\frac{7\,929}{23\,473} \times 100 = 34\%$

Machine income as a percentage of total sales: $\frac{820}{23\,473} \times 100 = 3\%$

2 The gross profit is first calculated as a percentage of the sales for each item:

Drink gross profit percentage: $\dfrac{7067}{14\,724} \times 100 = 48\%$

Food gross profit percentage: $\dfrac{5155}{7929} \times 100 = 65\%$

2 All other costs are calculated as a percentage of total sales:

Labour costs as a percentage of total sales: $\dfrac{5483}{23\,473} \times 100 = 23\%$

In order to make an initial judgement about the performance of this unit, we can compare these figures to typical performance figures for similar types of businesses. These could be national averages, or other units in the same brand.

Typical performance figures for this type of operation may be in the following ranges:

Drink GP	54–58%
Food GP	60–68%
Labour cost	15–20%

Active learning point

Do these performance norms seem reasonable to you?

Answer the following questions for this unit:

1 If you were managing this unit, would you be happy with the performance on this very basic initial analysis?
2 In what areas is the unit performance unacceptable?
3 What could be the possible causes of these poor performance areas?

If this were your unit, what other information would you want in order to be able to make a more reasoned judgement about the performance?

There may be a number of reasons for the poor performance of this unit. Whatever the cause, the overall problem is one of control. The weekly turnover and sales mix are in line with other similar operations. In general terms, they could include any or all of the following issues:

1 Poor production controls – portion control, production waste, pre-preparation volumes etc.
2 Customer/plate wastage
3 Theft of raw materials or prepared products
4 Give-aways – either as theft, promotions, or as recompense for poor quality service etc.
5 Too many sales at discounted rates as part of promotional activity
6 Low productivity through poorly trained staff, lacking resources, insufficient staff etc.
7 Low sales value per transaction – more effort is needed to make more sales, which generate lower sales each time
8 Misuse of equipment leading to increased repair bills etc.

These are not the only possible reasons for the poor performance of the unit. To know with more certainty requires specific data, more sophisticated analysis and a greater understanding of the situation of the business. Also, it can be dangerous to make big changes based on figures from one period. A comparison with previous periods – either with the last week or two or with the same periods last year – or budget will tell you more about the problems.

The first area of additional analysis we could consider is the cost–volume–profit analysis (C–V–PA). We explain the basics of this below, and then later in the chapter we show some examples of the kind of analysis possible.

Cost–volume–profit relationships ● ● ●

The basic principle of C–V–PA is that there are clear relationships between the volume of sales, the costs incurred and the level of profit achieved. These can be expressed using the formula:

$$S = VC + FC + P$$

where S = sales, VC = variable cost, FC = fixed costs and P = profit.

Variable costs rise as sales rise, and this relationship between sales and variable cost is pretty steady no matter what the level of sales. This means that when expressed as a percentage, the figure will remain stable. However, fixed costs remain constant and do not change with the level of sales, so when they are expressed as a percentage the figure will change as the levels of sales rises or falls.

The profit and loss report in Table 9.2 identifies the fixed and variable costs associated with this level of sales, and from this it is possible to identify the variable rate. This is the amount of variable cost associated with a unit of sale – in other words, the percentage of variable cost incurred every time a sale is made (Table 9.3). Remember that the examples discussed in the following pages are only meant to be a guide and that they assume that AWP/SWP sales do not change.

	£
Cost of sales:	
Drink	7657
Food	2774
Direct labour costs:	
Drink	1369
Food	804
Direct controllable costs:	
Drink	971
Food	570
Total variable costs	14145

$$\text{Variable rate} = \frac{\text{Variable cost (VC)}}{\text{Sales}} = \frac{14\,145}{23\,473} = 0.603$$

Table 9.3 Profit and loss report for the Big Six

Hospitality, Leisure & Tourism Series

As shown in Table 9.3, the variable rate is therefore 0.603, or 60.3 per cent. Expressed differently, for every £1 of sales there is 60.3 pence of variable cost.

The fixed costs are the total of all other costs associated with the unit:

Labour	3310
Controllable costs	2210
Non-controllable costs	2292
Total fixed costs	7712

This amounts to 32.9 per cent of sales.

For every £1 of sales that the business generates, £0.603 is taken up covering the variable cost. The remainder, £0.397, contributes to one of two things:

1 The fixed costs (it will do this until all fixed costs are covered)
2 The profit of the unit.

Analysis of cost–volume–profit data

Break-even level of sales

The important concept here is the break-even point. This is the point at which all fixed costs are covered by the contribution from sales, or in other words when total revenue is equal to total costs. Only after this point are there enough sales to begin generating a profit. This point, at which sales cover all fixed costs but are not yet generating sufficient contribution to produce profits, can be calculated by using the contribution rate. The contribution to fixed cost/profit from each £1 sales is equal to 1 less the variable rate. In the example above, this would be:

Variable rate   = 0.603
Contribution rate   = 1 − 0.603
Contribution rate   = 0.397

Given this, it is possible to work out the break-even point where sales begin to generate profit for this unit:

$$\text{Sales} = \frac{\text{Fixed costs}}{\text{Contribution rate}}$$

$$\text{Sales} = \frac{7712}{0.397}$$

$$\text{Sales} = 19\,426$$

With the current cost structure and controls in place, this operation must produce sales of £19 426 per week before costs are covered and it begins to generate a profit. Beyond this point, for every £1 in sales there is a contribution to profit of £0.39. This may seem like a dry academic exercise, leaving you asking the question 'so what?' How many operations have the aim simply to break even? However, it is not quite so simple, and there are a number of reasons why this knowledge is useful to unit managers:

1 If, before break-even is reached, individual sales are registered at prices below the variable cost level, they will fail to make any contribution to fixed costs and each sale will lose the business money.
2 Once break-even is reached, each sale generates a healthy contribution to profit – nearly £0.40 in the pound in this case. So profitability increases at a greater rate once fixed costs have been covered.
3 Every sale that is made beyond break-even contributes directly to profit, as long as it exceeds variable cost. This opens the possibility for price-based promotional activity aimed at increasing volume.
4 There is also a clear psychological point to be made from break-even. Beyond this point it is possible to see the effort being put in as contributing to profit, and therefore being somehow more worthwhile.

The concept of break-even can contribute to decision-making in a number of useful ways. At its simplest, it can enable you to work out the volume of sales you require in order to make a certain level of profit. It does this if you deal with the profit required as if it were simply part of the fixed cost. In our example, if we wanted to make a profit of £3500, then we could work out the sales needed as below:

$$\text{Sales volume for £3500 profit} = \frac{\text{Fixed costs} + \text{Profit desired}}{\text{Contribution rate}}$$

$$= \frac{7712 + 3500}{0.397} = £28\,242$$

(This is assuming the same price and sales mix.)

This is a simple example, but there are more sophisticated ways in which the CVP concept can help. When considering the contribution that CVP analysis can make to decision-making, it may help you to think about some of the questions that often need to be answered with regard to changed financial circumstances in your unit – questions such as:

• What impact will a change in the price of beer have on my profit?
• How much profit will be generated if sales rise or fall to a certain level?
• What level of sales do we need to cover the increased wage costs and maintain the current levels of profit?
• What will be the impact of a shift in sales mix from food to drink of 10 per cent?

This could be a never-ending list, but we won't go on. The impact of any and every change, variance or problem associated with one of the cost, profit or volume variables can be modelled using this technique. The technique will not tell you how to make the changes in performance happen, but it will tell you the impact the changes could have on the overall performance of the business. What this will do is enable you to set clear, realistic and measurable goals for which you will need to plan and implement appropriate courses of action.

Examples • • •

Below are a number of examples of the technique being used to answer important questions about the control of the business. All these examples are based on the formula version of the technique rather than the graphical version.

There is no time, in this text, to go into the detail of each question. If you need to see a more detailed explanation, we suggest you view some of the reading listed at the end of the chapter.

In all these examples we will consider our objective to be an increase in profit from £1616 to £3500 – that is, an additional £1884. This is quite a large change, and one that would be difficult to accomplish in the short term.

1 How much would we have to raise all prices, given the same level of sales?

$$\frac{\text{Increased profit}}{\text{Total sales}} = \frac{1884}{23\,473} = 8\%$$

An 8 per cent increase in prices would increase profit to £3500.

2 How much would we need to increase drink prices if the food prices remained the same?

$$\frac{\text{Increased profit}}{\text{Drink sales}} = \frac{1884}{14\,724} = 13\%$$

3 How much would we need to increase food sales?

$$\frac{\text{Increased profit}}{\text{Food contribution rate}} = \frac{1884}{0.477} = £3949$$

4 How much would we need to increase drink sales and food sales in a 70/30 ratio?

Drink:
- Variable cost – 9997 (7657 + 1369 + 971)
- Contribution rate – 0.321
- Contribution rate (0.321) × proportionate increase (0.7) = 0.23.

Food:
- Variable cost – 4148 (2774 + 804 + 570)
- Contribution rate – 0.477
- Contribution rate (0.477) × proportionate increase (0.3) = 0.14.

Therefore, average contribution rate for this sales mix = 0.23 + 0.14 = 0.37;

$$\frac{1884}{0.37} = £5091 \text{ in total.}$$

Therefore drink sales would need to be increased by £3564 and food sales by £1527.

5 What would the food cost percentage need to be reduced to?

$$\frac{\text{Food cost} - \text{Increased profit}}{\text{Food sales}} = \frac{2774 - 1884}{7929} = 11\%$$

We can see from this result that we are unlikely to achieve the desired profit increase through a reduction in food cost alone; a target of an 11 per cent food cost seems somewhat hopeful!

6 What would the cost of sales need to be if we increased drink sales volume by 20 per cent?

- Extra drink sales needed: $20\% \times 14724 = 2944$
- Cost of extra drink sales $20\% \times 7657 = 1530$
- Other costs associated with extra sales $20\% \times 2349 = 468$
- Total extra costs $= 1998$
- Extra profit from 20 per cent increase $= 946$
- Additional profit needed from reduction in cost of sales $= 1884 - 946 = 938$

New cost of sales percentage needed for drinks:

$$\frac{\text{Cost of sales} + \text{additional cost of sales from increase} - \text{additional profit needed}}{\text{Original drink sales} + \text{Additional drink sales}}$$

$$= \frac{7657 + 1530 - 938}{14\,724 + 2944} = \frac{8249}{17\,668} = 47\%$$

7 And finally, how much would sales need to increase to cover an increased fixed cost?

Assume profit stays the same.

$$\text{New level of sales} = \frac{\text{Old fixed cost} + \text{New fixed cost} + \text{Profit required}}{\text{Contribution rate}}$$

If we take the example of an increase in fixed expenses from hiring a DJ on Friday and Saturday nights, the answer would look like this:

Cost of DJ at £250 per night $= £500$

$$\text{New sales required} = \frac{7712 + 500 + 1616}{397} = 24\,756\ (-23\,473)$$

This is an increase in sales of £1283 to cover an extra fixed cost of £500.

It can be seen from this analysis that there are a number of possible ways of bringing about the objective of increased profitability. The requirements of each are clearly and simply identified, and some of them are more realistic than others! The key thing to bear in mind is that this is not an exhaustive list of alternative approaches, but some examples of tools and techniques that you can apply to any of your own circumstances. It is a tool that can help you to determine exactly what is needed in terms of changes in performance to achieve your financial goals. The use of cost–volume–profit analysis in this way can be a powerful tool in financial planning and control for your unit.

Active learning point

Choose a profit and loss statement from a unit with which you are familiar. The figures will be used as the basis for the calculations completed above, so check that all the necessary data are present.

Take each of the calculations described above and substitute the figures from your profit and loss account.

Make the calculations as directed. Do the results look reasonable?

What implications do the results have for the management of the unit in question? What actions would you consider as unit manager?

Conclusion

This chapter has attempted to provide an overview of the concept of control, and specifically financial control, as applied to licensed retail businesses. If a pub, bar or restaurant in the sector is to be a success, then there is a need to control the business on a day-to-day basis. The profitability that largely defines success for these operations can be achieved through generating sales and turning sales into profit, and this chapter has dealt with the second of these objectives. The focus of control, in this case, is achieving financial business goals.

The starting point for controlling the operation is an understanding of the control cycle and the role managers play in this. Unit managers must set targets, enable staff to perform as required, monitor the performance and decide upon and take corrective action as necessary. When considering financial targets, it is important to be aware of potential conflicts with other business performance aims. The difficulties caused by ignoring other business performance targets to focus solely on financial goals are discussed here, and it is clear that the licensed retail service sector has been guilty of this to an extent in recent times. The alternative, a balanced scorecard approach, is recommended.

Once the principles of financial control have been established, an understanding of the fundamentals of costs and sales is necessary. Costs can be classified as either fixed or variable, and it is important to be able to determine and measure the proportion of each in your business. The nature of controllable and uncontrollable and direct and unit or total costs are determined here, and similarly the nature of sales in the unit is described and a number of monetary and non-monetary measures proposed. It is important to have this level of understanding of costs and sales, as they are the building blocks of all the financial controls and techniques proposed as appropriate for pub and bar unit managers in Chapters 9 and 10 of this text.

The unit profit and loss statement is explained briefly as being an overall picture of how the unit has performed, in relation to sales and costs, over a given time period. This statement is the fundamental expression of the data necessary to carry out the financial analysis proposed for financial control of licensed retail businesses.

This chapter concludes with an explanation of the relationship between sales, costs and profit, known as C–V–P analysis. Brief details of this approach are discussed here, and the use of the technique in making financial control decisions is explained. This discussion begins with the basic calculation of break-even point and went on to ask more sophisticated questions about the relationship between cost, sales and profit by showing some worked examples based on a simple profit and loss account.

Chapter 10 will further develop the use of analytical techniques appropriate for financial control in pubs, bars and restaurants, and will conclude the discussion of financial control with a review of the budgeting process.

Reflective practice

Answer the following questions to check your understanding of this chapter.

1 Explain why a unit manager needs to be able to create budgets and measure performance against them.
2 Make the case for monitoring unit performance using a 'balanced score card' approach that relies on both financial measures and non-financial measures of performance.
3 Identify the range of monetary measures of performance that need to be used in your business or in a business known to you.
4 Analyse the difficulties faced in the non-monetary example given in this chapter. What corrective action could you take?
5 Explain the value of cost–volume–profit analysis. How can this technique be used to help you control and manage your business more effectively.

Further reading

Atrill, P. (2000). *Financial Management for Non-specialists*. Prentice Hall/Financial Times.
Atrill, P. and McLaney, E. (2001). *Accounting and Finance for Non-specialists*. Prentice Hall/Financial Times.
Coltman, M. (1999). *Hospitality Management Accounting*. J Wiley & Sons.
Harris, P. (1999). *Profit Planning*. Butterworth-Heinemann.
Jones, P. and Merricks, P. (1994). *The Management of Food Service Operations*. Cornell.
Kotas, R. (1999). *Management Accounting for the Hospitality Industry*. International Thompson Business Press.

On turning more profit

After working through this chapter, you should be able to:

- carry out and apply profit sensitivity analysis to identify the key determinants of profitability

- conduct sales analysis by reviewing sales patterns and applying the technique of menu engineering

- understand and contribute effectively to the unit budgeting process

- apply the results of all the analytical techniques to management decision-making for control and business development.

Further financial controls to improve business performance

You now have an understanding of the nature and importance of financial control in licensed retail units, and are aware of the key principles of financial control and the role of cost and sales data in the process. You have also begun to review simple analytical tools to help in your decision-making for control.

The CVP analysis conducted in Chapter 9 enables you to understand the relationship between costs, sales volume and profits. From this analysis you can identify the potential areas of concern with current performance and make some basic predictions about the impact of possible changes and strategies on future business performance.

This chapter extends the analysis to look at other techniques that will help you to make sense of the complexity of issues influencing your decision-making, and begins by looking in greater detail at what factors have most impact on the profitability of a pub, bar or restaurant. This involves the use of profit sensitivity analysis, and the aim of this approach is to identify the most effective future strategies for profit improvement – cost control or revenue generation – and which areas of costs to control. It goes on to look specifically at sales and the methods available to control and manage them effectively. The chapter concludes with consideration of the topic of budgets, the budgeting process and the effective use of budgets in control.

Following the structure identified in Chapter 9, we are concerned with the final two stages of the control cycle:

1 The analysis and interpretation of financial data for decision-making purposes
2 The preparation of budgets for future control and development of the business.

Profit sensitivity analysis

Improving profit is a key focus of all this management and control decision-making. Profit sensitivity analysis (PSA) can provide further useful guidance as to the most effective ways in which this can be done. Specifically, the objective of PSA is to identify the key factors that influence profitability in a business and determine their relative importance. A factor can be considered to be a key influence on profitability when a relatively small change in it brings about a relatively large change in profitability. You will no doubt already have opinions about which factors have the most impact on the profitability of your business, and it is also likely that these opinions are built from experience and maybe even a little prejudice. With PSA it is possible actually to measure the impact of different factors and therefore confirm or redefine these previously held views.

As this approach actually measures the impact of certain factors, the factors that you identify as critical must be measurable. You may well consider the number of customers coming into your pub to be a key factor in determining the level of profitability, and this may well be true. However, unless you have someone counting people as they enter, it will not be possible actually to measure the impact of this variable.

Applied learning activity

1 List all the factors that you think have an influence on the profitability of your unit. Focus on the financial and non-financial measures of performance or outcomes that are important rather than the management actions that you take – for example, the number of meals served or the average size of transactions over the bar.

2 Can you prioritize these from most influential to least influential?

PSA is related to cost–volume–profit analysis in that it is concerned with the impact of the cost structure of a business on its profitability. In very simple terms, differing levels of fixed and variable costs will mean that different factors have more or less influence on profitability. Generally, a business with higher fixed costs will usually be more sensitive to changes in critical factors than one with a higher level of variable costs. However, the potential rewards for the firm with higher relative fixed costs are greater.

It can be seen from the examples below that PSA has clear implications for management decision-making. In particular, PSA can give direction to the control strategy adopted by management. Businesses can broadly be classified as either cost-oriented or market-oriented:

1 *Cost-oriented* firms have lower relative fixed costs and a greater proportion of variable costs. In this situation, improving profits is more likely to be achieved through a strategy that focuses on controlling costs. Management decisions should always take this into account, and it can be a guide regarding where to place time, effort and resources for controlling the business.

2 *Market-oriented businesses* have higher levels of fixed costs and a correspondingly lower variable cost percentage. The strategies here will be more effective at profit improvement if centred on sales and revenue, concentrating on generating additional revenue in whatever ways possible.

Below we have illustrated the PSA concept with two examples, using the figures from the profit and loss statement in Chapter 9. Again, these are not intended to be an exhaustive blueprint for all that PSA can do, but they serve to illustrate the information that can be provided by the technique, and the relative simplicity of the analysis that provides the information.

The first step in doing a profit sensitivity analysis is to work out the 'profit multipliers' of the business. In order to do this, you must take the following steps:

- list out the key factors (from the previous active learning point)
- assume a standard change in each – in this case we will use 10 per cent for ease of calculation
- calculate the change in profit that comes about from the 10 per cent change in each factor (assume all other variables remain the same)
- use the change in profit to work out the 'profit multiplier' for each key factor
- use the profit multipliers to determine the relative importance of each key factor.

In the business that we are using as an example, the following have been suggested as two of the critical factors that influence profitability the most:

1 Average drink transaction over the bar
2 Food and drink cost of sales.

Average drink transaction over the bar. This is just a little more complicated, because an increase in the value of the average bar transaction may be due to people buying more each time (doubles instead of singles, for example) or it may be because they are trading up to premium products while still buying the same amount. For this calculation we will assume that both of these instances will increase variable costs by the same amount, so we don't need to account for them in the calculation.

A 10 per cent increase in transaction value gives:

Drink revenue	£16 196 (110% × £14 724)
Total revenue	£24 945
Variable cost increase	£1000 (10% × £9997)
New total cost	£22 857 (£21 857 + £1000)
New profit	£2088 (£24 945 − £22 857)
Increase in profit	£472 (£2088 − £1616)

Thus a 10 per cent increase in the value of the average bar transaction gives a £472 increase in profit. This works out as 29 per cent increase.

To calculate the profit multiplier for the average bar transaction:

$$PM = \frac{\% \text{ change in profit}}{\% \text{ change in key factor}} = \frac{29}{10}$$

Therefore, profit multiplier = 2.9.

This shows that, with the cost structure as it is currently, there is little to be gained from concentrating on drink sales. The profit multiplier is relatively low, and focusing on other areas could probably give greater gains.

Food and drink cost of sales.

Total revenue	£23 437
Food and drink costs	£11 474 (£10 431 × 110%)
Total costs	£22 900
New profit	£537 (£23 437 − £22 900)
Change in profit	£1079 (£1616 − £537)

To calculate the profit multiplier for food and drink cost of sales:

$$PM = \frac{\% \text{ change in profit}}{\% \text{ change in key factor}} = \frac{67}{10} \text{ (£1079/£1616)}$$

Therefore, profit multiplier = 6.7.

This is far bigger than the average drink transactions profit multiplier calculated above, and indicates that profits are far more sensitive to changes in costs of sales than they are to transaction value.

Further investigation of these figures would reveal a similar pattern, with the cost-oriented factors proving to have more influence over profit than the revenue-oriented ones. This situation indicates the difficulties facing this unit and the need to get the costs under control. If this happens, the cost structure and therefore profit sensitivities will begin to return to a more normal profile for a commercial business of this kind.

You may be thinking that this is all very well, but managers of branded operations are not in a position to influence a number of these key factors. This may well be true, but what you must be able to do is make effective control decisions. In order to do this, an awareness and understanding of these issues will mean that you are in a position to make better-informed and more effective decisions by identifying where to concentrate resources and effort.

Sales analysis

The control of sales, in its most basic form, is all about maximizing revenue and profit by:

1 Increasing sales volume – by having more customers, or existing customers buying more
2 Improving the sales mix
3 Increasing prices.

The manipulation of price is not really an option for unit managers in branded operations, so we have not considered this. Increasing revenue has been dealt with in Chapter 12. The remaining strategy is about the sales mix of the business – the combination of products that customers purchase.

Here we are concerned with the financial control methods that can be used to ensure that the sales mix is such that we get the best margin and net profit possible. In order to do this we have to be able to work out what this 'best' mix is, and then make decisions about how to achieve it. The techniques reviewed here will help you to do both of these.

Why sales mix? • • •

First we will answer the question, 'Why is the sales mix so important?'. The answer to this lies in the impact that it has on net profit. A change in the mix of products sold can have a major impact on the level of profit achieved, even though the total revenue, the number of customers and the direct costs remain the same. In other words, without changing the amount of revenue we make, the price we pay for our materials or the way we work, we can increase or decrease our profit.

Consider the simple example illustrated in Tables 10.1 and 10.2. The tables represent the same unit over a period of time; Table 10.1 shows the original performance, while Table 10.2 shows how performance changed over the period in question.

	Revenue	Direct costs	Contribution	Contribution (%)
Food	10 000	8000	2000	20
Drink	15 000	9750	5250	35
Total	25 000	17 750	7250	

Table 10.1 Sales and cost figures for sales mix analysis – original performance

	Revenue	Direct costs	Contribution	Contribution (%)
Food	15 000	12 000	3000	20
Drink	10 000	6500	3500	35
Total	25 000	18 500	6500	

Table 10.2 Sales and cost figures for sales mix analysis – change in performance

We can see that the only changes over the period have been to the mix of sales, where the emphasis has changed from drink to food. The total revenue and the costs and contribution percentage from each product category have remained the same. Despite this, there has been a £750 drop in contribution – which, if all other factors are equal, means a £750 drop in profit; a reduction of 10.3 per cent.

If the profit can suffer so clearly with a change in mix, it is equally apparent that if the mix is managed effectively, then profit will benefit from this.

Unit managers require an awareness of the varying contributions to profit of the different elements of the sales mix in order to improve the quality of their decision-making. This does not just mean understanding the difference between food and beverages. It is possible to look at the sales mix on the basis of different categories of products. These categories would traditionally be based on standard ones prevalent in the industry for years, such as:

1 Drinks
   • beers – ales and lagers
   • wines
   • spirits
   • soft drinks
2 Food
   • starters
   • mains
   • sweets
   • side dishes.

Whilst there is no implied criticism of these in their own right, there has been an over-reliance on them as the focus for understanding the sales mix. This could be

Hospitality, Leisure & Tourism Series

because of the ease with which data for these categories can be collected and analysed; it is also easier to work with these categories for drinks purchasing and supply purposes. It may well be worth considering some other categories as a more effective focus for improving the sales mix. We will examine the technique of *menu engineering*, which can be used to do this, but you could also consider categories or groups based on:

- service – all pre-plated food items
- packaging – all bottled products
- customer perception or usage – all 'getting me drunk' products
- promotional activity – all brands receiving heavy national promotion.

Any category that is meaningful for management decision-making and is measurable can be considered as a basis for sales mix analysis.

Applied learning activity

In your unit, or a unit known to you, identify the product categories/groups that you could use as a basis for sales mix analysis.

Without calculating anything at this stage, which of these groups do you think is likely to have the most and least impact on profit if the sales mix changes in their favour?

Reviewing sales patterns

Your sales mix analysis does not have to stop at product categories; it can be as specific and precise as individual brands or products, if this is relevant. Later in the chapter we will discuss a technique called *menu engineering*, which is designed to enable you to review the performance of each individual item on your menu (food and/or drink). Before this, however, it is necessary to look at the broader pattern of sales in the unit – not confining ourselves to particular products or categories of products, but considering such fundamental questions as:

1 When are the busy and quiet times?
2 Are sales patterns the same at busy and quiet times?
3 Are particular products popular at certain times?
4 Are there any trends (particularly growth or decline) in sales patterns?
5 What periods represent sales growth opportunities?

Answering these questions begins with a system for recording the data about sales. All sales analysis requires historical review – in other words, looking at patterns from the past and trying to pick out key elements of these. If this is to work, there must be an accurate, clear and simple method of storing and reviewing these data.

The timing of these records is again important. Records have to represent a long enough period to avoid one-off blips or deviations caused by freak circumstances, but they must also be recent enough to make control activities possible. This will be a decision that you will need to make as a unit manager, as it will be as appropriate for the particular business and circumstances. However, it is unlikely that weekly analysis will provide sufficient data to reliably identify trends or important issues, and conversely, anything over three months is leaving control a bit late. There is a place for longer-term analysis, even comparing back to previous years, but this is more likely to be part of planning and strategy development rather then control.

Table 10.3 gives a very simple sales analysis of the patterns of trade over the previous week. This record looks at the patterns of trade over three key periods of each day – P1, which is 11 am–2 pm; P2, which is 2 pm to 6 pm; and P3, which is 6 pm to 11 pm. These periods were identified as the key breakdown for this unit; yours may well be different, and a brief review of trading patterns should identify the key periods in your unit.

	Week 1				Week 2			
	P1	P2	P3	Total	P1	P2	P3	Total
Sunday	400	200	600	1200	450	200	650	1300
Monday	550	150	400	1100	550	100	400	1050
Tuesday	250	100	450	800	300	70	400	770
Wednesday	300	150	550	1000	350	80	650	1080
Thursday	450	350	1700	2500	500	200	1700	2400
Friday	500	400	3600	4500	550	250	4000	4800
Saturday	600	600	4800	6000	650	400	4300	5350
Total	3050	1950	12 100	17 100	3350	1300	12 100	16 750

Table 10.3 Example weekly sales figures by period

There are two things that are immediately apparent from these figures:

1 Afternoon trade appears to be declining. If this is the first time that you have noticed this result, then it is probably not yet necessary to begin taking action; however, it does warrant further attention in next period's figures. Also, it may be worth looking at this period last year to see if similar trends were evident. If this is something that is longer established, it definitely requires action – first to research what is causing it to happen (has anything about the product or service changed over the same period? Is there some new competition?), and secondly to prepare strategies to deal with it. Alternatively, you may feel that it is not a key issue and that reducing costs to maintain margins over this period is sufficient action.
2 Monday lunchtime figures stand out as being relatively high. Compared to other sessions in this unit, but also in general, this is a good level of trade. Certainly this pattern of trade on early weekday lunchtimes is not a common occurrence. Do you know why this is happening? Can you do anything to capitalize on it for other, quieter periods?

The level of detail and time period that your records cover can vary according to your objectives and the data you have. Similarly, you may wish to consider other factors rather than particular sessions of each day, such as:

- comparisons of your trade with the averages for this brand (Table 10.4)
- average spends at different times (Table 10.5)
- sales for different weather conditions etc. (Table 10.6).

When recording and analysing sales patterns, always remember:

1 It is likely that a good deal of the data you need for these kind of analyses will be provided from the brand accounting system. This may well be through the EPOS system that operates your tills and food ordering system, for example. Make sure that you are fully aware of what data this system can provide, and that you make

	Average spend				Variance (±)	Comments
	Unit – food	Brand – food	Unit – drink	Brand – drink		
Mon						
Tue						
Wed						
Thu						
Fri						
Sat						
Sun						

Table 10.4 Average spend brand comparison

Time	Actual volume of sales	Percentage of daily sales
9.00 am–12.00 noon		
12.00 noon –2.00 pm		
2.00 pm–4.30 pm		
4.30 pm–7.30 pm		
7.30 pm–10.00 pm		
10.00 pm–1.00 am		

Table 10.5 Daily breakdown of sales

Month	Mon	Tue	Wed	Thu	Fri	Sat	Sun
January							
February							
March							
April							
May							
June							
July							
August							
September							
October							
November							
December							

Table 10.6 Yearly planning review of sales

the most of this before starting to develop your own recording and analysis systems.

2 Collect and analyse data that are relevant to your aims and objectives. Don't be content with dealing just with the information that is readily to hand – having the wrong data and then acting upon it is worse than having no data at all. If what you need is not available from the head office system, and you think it is important enough for other units too, then be a pest and bother head office until the data are made available!

3 Record unusual conditions or occurrences that could have had an impact on the level of sales. This will help to ensure that you don't misread trends that are not real, ascribing increased significance to figures that are affected by one-off events. It will also help you to plan ahead if these events are likely to occur again.

This analysis should give you some ideas about specific areas where sales growth is possible and the type of growth that is desirable, which will give you some explicit objectives for sales growth. As with any other objectives, you should always identify these in SMART terms.

Menu engineering

So far we have analysed sales on a fairly simple level, looking at the numbers sold in comparison with other variables such as time. We have made the basic assumption that a higher level of sales is good and a lower level is bad. This seems a perfectly acceptable view to take, and this analysis does produce valuable information. However, it is also somewhat simplistic, and this can be seen if we look a little more closely at sales.

Earlier we mentioned the menu engineering technique as a means of evaluating the performance of each individual item on the menu. This can be an extremely powerful tool and one that can provide very valuable information when making decisions about product and promotional strategies and tactics, among other things. It should be pointed out that in this case the term 'menu item' is used to mean both food and drink products.

The concept of menu engineering was developed in the early 1980s by Kasavana and Smith (1982). It was derived after a long search for a way of analysing menus to find the most profitable items – those that make the best contribution to the performance of the business. Basically, the technique uses principles of 'portfolio analysis', assessing items based on two measures and putting them into a matrix with four categories. With this method you can compare the performance of menu items on the basis of the gross profit (contribution margin) they provide and their popularity (sales volume). The technique deals in actual money values, rather than percentages, as this gives a real picture of their contribution and not just a 'relative' one.

The two measures are assessed against the average performance of all items, and are then classified as either high (above average) or low (below average). As with any tool or technique of this kind, the use of menu engineering requires you to make judgements and assumptions based on your experience and knowledge of the business. This means that the accuracy of the results is dependent, to some extent, on your own judgement; this is not a scientific process. What this does do, though, is provide a wealth of information that all has the same basis and allows real comparison and better decision-making.

The process of menu engineering requires collection of a lot of data regarding all the items on your menu. It is a simple process, but one that has a number of steps and that must be followed precisely if it is to work.

Before beginning the process, some preparation is necessary:

1 Decide over what period you are going to carry it out. A week is probably the shortest feasible period of analysis, but even then the results may well be limited.
2 Decide which categorie(s) you are going to evaluate. It is only really possible to compare items from one category at a time because of the differences in prices and costs between different categories.
3 Prepare a sheet for the analysis so that all the data can be recorded easily and calculations can be readily completed.

The analysis sheet needs to contain the following information (letters refer to the appropriate column in Table 10.7):

1. Menu item	A	All the items from the category being analysed
2. Menu mix	B	Number of each item sold over the period of the analysis
3. Menu mix (%)	C	This converts the number of items sold into a percentage of all items sold

4. Food cost   D   Food cost of each item

5. Selling price   E   Full price of each item, as presented on the menu

6. Contribution margin   F   Gross profit of each item, i.e. selling price minus the food cost (E − D)

7. Total costs   G   The total cost for each item in the analysis, i.e. volume of sales for an item multiplied by its food cost (B × D)

8. Total sales   H   The total money value of sales for each item, i.e. the total number sold multiplied by the selling price (B × E)

9. Total contribution   I   The total gross profit contributed by each item – sales number multiplied by contribution margin (B × F)

10. Contribution margin class   J   Identifies whether the contribution margin for each item is above (H) or below (L) average

11. Menu mix class   K   Identifies whether the menu mix is above (H) or below (L) the average menu mix achievement rate

12. Menu item classification   Identifies the category into which each menu item falls (star, plough-horse, puzzle, dog)

Unit: The Big Six   Category: Food – Mains   Date: 05.03.02   Period: 2 weeks

A	B	C	D	E	F	G	H	I	J	K	L
Steak	360	36%	3.00	7.00	4.00	1080	2520	1440	H	H	Star
Chicken	420	42%	2.95	5.95	3.00	1239	2499	1260	H	L	Plough-horse
Balti	70	7%	2.45	4.95	2.50	172	347	175	L	L	Dog
Salmon	150	15%	2.00	6.50	4.50	300	975	675	L	H	Puzzle
Total	1000	100%				2791	6341	3550			

Menu mix achievement rate 17.5%   3.46 Average contribution margin

Table 10.7 Menu engineering data record sheet

The menu item classification is described below (see also Figure 10.1).

There are two other calculations required to prepare the menu engineering analysis:

1 *Menu mix achievement rate.* This represents the average sales of all items on the menu. In this case, four items with total sales of 1000 should give an average sale of 250 units per item. However, Kasavana and Smith (1982) state that it is not realistic to expect items to reach this level. By definition, some have to be lower for

some to be higher. To make the figure realistic, it is tempered with a weighted multiplier of 0.7 (70 per cent). Thus an item is expected to sell 70 per cent of the average item sales to be performing at an acceptable level, and in our example this is 17.5 per cent, or 175 items.

2 *Average contribution margin.* This is simply the average gross profit of all the items being analysed. Remember that it is the actual contribution achieved and not just the potential, so it takes into account the sales (menu) mix as well as the margin for each item. In this case, it is £3.55.

Analysing the menu engineering data

A review of the results from this activity classifies each item as being a plough-horse, star, dog or puzzle (see Figure 10.1).

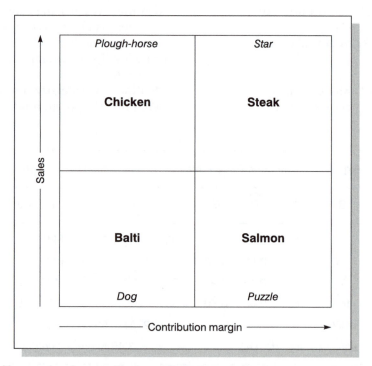

Figure 10.1 Menu engineering classification of items

Each category has a specific meaning, which helps to define the strategies for each item within that category.

Stars are the items that are performing the best. An ideal menu would be made up entirely of these – if this were not technically impossible! They make a better than average contribution to fixed cost and profit, and sell at a rate above that defined as good performance. They are popular with customers and contribute well to the business.

Dogs are products that do not make much money and are not popular with many customers.

Plough-horses are items that are popular with customers and have a high level of demand. However, they do not make much contribution to profit. Usually the aim is to increase the margin, and therefore the contribution, without reducing the level of demand.

Puzzles are indeed puzzles! These items make an above average contribution, yet not enough of them are sold. They have the potential to be good earners, yet lack something. We would clearly like them to be more popular.

Strategies for stars ● ● ●

These items will pretty much always be left on the menu. In most cases, stars will be actively promoted to ensure that they maintain their position. Promotion might involve positioning on the menu, and effective merchandising. They should never be promoted with price reductions of any kind – at least not as part of their own development strategy. It may occasionally be appropriate to price-promote stars for the good of the operation overall, for example when considering a 'reward' for loyal customers with a view to encouraging further loyalty. If anything, though, the price of star items can be increased. This tends to be the least price-sensitive category and is therefore able to maintain demand at higher prices. With this in mind, promotional activity for stars may well attempt to emphasize their added value and quality elements. Operationally, because of their importance, it is wise to make doubly sure that control of product and service delivery quality for these items is a priority.

Strategies for dogs ● ● ●

The initial reaction is that we don't want dogs on the menu, and if they have to be there we want to them hide them away as far as possible. However, it is worth noting that because of their current position there is not much that we can do to harm them, and therefore it is possible to employ some outrageous strategies to increase demand or margin, which just may come off! This is a long shot, though, and it is more likely that these items will be replaced in the long term. In a similar vein to puzzles, there may be a small band of loyal followers who make a good case for retaining the product as it is. Alternatively, a product may perform some other function that reduces its need to contribute in the traditional way (see Box 10.1).

Box 10.1 *The Big Steak Brand*

When the Big Steak brand was in its second stage of development in the early 1990s, there was an item on the menu that fitted the 'dog' category to a tee – the 32-oz rump steak. It was 50 per cent more expensive than anything else on the menu at £9.99, yet it's contribution margin was poor. Because of its price (and possibly size!) it was also very unpopular. However, it was retained on the menu because of its marketing function. A steak this size was a talking point with nearly all customers, especially if they were tackling it! It gathered publicity from a number of unlikely sources – of the 'you can't buy steak in the supermarket for this price' variety – and generally performed an excellent awareness and interest-raising function. As a revenue and profit generating item in its own right, it was hopeless!

Hospitality, Leisure & Tourism Series

Strategies for plough-horses ● ● ●

The obvious strategies for plough-horses would seem to be price-based – i.e. increasing selling price if price sensitivity is not high. Alternatively, an option may be to look at reducing the costs of producing the item – for example, by using different ingredients or portion sizes. There seems to be a need to retain these items on the menu because of their popularity, so if it is not possible to raise margins through the strategies mentioned, it may be necessary to attract customers' attention elsewhere. Put these items out of sight, distract customers' attention from them, and dissuade people from purchasing them.

One thing to mention here is the need to consider the total contribution as discussed above. Plough-horses are often in the category of having a seemingly poor classification but contributing a great deal to the profit overall. Always be aware of this in your decision-making.

Strategies for puzzles ● ● ●

Owing to their potential for improvement, puzzles perhaps warrant more attention overall than the other categories, beginning with an effort to understand why they are not more popular. This could, for example, be because the price is too great or the level of quality is not sufficiently high. Either of these could explain both the high margin and the low popularity. It seems reasonable to assume that we would want to keep these items because of their potential, and usually this is a reasonable conclusion. However, if they remain resolutely unpopular after a concerted effort to increase demand, there is a case for removing them from the menu.

Particular strategies could include re-presenting the product on the menu, high-profile promotion, which could include price reductions (the margin can support this), effective merchandizing and strong personal selling from staff.

There is a very particular case when it may be possible to increase the price of puzzles even further. This is if there are a number of highly loyal consumers for this product – for example, a particular imported bottled beer. In this case it may be necessary to admit that the product will never have widespread popularity and resign yourself to maximizing the contribution from the existing level of demand.

Summary ● ● ●

We can see it is possible to identify some generic strategies for products in the different categories. While these are valuable as guidance, or a starting point for developing sales strategies, it is dangerous to stick to them too closely at the expense of your interpretation and your own creative input.

A number of the strategies identified may well fall outside the scope of responsibility for most unit managers. This does not make them invalid for discussion here. You need to be aware of the objectives and possibilities for all your products so that all factors can be taken into account when making decisions. Also, it is in the interest of the brand as a whole to consider these strategies, and therefore the more you can contribute to this process, the better the potential benefit all round.

Active learning point

Carry out a run through of the menu engineering process, using sales figures from a unit known to you. If possible, choose one where you are familiar with the figures and are able to make a reasonable assumption as to the classification of menu items – either food or drink.

Choose a category of items on which to base your analysis. This could be draught beers or ales/lagers, or perhaps starters. If it is a big group with a lot of items in it, look at just three or four to begin with.

Carry out the analysis using the table format given above (Table 10.7) or by any other means you feel comfortable with. Finish by classifying the items as stars, dogs, plough-horses or puzzles.

Given the need to maximize the profitability from your sales mix, and knowing what you do about this unit and its customers, what would your strategy be for each of the items in your analysis?

Budgets

Chapters 9 and 10 have so far considered the meaning, objectives and techniques of financial control in pubs, bars and restaurants. What has not yet been considered is the concept of budgets and budgeting. A budget is a financial representation of the unit manager's goals and objectives for the coming period. At their simplest, budgets control money, setting limits and controls for the access to money and for the amounts that should be generated. They may well limit your ability to get the money you need for development in your unit, and they will undoubtedly have an impact on the reward you receive for managing your business.

Types of budgets

There are three fundamental kinds of budgets – capital, cash and operating budgets. All three are combined to form the master budget. Capital and cash issues have limited relevance for management at a unit level, so the focus here is on operating budgets.

Operating budgets may in fact have two specific and distinct functions – planning and control. The distinction between these is as much to do with timescale as with any discrete content or approaches to management. Planning budgets will usually be for the longer term – a year and upwards – while control budgets, if they are to be any use in control, have to be over shorter time periods – usually up to a maximum of a year. If you refer to the discussion about the nature of control at the beginning of Chapter 9, then you can see that the fundamentals are knowing what should be happening, monitoring what is happening, identifying where things are not as planned, and taking action to put things right. This is essentially the budgeting cycle in a nutshell. Specifically, budgets are about setting and monitoring financial targets, followed by any necessary corrective action that results. It is likely that unit managers' responsibilities for budgets will be much more to do with evaluating performance against budget and initiating corrective action than with preparing and setting the targets. However, it is important that you understand all aspects of budgeting if you are to contribute fully throughout the cycle. This is perhaps more the case if you operate in an environment in which budgeting still takes a gladiatorial approach.

Conflicts in budgeting

Budgets have long been an area of potential contention and conflict in licensed retailing. From a unit manager's point of view, these difficulties have included budgets enforced on unit management that are perceived as unrealistic or even punitive, budgets being changed without notice or reason, and, perhaps most worrying, rewards payable against budgets being withheld or withdrawn altogether for no suitable reason. For these reasons the word budget has been almost guaranteed to produce, at the very least, a wry smile on the face of the most experienced and successful operators, and at the worst a bout of anguish and panic of dangerous proportions.

Fortunately it need not be this way and things are improving. There are an ever-increasing number of firms with an enlightened approach to budgeting, with numerous examples of good practice of the type discussed here. These firms are the ones that have recognized two key elements of the budgeting process:

1 Budgets can be a very powerful management tool if prepared and used properly
2 Probably the most important factor in budgeting is the human element. Budgets will not be worth the computer memory they take up if they are not understood, believed in and committed to by the people who are responsible for making them work. In our case, this means you . . .

The people factor • • •

Budgets have the power to be a force for good or bad in pubs, bars and restaurants. They can be an effective motivator for unit management, guiding and influencing behaviour toward achieving targets never thought possible. This text has on many occasions discussed the benefits of involvement, participation and empowerment for managers and staff alike. The preparation of budgets is no different when it comes to these issues; they are equally important. Alternatively, budgets can create problems, causing managers to be inefficient, to focus on irrelevant matters or to neglect completely the important targets set by the budget. In short, the budget can be perceived as a challenge to be met and defeated or as a threat to be neutralized or avoided, and which of these it is depends to a certain extent on the actual content of the budget. More important than this, though, is the way in which the budget is prepared and administered. It has to be remembered that the budget for an individual unit is only a single part of the budgeting process for the brand as a whole, which in turn is one part of the company. This means that, by definition, there has to be a large element of top-down input into the budgeting process. Unit managers will never be in a position to prepare their own budgets without reference to the company as a whole. In budgeting terms, individual units are responsibility centres. More precisely, they are profit centres where the manager is responsible for revenue and costs and the profit generated from them. Some organizations, however, try to exert cost centre control over units as well, and this is often an area of conflict – when a brand tries to exert control directly over managers' spending instead of allowing them the authority to manage profit as well as the responsibility for achieving it. It is only realistic, however, to make managers responsible for costs that they can actually control. This is a difficult idea to put into practice. As we saw in the previous chapter, it can be difficult to apportion costs accurately. In principle, responsibility for a cost should rest with those who have significant influence over it – whether in actually spending the money (e.g. ordering food for the kitchen) or in determining how the materials are used (cooking and preparing – and wasting? the food). Thinking back to the previous chapter, we are talking about controllable and non-controllable costs. It is not appropriate for unit managers to be responsible for non-controllable costs.

The principle of authority and responsibility for budgeted costs applies equally within the unit as it does between the unit and head office. The manager will not be able to ensure compliance with all budgeted targets single-handedly, so a good manager may choose to devolve some of the responsibility and authority for costs to those directly responsible for achieving them – for example, the chef/cooks may be made responsible for food material costs. This devolved responsibility can be located with teams as well as individuals.

Preparing and using the budget

The concept of the budget cycle, illustrated in Figure 10.2, is a useful one in helping to understand how we can best prepare and manage a budget, and the parts of the cycle are discussed below.

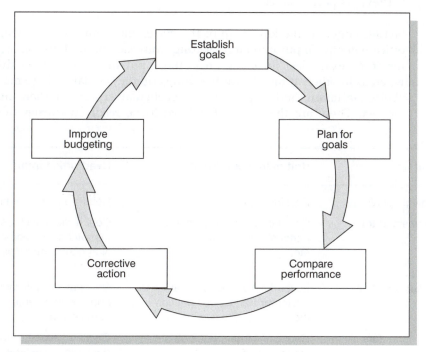

Figure 10.2 The budget cycle

Establish goals ● ● ●

The purpose of budgeting is varied. There may be a number of benefits sought that go beyond basic target setting, and these include:

- bringing direction to the business – encouraging forward thinking, and a clear focus for everyone to aim for
- encouraging coordination – this requires communication and integration when preparing and implementing budgets
- promoting planning – this requires clear ideas about how things will be made to happen, including consideration of alternative courses of action and the impact of external factors
- offering measures of performance – this allows a clear and widely accepted view about how well the business is doing, both overall and in specific areas
- facilitating control of the business
- motivating and challenging people to achieve or exceed a target.

The specific targets in any budget must be developed with the purpose of that budget in mind. Equally they will be based on a number of different criteria, which can be grouped under five headings:

1 Strategic goals
2 Brand standards
3 Market conditions
4 Limiting factors
5 Previous performance.

Setting targets is the key stage of the cycle, and both unit management and head office will have input into target setting from each of these five areas (see Table 10.8 for some examples). In some areas the input may well be on different criteria, whereas in others it may be on the same criteria. Similarly, there may be agreement about the nature and importance of particular criteria or there may be areas of conflict. These are the issues that have to be resolved during the target setting

Input	Unit managers' input	Head office input
Strategic goals	Position against competition	Return on investment
Brand standards	Cost targets such as labour and material costs, consumables etc.	Cost targets such as labour and material costs, consumables. Non-controllable costs, pricing policy etc.
Market conditions	Local developments, local customer trends, competition etc.	National and international trends and developments, brand level competition
Limiting factors	Capacity, labour, equipment, systems and materials	Capital, capacity, labour, equipment, systems and materials
Previous performance	Unit statistics and details of prevailing local conditions	Unit and brand statistics, national/industry averages

Table 10.8 Input into the setting of budget targets

discussions. If there is no genuine agreement at this stage, it will be much harder for the budget to achieve its purpose.

There is no discussion here regarding when and how each of these areas is brought into the target setting process. Neither is there consideration of any events taking place outside the budgeting process that are likely to have an impact on the outcomes of the process. For example, the availability of sufficient suitable labour is often a constant limitation on the revenue-generating capacity of some licensed retail operations, especially in the south east of England for example, where local labour markets are very competitive. Target setting and the rest of the budgeting cycle will take the labour situation as it is and ignore any steps being taken outside the budgeting cycle to deal with this issue.

To maximize the effectiveness of your contribution to the budgeting process, it may be useful to perform a simple review of costs and revenues, as follows, to come up with your forecasts for this round:

1 Check past performance
2 Itemize key costs and revenues
3 Identify potential impacts on each individual cost or revenue stream
4 Assess the likely changes to each cost/revenue stream
5 Compile this back into a forecast budget.

Plan for goals ● ● ●

At this stage in the process you must determine how you will actually achieve the budget targets set. Clearly there are numerous factors that come into play when making decisions about how you will run your business, and this book has talked about a number of these. What you must do, as part of the budgeting process, is be aware of the implications of all your actions for the financial targets you are seeking to achieve. Each and every decision you make and each activity you undertake will impact on your ability to meet your targets, and you must consider all these when planning your operation. The cost–volume–profit and profit sensitivity analysis techniques discussed earlier are helpful in understanding the likely outcomes of different courses of action and therefore in planning the most effective ways of meeting targets.

Compare performance ● ● ●

This is the part of the cycle that actually enables you to understand what is going on in your business. Previously, financial control has asked a lot of 'what if?' questions to help you plan, or 'what?' questions to describe what is happening at a certain time or in a certain situation. Comparison of actual performance against budget enables you to identify where there are differences between what is and what should be, and to ask the question, why?

Take, for example, the situation where the net profit performance for drink sales this month is less then the budget but is nonetheless much better than last month and than the same period last year. Performance has obviously improved, but not sufficiently. We need to ask if the failure to meet targets is due to a shortfall in sales or a change in sales mix, or if costs have increased more than expected for some reason. If it is down to an increase in costs, which ones have risen, by how much, and why? Effective comparison of actual performance against budget can help you to answer these and other important questions.

This kind of comparison is called *variance analysis*. This is a detailed and sophisticated area of study in its own right, which we cannot cover in detail in this text. For more information we suggest you refer to the texts recommended at the end of the chapter. There are a number of potential variances (differences between actual and target performance) that you should monitor. The first thing to note is that a variance can be:

- favourable (F), where the actual performance is better than the budget
- unfavourable (U), where the actual performance is worse than expected.

A cursory examination of actual performance will reveal basic favourable or unfavourable variances, while a deeper and more detailed look will be required to identify the specific reasons. The basic variances to be considered are either revenue- or costs-based:

1 *Revenue variance* is affected by
   - price – where there is a variance against budget in revenue generated due to the price charged being different; for example, the revenue from beer sales being greater than expected because of a price rise to meet duty changes
   - volume – where there is a variance in revenue generated caused by the actual number of sales being less than expected or by customers spending less
   - sales-mix – where there is a variance in revenue generated as a result of the mix of sales being different to that predicted; for example, greater sales of low GP products like bottled beer promotions at the expense of higher GP products.
2 *Cost variance* is affected by:
   - price – where there is a variance in the cost accrued due to prices paid for materials being higher than expected; for example, an increase in duty could cause this
   - volume – where there is a variance in performance due to the increased costs of more materials being bought than were budgeted for
   - standard costing – see below.

Standard costing is a specific kind of variance analysis that provides even more information for budgetary control. Standard costing techniques can be applied in businesses where it is possible to specify standard ingredient prices and quantities for all the products being sold. In the systematic and standardized operations of branded licensed retailing, this should definitely be possible. The combination of standard material price and quantity gives a standard cost for each meal or drink sold. This allows any variances in costs to be further broken down into variances of price or usage of materials (deviation from standards of performance), giving further guidance regarding the nature of corrective action.

Corrective action

The variances that you identify do not, in themselves, determine the corrective action required. This is your job as manager. However, it is made easier by effective analysis of the variances from budget that has highlighted the possible problems and/or causes that need further consideration. Sometimes budget variances are caused by factors outside unit management control – the earlier example of a change in duty being one such case. In these circumstances it is still important that you know what influenced the variance and how, so that you more easily understand what is within your control.

More often the causes of variances are controllable. In highly standardized operations such as licensed retailing, variance from budget often denotes a deviation from the operating standards and specifications laid down. In most cases this will be your first consideration for corrective action – looking at staff performance in relation to standards, and instigating corrective coaching or retraining as required.

Improve budgeting • • •

It is in your best interests and those of your business to ensure that the budgeting process is as accurate as possible. This requires constant improvement to the process itself and to the information used within it. For example, an understanding of the factors outside your control that caused variances from budget is important, as the information can be fed into future forecasting and budgeting processes to make the outcomes more accurate.

Budgets are one of the key areas of your role as unit manager. The situation where managers are passive recipients of budgets and view them as constraints or, worse, as insignificant factors to be ignored, is all too common. You must make it a priority to be involved in all stages of the budgeting process, from developing the standards through evaluating actual performance against standard to feeding information into the next stage of the process. Effectively used, the budget is one of the most powerful tools in your armoury for controlling and developing your business.

Conclusion

This chapter has further developed the ideas of the financial control cycle introduced in Chapter 9. It concentrates on the analysis and interpretation of data and the budgeting process. The focus on non-management decision-making – how financial data can be collected and analysed to enable more effective management decision-making. A number of techniques for analysing financial data have been discussed, and all of these have clear implications for the way in which unit managers manage their businesses in branded licensed retail operations. The discussion has created a context for these techniques and identified how they can support the management decision-making process.

It is now clear how you can make use of these techniques, and it is up to you to look at your own operation and identify where you can get the most out of them. It is beyond the scope of the text to go into detail about how to do all the calculations, and their specific meanings and derivation. It is strongly recommended that you apply the techniques to figures you are familiar with, and that you read about them further, even if you don't have any problem with carrying out the analysis.

The techniques discussed include profit sensitivity analysis, which is a means of identifying and understanding the key drivers of profitability and of focusing efforts on improving profitability. Also covered is a general review of sales patterns and the specific analytical technique of menu engineering, which is a means of identifying and prioritizing possible strategies for the improvement of the sales mix of both food and drink items.

The chapter concludes with an overview of the budgeting process and reinforces the need for unit managers to understand and contribute to the process fully, in order to develop and maintain commitment to the targets set and to communicate this throughout their operations.

Reflective practice

Answer these questions to check your understanding of the chapter.

1 What is the purpose of the profit sensitivity analysis (PSA) technique? How might the information gained from PSA be used to support management decision-making in licensed retail units?
2 Why is the sales mix important for the profitability of licensed retailing businesses? What are the possible categories for use in analysing the sales mix of pubs, bars and restaurants? Critically evaluate these categories, with reference to a unit known to you.
3 For a business known to you, critically evaluate the sales mix currently achieved in the categories identified as important. Propose and justify strategies to improve this sales mix.
4 What is the value of analysing the sales patterns over time of a licensed retail operation? Over what periods of time would this analysis take place for the purposes of planning and control? How can you ensure that the analysis of sales patterns provides information useful for management decision-making?
5 Describe the process for the preparation of budgets in a business known to you. Critically evaluate the implications of this process for the effectiveness. How does the process impact on the operation of the business overall?
6 In the same unit, describe and critically evaluate how the actual performance of the business is compared to budget, and how the variances are identified and analysed. How could this be improved to provide better information for the management of the unit?

Further reading

Atrill, P. (2000). *Financial Management for Non-Specialists*. Prentice Hall/Financial Times.

Atrill, P. and McLaney, E. (2001). *Accounting and Finance for Non-Specialists*. Prentice Hall/Financial Times.

Coltman, M. (1999). *Hospitality Management Accounting*. J. Wiley & Sons.

Harris, P. (1999). *Profit Planning*. Butterworth-Heinemann.

Jones, P. and Merricks, P. (1994). *Managing Foodservice Operations*. Cassell.

Kasavana, M. and Smith, D. (1982). *Menu Engineering: A Practical Guide*. Hospitality Publishers.

There's more to it than cutting wages

After working through this chapter, you should be able to:

- recognize and manage the elements of labour costs
- calculate effectiveness by measuring productivity
- undertake scheduling and staffing to ensure a number of service goals
- monitor performance against standards and budgets.

Labour cost management

Earlier chapters introduced some of the costing and managerial problems associated with labour costs in licensed retail service operations. Traditionally, labour has been regarded as a fixed cost in licensed operations – that is, an expense that has to be met, with little direct linkage to the costs of producing individual sales. More recently many have started to refer to labour as a semi-variable cost, because the amount of labour can be varied to meet different levels of expected sales. The key problem is that labour is frequently treated as a cost to be minimized, and too many licensed organizations keep wage levels down and reduce the number of staff on duty.

This tendency to see labour chiefly as a cost results in two problems:

1 It fails to recognize that employees deliver the service, and that insufficient staff on duty, or poorly trained staff, can result in service breakdowns and customer dissatisfaction.
2 It fails to recognize that the wage cost to the employer is also a source of income to the employee. Attempts to cut pay rates or hours worked reduce the employee's income and can cause employee dissatisfaction, leading to staff turnover and other problems.

Part of the problem lies with the limited information systems used in the past. The trading account and the profit and loss account generally only register labour as a cost, and there has been no tradition of costing other labour costs – such as staff turnover, or reduced productivity for inexperienced staff. Similarly, there have been few, if any, attempts to see labour as an asset to be developed. Thus an investment in training that improves employee effectiveness and productivity is mostly regarded as a cost, and there is no attempt to value the benefit of the trained employee.

Elements of labour costs

The 'labour as cost' model is powerful because in most licensed retail operations labour represents a considerable part of the operating costs. In a simple licensed operation labour is likely to represent 15 per cent of total sales revenue, and in complex operations it represents over 30 per cent of sales income. It is perhaps not surprising that managers have tried to reduce the labour costs as a way of increasing profits.

Under the pressure of commercial objectives, it is easy to forget that labour costs to the unit represent income and a key motive for working for the employees. Before going on to look at the compensation and reward package that makes up 'cost' and 'pay', we need to consider the different time relationships involved in employment.

Full-time employees are employed for a fixed number of hours for a set weekly wage. Typically the hours are fixed at, say, forty hours, and work beyond this entitles the employee to over-time pay. The employee has protection against a maximum number of hours, and is regarded as permanent until such time as one or both parties decides to end the relationship.

Part-time employees work for a variable number of hours per week. The relationship is semi-permanent in that employees still have protection under the law – in other words, there is an expectation that hours will be provided. Most part-time employees expect a reasonably predictable number of hours, because this helps them to plan their income and domestic lives.

Casual employees are employees who work irregular hours. Usually they are brought in for a special job, say a banquet, or to cover a temporary shortage. The relationship is less regular, but employees may still need some training to be effective in their role.

Agency or contract staff are those employed to fill gaps in emergencies. They are used particularly in the skilled jobs in the kitchens or in some of the administrative and management jobs. Usually the rates paid are higher than for employees, but the contract can be terminated with no notice.

When managing employees as a cost, the temptation is to treat each type of employee differently, because each represents a different cost relationship. In the case study described in Chapter 5 (see Boxes 5.1, 5.2), managers at the The Bird in Hand:

- made full-time employees work shifts longer than their contracted hours in sessions where there were not enough staff on duty
- brought in part-time employees who were then sent home if the unit was not as busy as predicted
- employed casual employees only for special events, or in emergencies
- used agency staff as a 'quick fix' to a desperate situation.

Employee reward and payment

All employees are paid wages, although the reward package can be made up of several elements. Figure 11.1 provides an overview of the various elements that

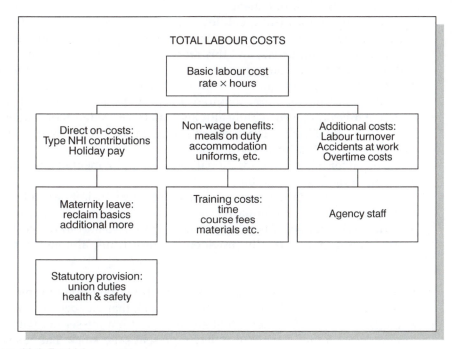

Figure 11.1 Total labour costs

make up the direct, statutory and indirect elements of the total costs of labour. As we have seen, traditional approaches to labour costs management have been to regard these as a semi-variable and related to the costs of sales in calculating the gross profit. This view causes problems because:

- often it fails to allow for the fact that various legal responsibilities add to the cost of employing people
- it fails to recognize there are additional non-wage benefits given to employees, and these are a direct cost of employment
- it fails to show that training is a necessary additional cost that can produce benefits to the employer through the improved outputs from staff
- additional costs are caused by high levels of staff turnover.

The basic labour cost is the standard pay rate multiplied by the number of hours worked. Full-time employees may be paid a standard wage at a fixed amount per week, and this represents an agreed number of hours – and thereby an agreed rate per hour. Both part-time and casual staff are paid at an hourly rate. In most countries the standard rate is regulated by law, in that there is a rate below which pay cannot drop. In the UK, this law is known as the national minimum wage. It is common practice in many bar, pub and restaurant firms for the rate to be fixed at the statutory minimum, although some firms (e.g. McDonald's) aim to pay above this amount. In addition, local labour market conditions have an effect, and competitor employers may pay above these rates, thereby forcing licensed retail employers to pay more.

In addition to these direct wage costs paid to the employee, employers in the UK have to pay a contribution to the National Health and Insurance provision, as well as towards holiday pay entitlements and, in many cases, pension funds. These are additional costs of employment.

Female employees are also entitled to Statutory Maternity Pay, although the basic rate can now be reclaimed from the State by the employer. In some cases these rights are extended by employers, and this represents an additional set of costs associated with employment; although they are not directly associated with the costs of sales, they are costs to be met and are additional to the basic wage cost.

Similarly, employers are required to provide paid time off for employee representatives involved with health and safety, or trade union duties, to attend to their duties. Again these represent an indirect cost of employment, but they are a cost to be accounted for nevertheless.

It is usual for the various additional costs of employment to amount to an extra 25 per cent on the basic wage bill.

As well as the payments associated with legal responsibilities and duties that have to be paid either to the employee or to the State, licensed retail employers often provide additional benefits to employees. These also add to the cost of labour.

Meals on duty are usually provided by most firms, although the arrangements vary:

- in some cases, the staff choose menu items from the restaurant menu; these items must be accounted for because they are stock that has been used
- in other cases, staff eat items that are left over from the service period; again these must be accounted for because they represent sales stock that has not resulted in sales

- in other cases, special meals are prepared for the staff as separate menus and costs; again, costs are controlled, but they do not relate to stock that has not been used to generate sales.

Each of these approaches to providing staff meals can result in benefits and difficulties. There are clearly benefits, from a training point of view, in letting staff sample the meal they are serving, though controls are important so that you know what has been used for sales. Similarly, using up left-over items for staff meals may help reduce wastage loss, but may cause staff dissatisfaction because they have to eat unpopular items. Prepared staff meals are easier to isolate and control, but staff may not like the food prepared, considering it low quality.

Accommodation is another benefit provided to employees in some businesses. Some pubs provide accommodation for full-time employees, and this is seen as a benefit for the employers because employees are available on the premises when needed. For employees, the provision is something of a mixed blessing. It is useful to have accommodation, but availability to the employer – even during days off – is seen as a major disadvantage. Increasingly, licensed retailers do not provide accommodation – particularly where the units are in tailor-made buildings.

Where accommodation is provided it is usual for the employee to pay some form of rent, and there are a number of different ways of charging this. Usually, the rent is deducted from the employees' pay, and building costs etc. are covered as an overhead cost deducted after gross profit. Accommodation is an indirect cost of employing employees.

Uniforms are provided in many licensed retail operations. Staff uniforms are one of the means by which brand identity is established. The provision of uniforms involves two types of costs:

1 The purchase of the uniform – in some cases employees need more than one set
2 Cleaning and maintenance of the uniform.

Uniforms for all new employees can cost anything from £30 to £80 per set. It is not unusual for employees who leave the company to take the uniforms with them, thereby adding to the costs of staff turnover. Usually, the costs of these are borne through the overheads and represent an indirect cost of employment.

Uniform cleaning is charged to the unit as part of the general laundry and cleaning function in the overheads. Again, uniforms are regarded as indirect costs of labour.

Staff training provision varies in the scope and cost to the organization, and training may be off or on the job:

1 Training off the job is where employees are paid to do a college course or even an in-company programme. Their wages for the time away from work are counted as a cost of training. Even if employees attend the course on their day off, the costs of course fees and other expenses such as books may all involve charges to the business.
2 Training on the job also involves costs. Even in lightly structured approaches to training employees, there will be costs associated with training that should be accounted for. The trainees' time during instruction, the time of the instructor, the

cost of materials used in demonstrations, the cost of wastage during learning, and the cost of any other printed documents all involve direct costs.

As well as these direct costs, indirect costs occur through lost productivity, customer dissatisfaction and added employee stress as the trainee is learning. These all add to the true cost of training.

Where training is taking place off the job, it is not unusual for the cost to be substantial, once all the fees and time away from work are taken into account. Even in situations where the training occurs at work, direct costs can be high. A recent study at McDonald's (Eaglen *et al.*, 1999) suggested that on average these costs amount to just under £600 per head.

Traditionally many licensed retail organizations have regarded training as a luxury; with a few exceptions, they have tended to cut training budgets when trading situations were difficult. Yet a recent study at McDonald's showed that the best training units outperformed the worse training units through:

- higher productivity per labour hour
- registered higher service quality grades
- better employee satisfaction scores
- a more flexible workforce, because more staff were available to work in all sections of the restaurants
- lower levels of staff turnover, and lower costs associated with staff replacement.

Although these and other studies show that training is an essential element of running a licensed retail brand, many managers continue to treat training as an expensive luxury to be trimmed when times are hard and costs have to be cut. There are several reasons for this:

1 Current accounting methods often only account for labour as a cost to the business
2 Comparisons are only made with sales revenues in total amounts
3 There is little consideration of productivity through transactions or sales per labour hour per employee
4 Training benefits are rarely recognized and accounted for in performance
5 The costs of *not* training are never calculated.

This latter point needs some expansion. The costs of not training include:

- absolute productivity loss
- productivity loss from reduced learning speed
- increased staff turnover costs
- increased levels of wastage
- reduced service quality
- reduced employee satisfaction
- an increased employee accident rate
- limited flexibility
- resistance to change.

People do eventually learn from experience and by trial and error, but this approach is not cost-free; it is just not recognized. The productivity levels, as measured by output, are lower for untrained employees. They are also more likely to leave their jobs more quickly, produce higher levels of wastage, have fewer satisfied customers, be more dissatisfied at work, have more accidents at work, and be less flexible in their working practices and more resistant to change.

Furthermore, training is one of the key techniques for managing a brand in licensed retail operations. Training helps employees to:

- deliver consistent brand standards
- establish portion, quantity and cost controls
- deliver quality goods and services
- meet customer expectations
- increase sales and profitability.

'Hidden' costs • • •

As well as the costs of labour that are a direct consequence of the employment relations, and the additional costs incurred through the package of non-wage benefits and the need to train employees, there are some other and often hidden costs of employment. These are costs that come about from the need to recruit and cover employee shortages through the use of over-time payment, or the employment of agency staff in times of shortage. Sometimes these costs are a result of unforeseen high levels of customer demand or staffing difficulties because of illness. More often than not, however, they are the result of staff turnover. Chapter 5 deals with the causes and remedies for staff turnover in detail, but the following focuses on some of the key costs involved in replacing staff in licensed retail operations.

Staff turnover

It is not unusual for individual licensed retail businesses to have no detailed records of unit-by-unit levels of staff turnover, and it is almost unheard of for the firm to account for the costs of losing and replacing staff.

Recent research conducted by staff at Leeds Metropolitan University suggests that the direct costs are between £400 and £500 per person. The direct costs only take account of the immediate expenditure involved in:

- advertising for replacements
- management time spent recruiting, interviewing, selecting, inducting and training
- recruitment agency fees
- travel expenses for interviews
- postage and stationery
- induction and orientation
- training
- over-time cover
- agency staff cover
- processing new recruits' documents
- processing ex-employees' documents
- uniforms.

These various cost headings may not apply to all businesses, but many of them are likely to be common to every licensed retail operation. In addition there are considerable indirect costs; these are more difficult to count, but nevertheless are costs to the business. These can easily add another 50 per cent to the cost of staff turnover, and include:

- lost investment in training
- lost staff expertise
- reduced service quality
- reduced productivity
- increased wastage and costs
- customer dissatisfaction
- the negative impact on remaining staff
- the opportunity cost of lost management time.

Usually, the most highly trained employees are the first to leave the unit, and when they leave their skills and talents go with them. Whilst it is possible to calculate the cost of training an individual, the additional talents and expertise developed are difficult costs to calculate.

Similarly, it is not easy to calculate the cost of lost customers; however, Chapter 7 suggests that this could easily represent thousands of pounds.

Finally, the lost opportunities of management time involved should not be underestimated. If managers are spending time recruiting new staff, they are not doing other things that could be developing the business.

Bearing in mind these points, it is not unreasonable to see that the true costs of staff turnover can easily be double the direct costs. Certainly the IPD figure of £735 per person for 'unskilled routine labour', given in Chapter 5, is not unrealistic.

Box 11.1 provides an example.

Box 11.1 *McDonald's Restaurants – the costs*

McDonald's is an example of a hospitality retail organization that has had a poor reputation for staff turnover in the past, but has made attempts to manage it with successful results. Staff turnover in the past has been similar to that in many other licensed retail organizations – an average rate of about 150 per cent per year was quite normal for the group, with some large variations across units.

Recently the company has adopted policies designed to bring these rates down. The average rate in 1998 was below 90 per cent, and the company has a national target to reduce the rate to below 70 per cent. Key to this approach has been recognition that staff turnover is a problem that can be managed, and that unit managers make a considerable impact on staff retention. Performance monitors for every unit in the group include a monthly staff turnover rate calculated for the preceding twelve months. Unit managers' performance reviews include staff turnover targets, and performance bonuses are only paid if these targets are met.

As yet the company does not account for the cost of staff turnover in each unit, but staff at Leeds Metropolitan University recently estimated that the direct cost of staff turnover averaged £450 per person. A sample of restaurants showed the extent of these extra costs. Table 11.1 highlights the rates in two clusters of restaurants based on their training activities. The Beta group of restaurants were lower than average trainers and had higher than average staff turnover rates. The key point is that the extra costs of staff turnover added considerably to operating costs. For example, in 1997 the number of staff employed in directly managed restaurants totalled 42 982; based on an average of 90 per cent staff turnover and a direct cost of £450 per head, staff turnover of crew alone cost £17,407,710.

Restaurants	Headline rate (%)	Rate after temporary staff (%)	Temporary staff leavers	Leavers after temporary staff	Cost of staff turnover in restaurant (£)
Alpha1	42.07	42.07	0	14	6300
Alpha2	52.57	46.88	4	33	14 850
Alpha3	74.09	74.09	0	23	10 350
Alpha4	60.06	60.06	0	38	17 100
Alpha5	74.03	67.35	3	33	14 850
Alpha6	78.80	43.01	15	18	8 100
Av Alpha		55.57			11 925
Beta1	128.10	118.60	7	87	39 150
Beta2	158.00	152.40	2	55	24 750
Beta3	175.00	166.10	5	93	41 850
Beta4	128.40	126.00	1	54	24 300
Beta5	176.10	155.50	9	68	30 600
Beta6	169.70	118.20	27	62	27 900
Av Beta		139.46			31 425

Table 11.1 Staff turnover in a sample of McDonald's restaurants

Agency staff

The use of agency staff can fill an immediate gap in staffing, particularly in replacing skilled kitchen workers. However, agency staff are considerably more expensive. The hourly rates are frequently three or four times the normal wage, and, in addition to the extra hourly rate, agency staff can also cause added indirect costs in that:

- they are unlikely to understand the immediate brand standards and operating procedures
- they are not part of the permanent team, and may cause friction with other staff
- they are not as committed to the business and its goals in the long term.

Summary

This section has shown that staff costs account for more than just the hourly rate and the broad variable cost of traditional management approaches. Some costs, such as National Health and Insurance and pension costs, are directly related to hourly rates and payment for work done. Other costs are more indirectly linked to providing staff with an array of other benefits, such as meals on duty, and costs of ensuring effective performance through training and employee development. Finally, some costs result from mishandling staffing and labour costs. The added costs due to staff turnover and staff shortages are neither direct costs of producing licensed retail goods and services, nor indirect costs of employing people; they are extra costs that arise from not managing labour stability and ensuring that the right staff are available as and when needed. As we have seen, these costs are rarely accounted for and recognized, but they do add to real operating costs.

Measuring staff costs

At its most simple and crude, the measurement of staff costs involves solely the consideration of the amount of hours bought and the rate paid. Using this approach, attempts to control labour costs involve strategies that:

- keep the rate paid per hour low
- reduce the number of hours paid for
- make employees work without pay for additional hours
- increase the work rate of those who are employed.

Managers at The Bird in Hand (see Boxes 5.1, 5.2) followed all these strategies. They paid the lowest rate possible; they minimized the hours for part-time staff, even sending staff home after just one hour; they made full-time staff work longer hours than the agreed forty-hour week; and they made full-time staff work with lower staffing levels. As we saw, they also generated high labour turnover and the extra costs associated with replacing staff. Like many other licensed operators, because they didn't ask the questions about these costs, they had no idea about the real cost of their actions.

Labour performance indicators

As in many other aspects of management information, failure to ask the right questions means that you have an unsound basis on which to make decisions – you do not even know what decisions have to be made.

Given the team nature of much of the licensed industry work, it is not always possible to measure the precise output of every individual. In particular, kitchen work cannot always be linked to individual efforts, and the work of ancillary workers such as cleaners, storekeepers and administrators is also part of the operational need but is not directly linked to particular levels of output or sales. In these circumstances, it is possible to aggregate employee performance and apply some general ratios. Table 11.2 explains some of these, with reference to the pubs mentioned in Table 11.3.

Sales per labour hour	The sales take is divided by the number of labour hours purchased in the period. For example, if the Leeds pub takes £900 000 and employs 24 137 hours of labour during the year, this averages £37.28 per labour hour. This can be compared to £32.60 per labour hour in the Nottingham pub (Table 11.3)
Transactions per labour hour	The total number of transactions for the period is divided by the total number of labour hours. For example, in the Leeds pubs there were 56 250 transactions delivered through a total of 24 137 labour hours. This gives an average 2.33 transactions per labour hour, compared with 2.1 transactions per labour hour in Nottingham
Transactions per customer	The total number of individual customers or covers, divided by the labour hours. The Leeds pub serves an average of 6.52 customers per labour hour, as opposed to 5.88 in Nottingham
Sales per transaction	The average sales revenue from each transaction – i.e. the total sales figure divided by the number of transactions. The average transaction sale was £16.00 in the Leeds pub and £15.50 in the Nottingham pub
Training activity	There are a number of ways of measuring the training activity in different units. McDonald's restaurants have specific performance indicators and monthly audits of training. In other cases, the activity may be measured through a simple calculation of the cost expressed as a percentage of direct wage costs
Labour turnover rate	There are a number of indices of staff turnover and retention, but the simplest measure is to express the number of leavers over the year divided by the normal establishment (see Chapter 5). These can also be expressed for different job categories, levels and departments
Labour turnover cost	The number of job leavers in the period priced out at a rate per head. This may vary between different types of employees and managers – for example, skilled kitchen staff will be more expensive to replace than unskilled routine pub and bar workers

Table 11.2 Employee performance indicators

Using these global labour ratios, it is possible to focus on different approaches to managing the labour budget. Table 11.3 lists some of these measures for two pubs in Leeds and Nottingham, and this shows that although the labour budget appears higher in the Leeds pub, labour productivity is higher, and the staff generate higher sales, lower operating costs and ultimately greater profitability. The Leeds manager allocates £20 000 per annum for staff training, and this represents an additional 10 per cent on the labour budget. The Leeds pub, however, generates more sales per labour hour, more transactions per hour and more sales per average transaction. In addition, the unit is able to operate a lower cost of sales ratio and has lower levels of staff turnover and all the costs associated with staff replacement. Moreover, the

Hospitality, Leisure & Tourism Series

	Leeds pub		Nottingham pub	
Sales for year	£900 000		£950 000	
Labour cost	£216 000	(24%)	£218 500	(23%)
Training	£20 000		0	
Net labour cost	£196 000		£218 500	
Pay rate averaged +25%	£8.12		7.50	
Labour hours	24 137		29 133	
Transactions	56 215		61 290	
Average transaction	£16.00		£15.50	
Transactions per hour	2.33		2.1	
Average sales per hour	£37.28		£32.60	
Normal establishment	25 (full-/part-time)		30 (full-/part-time)	
Leavers in past year	10		54	
Staff turnover rate	40%		180%	
Cost of staff turnover:				
• direct (£500)	£5000		£27 000	
• indirect (£800)	£8000		£43 200	

Table 11.3 Labour performance indicators for the Leeds and Nottingham pubs

pay rate averaged over all staff categories is higher in the Nottingham pub, yet profitability is greater.

The Nottingham pub is superficially more successful, because the manager has generated more sales and operates with lower labour costs. Yet despite operating with lower wage levels and cutting out training, the manager needs to employ more labour hours, because the labour productivity is lower:

- working at the same number of transactions per hour as the Leeds pub, the Nottingham pub could have served the same number of customers with 26 647 labour hours – a saving of 2486 hours, or £18 645
- similarly, if the average sales per transaction of the Nottingham pub matched those in the Leeds pub, the business would have generated another £30 645
- finally, the staff turnover costs could be brought down to £6000 if the rate at the Nottingham pub matched the Leeds pub, making a further saving of £21 000.

These savings do not take account of the differences in the costs of sales in the two pubs, where staff training and staff commitment are important factors.

Active learning point

Using figures from a restaurant, bar or pub known to you, explore the real staff costs by investigating the wider range of measures given above. Is there potential to provide better wages and training as a result of saving on staff turnover costs and other gains in performance?

Locations	Inexperienced		Experienced		Difference	
	Served	Sales (£)	Served	Sales (£)	Served	Sales (£)
Community pub – Lancashire	1. 173	590	198	665	24	75
	2. 175	560	198	665	2	43
City centre bar – Manchester	147	448	234	712	87	264
Country pub – North	71	254	88	313	17	59
Country pub – North	75	304	111	458	36	154
City centre bar – Liverpool	1. 154	495	218	689	64	194
	2. 178	584	287	859	109	275
City centre bar – Manchester	164	450	221	621	57	171

Table 11.4 Comparison of experienced versus inexperienced staff

In addition to the broad performance indicators that you can use to compare your employee's general performance with those in other pubs, or in the group as a whole, electronic point of sale (EPOS) systems allow comparison of individual employees in selling roles. Thus a comparison of frontline staff in bars and pubs is much simpler using EPOS.

Table 11.4 gives an example of different levels of staff performance, depending on whether the employee was experienced in bar work or not. The data were collected from a range of different pubs in different settings over one shift period. These figures show considerable differences, and highlight a need to ensure that inexperienced staff climb the learning curve quickly. Training and coaching is an essential technique in ensuring that the learning stage is short.

As well as the statistics given under customers served and sales made, it is also possible to explore differences in sales mix and the achievement of targets to feature certain products.

This section has attempted to show that the traditional approach to managing labour costs tends to focus on the cost of labour, but this approach is limited because it fails to consider wider aspects of cost associated with employing staff. It's not so much what labour costs, but what labour does:

- the skills that staff bring to their work
- the ability of the staff to work within cost targets
- the numbers of customers that can be served.

The revenue gained from each transaction and additional costs generated by staff replacements are also important considerations.

Adding to staff income

In addition to the basic wage paid to staff, there are a number of other means by which their income can be increased. Tips from customers and a set service charge are both additional payments made by customers. Commission is paid by the employer and is directly linked to some additional incentive – typically sales, although several organizations make additional payments based on other aspects of performance. All of these arrangements can be seen to have strengths and weaknesses.

The assumption that they all share is that money is a prime motivator and that employee effort will be directed to earning the maximum income. There are several problems with this view.

1 Money is only a motivator if the individual is generally dissatisfied with the level of pay, or needs to maximize income for some other reason. In Herzberg's terms, it is a 'hygiene' factor but not a 'motivator'. In other words, money can be the cause of dissatisfaction and can lead employees to leave the firm, but in the long run money is not a primary motivator.
2 Whilst it is possible to identify individual contributions in some cases, licensed operations are generally based on team working, and several different individuals contribute to producing the goods and service supplied to customers.
3 Where money rewards are low, individuals may say that they are not worth the extra effort.
4 Money rewards can be the source of envy and conflict, which add further to employee stress.
5 When ranking issues important to their subordinates, managers frequently over-estimate the value of material (extrinsic) rewards (see Chapter 3).
6 Any one approach – tips, service charge, commission – and the incentives vary considerably, and there needs to be a clear understanding of the aims of the incentive scheme.

Tips from customers

Although a widespread practice in service businesses, tips from customers present both employees and customers with many anxieties. In the UK in particular, the rules about tipping – when to tip, how much to tip, the reasons for tipping (a norm or for excellence?) – are not culturally shared and there are different expectations between staff and customers, and between staff and staff. Apart from these confusions, arrangements for dealing with tips vary and can represent different benefits to the individuals and teams involved.

Individualized tips are those received by service staff in the pub or bar from customers, and are the property of the person receiving them. This is probably the most widely practised method in licensed retail operations. In some units, staff can double or treble their wages through tips. Although individualized tips benefit individuals and in theory make them more concerned about service quality, the practice can be divisive amongst employees. Competition for the 'best' tables and customers, as well as jealousies between kitchen and restaurant, can be counterproductive.

Shared tips are those tips received and shared out amongst the staff as a whole. This method removes some of the jealousy, but it is difficult to police, and a lack of trust might lead to tensions amongst staff. It may also challenge the supposed incentive to good service. There are a number of variations to this approach – for example, a points system may weight the benefits to different groups.

Service charges

When the management sets a service charge, it levies a set charge on all bills for the service given. This removes some of the uncertainty about what to give and when to give the tip, but it can cause customers stress, particularly where the service has not been satisfactory. The arrangements for paying the charge levied are also somewhat vague. Is the charge paid in addition to the basic pay, or does it in part meet the cost of basic pay? Many firms use the charge to help meet labour costs, and so it is not an extra payment. Differences in arrangements make the service charge of variable benefit to employees. If staff will be paid the service charge in any case, it is unlikely to motivate staff to give priority to service quality. Nor will it be an incentive if the charge is being used to meet basic pay.

Commission on sales made

Some organizations pay staff a basic pay and then add a bonus related to the customers served and sales made. It is assumed that staff will work to maximize their income by 'up-selling' to customers.

TGI Fridays use this approach. Service staff are paid 3 per cent of all sales made in the evening, and kitchen staff get 6 per cent. The restaurant and bar staff are paid the commission on the sales they individually make, whereas kitchen staff are paid a commission for the session shared equally amongst those on duty. On a regular basis, managers select the top ten service workers and they are allowed to choose the shift periods and the restaurant areas they work.

Again, there is a fine line between individual incentives and setting up reward systems in which some people will always have to lose. Where there are winners there are also losers, and in this situation employees not earning the best commissions may become demotivated.

Extra payments for performance

Several licensed retail organizations use some form of additional payment related to performance or the achievement of a desired goal. One approach involves monitoring employee performance over a period, and then paying an extra amount to staff who achieve a particular performance level. One example worth considering is McDonald's Restaurants. They evaluate staff performance through the observation checklist (OCL). Crew who achieve scores over 90 per cent in all the OCLs in a six-month period are paid £0.15 per hour extra during the next period. This scheme reinforces the 'one best way' of operation, because it rewards payment for a consistent adherence to the company's standards.

Other organizations link the extra payment to the achievement of a specified training standard or award. Usually the extra payment is made as an added hourly rate, paid once a person has achieved the required training level. For example, Harvester Restaurants link an extra £0.20 per hour bonus to the achievement of the 'Silver Badge'. It is paid on the achievement of at least eight of the team's key skills related to the team's accountability.

Whilst the extra amounts that can be earned by staff are relatively small, they do at least reward the achievement of a desired company objective and send a message to staff about the priorities. Extra money rewards can benefit employees and create an incentive pay structure that encourages them to aim at the priorities set by management. However, there can be problems where the additional pay is marginal and does not compensate for the added effort involved. In some cases, these schemes can be divisive and lead to harmful competition between employees.

Scheduling employees

The preceding sections have shown that the calculation and management of labour costs is more complex than the mere calculation of cost of labour to the organization. It is equally important to consider the outputs from labour – that is, it is as important to ask 'what does labour do?' as it is to ask 'what does labour cost?'. Concern with productivity, skills, service quality, and customer satisfaction are crucial. Having the correct number of staff on duty to meet customer demand is clearly a matter related to these issues – too few staff creates a threat to customer service targets and service quality, whereas too many staff increase costs and reduce profitability.

Staff scheduling has to take into account the staff needed on each day, at various times during the day, and at the same time ensure that part-time employees, in particular, have sufficient hours to ensure a reasonable pay level for their period on duty.

The case study in Chapter 5 (see Boxes 5.1, 5.2), together with comments made earlier in this chapter, show that there is a temptation to treat full-time and part-time employees differently. Part-time staff are frequently treated like a water tap to be turned on and off as customer demand dictates. A lack of sensitivity to their income needs can have motivational and staff turnover consequences that are counter-productive and ultimately more expensive.

A thorough analysis of past sales together with a consideration of influencing factors such as the following is essential:

- weather conditions
- competitor activity
- special promotional activity
- general sales trends
- macro-economic activity.

Using these sources of information, it is possible to develop a reasonably well-informed estimate of likely sales levels over the next months, weeks, days and hours of the day.

This task is made simpler through the use of information technology. Electronic point of sale (EPOS) information can produce sophisticated data about sales that then help to build an estimate of the employees needed on duty. Figure 11.2 provides an example of a typical sales pattern over the days of the week. The number of customers (mean individual portions) is probably a more accurate measure than transactions, although the transaction count needs be studied as well, because there may be implications for the numbers of service staff required.

Similarly, an analysis of sales by hour through the day can help to identify the staff cover required in order to be able satisfy the different levels of sales at different times during opening hours. Table 11.5 lists the number of customers served in a themed restaurant for just one day. As stated earlier, the records must keep some account of the weather conditions and competitor activity, and promotional activities such as 'early bird' promotions, or other activities that influence sales at a particular time of day, can be factored in to the calculations.

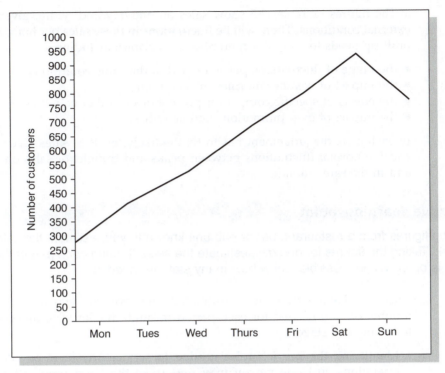

Figure 11.2 Number of customers served per day

Hourly period	Customers served
Weather: fine and dry	**External factors:** low competitor activity
11.00 am–12.00 noon	33
12.00 noon–1.00 pm	90
1.00 pm–2.00 pm	89
2.00 pm–3.00 pm	51
3.00 pm–4.00 pm	6
4.00 pm–5.00 pm	7
5.00 pm–6.00 pm	45
6.00 pm–7.00 pm	78
7.00 pm–8.00 pm	95
8.00 pm–9.00 pm	95
9.00 pm–10.00 pm	73
10.00 pm–11.00 pm	48

Table 11.5 Hourly business volumes in the pub (Friday xx/xx/xxxx)

The figures in Table 11.5 show sales on one day and within given internal and external conditions. There will be fluctuations in these sales per hour, and the model built up needs to allow for a number of variables including:

- the range of fluctuations per hour within the same conditions
- the impact of weather on sales in each hour
- the effects of specific competitor promotions or other activities
- the impact of own promotions and activities.

In each case, the judgement has to fix the likely levels of sales given the variables, and the normal fluctuations between peaks and troughs of sales on the same day and in the same month.

Active learning point

Using figures from a restaurant, bar or pub unit known to you, estimate the sales levels for a week. Taking the figures for one day, estimate the sales through each part of the day that the unit is open. Where possible, show how many staff are needed.

Once you have arrived at an estimated sales volume, you need to calculate the number of staff needed for each period through the day. The process involves the following key stages:

1 Identifying the key job roles needed to service any level of sales. For simple operations, just one person may undertake the 'food preparation' and service during quiet periods. In the more complex settings, it is likely that several posts are needed to prepare, cook and serve the food.
2 Matching the job with the normal output level and the estimated sales for each period during the day. Table 11.6 gives an example for the pub service staff needed for the sales levels indicated for the day given in Table 11.5.
3 Comparing the staffing requirement with the skill profile of each member of staff. Typically, these might be available solely for specific jobs, though increasingly staff are being trained to be multi-skilled and thereby available to work in several areas. Staff at McDonald's Restaurants, for example, are trained to do the full range of production and service jobs.

In the example in Figure 11.3, the schedule allows for two staff to be on duty to set up before service commences and then for two staff to be on duty after service. To increase flexibility, the schedule uses four full-time and three part-time staff. Three of the full-time staff are scheduled for split shifts. Part-time staff need to have sufficient hours to ensure an agreed income level. In the above case, it could be possible to have employee B do the work roster of employee G if needed. Some employers prefer to employ mostly part-time staff because it enhances flexibility and the potential to minimize costs. On the other hand, some employers see the value of employee commitment and employee skills, and prefer to maximize the use of full-time staff.

In modern licensed retail organizations, a computer program can be used to calculate the potential sales and staff needed. Whilst most unit managers prefer to use their own knowledge and judgement about how best to staff the pub and use the skill profiles of individual employees, this type of program provides valuable support.

Hours of operation	Estimated sales levels	Staff required
10.00 am–11.00 am	–	2
11.00 am–12.00 noon	33	2
12.00 noon–1.00 pm	90	5
1.00 pm–2.00 pm	89	5
2.00 pm–3.00 pm	51	3
3.00 pm–4.00 pm	6	1
4.00 pm–5.00 pm	7	1
5.00 pm–6.00 pm	45	3
6.00 pm–7.00 pm	78	5
7.00 pm–8.00 pm	95	5
8.00 pm–9.00 pm	95	5
9.00 pm–10.00 pm	73	4
10.00 pm–11.00 pm	48	3
11.00 pm–midnight	–	2

Table 11.6 Staffing needs in the pub (xx/xx/xxxx)

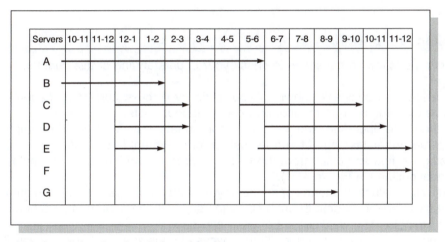

Figure 11.3 Sample hourly schedule for pub staff

Conclusion

This chapter has shown that managing labour costs in licensed retail operations involves more than a narrow concern with wage rates, hours worked, and keeping the labour account within budget. These direct costs of staffing are only part of the story. Labour costs also include some indirect fees, for example to meet tax, pensions and National Insurance responsibilities. In addition there are costs associated with other employer responsibilities, such as providing time off for union or health and safety duties.

Additional costs are incurred when providing non-wage benefits such as meals on duty and uniforms. These are rarely taken into account as part of the direct costs of employment. Similarly, the cost of training is not shown as part of the direct costs of employment, if it is shown at all. More often than not, training is treated as a luxury that can be cut in bad times. Yet training is a fundamental feature of brand management. Without adequate training it is impossible to meet the brand standards and meet customer expectations. At the moment, firms in the sector do not calculate the costs of not training. Lost productivity, reduced customer satisfaction and added wastage all increase cost for the firms who do not train. Another related aspect of these hidden costs in licensed retail operations is in labour turnover. The cost of losing and replacing staff is high, particularly when the excessive rates of staff turnover are considered.

When these additional costs of staffing are taken into account, the old certainties of licensed business management are brought into question. An organization that cuts wage costs, shaves employee hours and eliminates the training budget, finds that staff productivity is lower, customer satisfaction is reduced, wastage is increased and staff turnover costs are raised. Often these organizations are saving money with one hand and throwing it away with the other.

As a licensed retail operator, you need to adopt more searching approaches to labour cost management. The approach must take into account these wider issues. The added costs produced by shortsighted management practices have to be calculated. Paying higher wages, providing employees with a decent wage, ensuring that training and career progression are built into normal management practices, and calculating labour turnover, adding this to costs and recognizing it as a real cost need to become the norm in licensed retail businesses.

Reflective practice

Answer the following questions to check your understanding of this chapter.

1 In a licensed business known to you, critically discuss current management information systems being used to monitor and control labour costs.
2 In the same operation, suggest how the information systems could be improved to give a broader understanding of the true costs of employment in the unit.
3 Using the figures gained from the unit, calculate the added costs of employment (use the model outlined in Figure 11.1).
4 Critically evaluate the forms of added payment that employees receive in the unit. If staff are not given added income through tips, etc., suggest some alternative schemes and discuss the strengths and weaknesses of each approach.
5 Using the same unit, describe different ways of considering labour productivity. What is the range of productivity rates for staff doing the same type of work, say in the bar, restaurant, accommodation and reception? What would be the effect of all staff working at the rate of the best? How might that happen? Discuss ways of increasing employee productivity.
6 Calculate the likely sales level within the unit, and work out the staff roster for one day. Explain your answer.

Further reading

Coltman, M. (1998). *Licensed Management Accounting*. J. Wiley & Sons.
Dittmer, P. R. and Griffin, G. G. (1999). *Principles of Food, Beverage and Labour Costs Controls*. J. Wiley & Sons.

Meeting and exceeding customer expectations

After working through this chapter, you should be able to:

- state the importance of a full and accurate understanding of customers and identify the key characteristics of this understanding

- identify the market segments appropriate for a particular unit, and put existing and potential customers into the correct segment(s)

- explain the nature and importance of customer occasions and accurately define the occasions for particular customers and/or units

- identify and collect the necessary customer information to be able to achieve the other objectives.

Marketing – understanding your market

As discussed earlier in the book, the market in which branded licensed retail units operate is fiercely competitive, with consumers having a large choice from a number of competing propositions and brands. In this situation, developing and sustaining a competitive advantage for your business becomes even more important. The difference between these brands can be great – no one will ever get confused between the offers of All Bar One and Brewsters, or between Wetherspoons and Tiger Tiger. However, within the market there are also a number of brands that target the same customers with very similar offers, and the difference between these brands can be infinitesimal. Customers often cannot, or will not, take the time to differentiate between these offers. Without overt signage and merchandising, all but the most sophisticated customers may well find it hard to differentiate between a Rat & Parrot and a Yates' Wine Lodge, or between Chef & Brewer and Vintage Inns.

In cases such as this, the competitive advantage of one unit over another is not built into the brand itself. Alternatively, an advantage that was designed into the brand originally may have been eroded over time by copycat developments from competitor brands. This situation is made more complicated by the growth of independent businesses that also provide similar offers and target the same customer groups as some brands. As competition between units for customers is largely at a local level, these independent operations can have a significant impact on business performance. For branded units that have very similar competition to be successful, they not only have to deliver the brand standards as required but must also be able to develop some advantage over the competition. Opportunities for developing this competitive advantage may be greater at unit level because of the largely 'local' nature of the market and competition.

A successful competitive advantage is something that sets you apart from the competition – something that you do better than them. The result of this is that you either operate with lower costs and therefore generate greater profits from similar levels of turnover, or generate greater levels of sales and revenue.

Other chapters in the book have considered possible strategies and tactics that may generate competitive advantage. These could include managing people more effectively, ensuring that the quality of products and services is better than competitors, or operating more efficiently. These issues are not usually presented as means by which a competitive advantage can be generated, but in the right circumstances they can be extremely effective in achieving this goal. Before a particular route to competitive advantage is chosen, it is necessary to understand the position of the business in the market – that is, the position of the business relative to competitors, to customers and to the rest of the sector.

Developing an awareness of the position of your business requires that you have knowledge and understanding of the operating environment, including:

- customers
- competitors
- the local, national and international conditions and developments.

This awareness of your position enables you better to understand where your potential competitive advantage lies and how best to achieve it.

It is unlikely that unit managers will know the fine detail of competitors' operations or be able to respond directly to global or even national trends in business or markets. This kind of information is more likely to be considered at head office and will inform the focused strategy developed at this level, and you as a unit manager will have responsibility for implementing this at unit level. It is more likely that you will seek to develop and maintain competitive advantage through more localized marketing activity.

This chapter will consider how you can develop the required awareness and understanding of your unit's position, with a particular focus on customers, and how to identify potential advantages from this. Chapter 13 will go on to cover the communication strategies and tactics that can be used to turn this knowledge into a marketing advantage for your unit.

A customer focus

Throughout this book, the importance of customers has been made clear. This is because of the direct relationship between satisfied customers and business performance. Consistently providing products and services that satisfy customers and persuading them to consume these items has been presented as the purpose of all activity for branded licensed retail unit managers. The customer is therefore the ultimate focus for all decisions made in the unit, for all the business policies and procedures, and for all the systems and processes used to operate the unit. All of these have to be concentrated on satisfying customers.

Satisfying customers means providing them with the products and services they require at the time they want them, to the standard they expect and at a price they feel is reasonable. As a unit manager, then, you must make decisions that are based on a thorough understanding of what it is that your customers expect, and this can only be accomplished if you have a clear and detailed understanding of them.

This customer understanding not only enables you to provide the correct products and services; it also helps you to understand how you can influence their behaviour in a number of other ways that could be beneficial to your unit. To understand customers you must be aware of:

- the number and type of customers using the business
- the usage patterns of consumers – when they visit and how often, how long they stay etc.
- their consumption patterns – average spend, product mix etc.

Customers can be put into four basic categories according to whether they currently use your unit, and whether you want them to use it or not (Figure 12.1). You may wish to influence the behaviour of some or all of these categories at one time or another.

There will be different goals and strategies associated with each of these categories. In general, you will probably have the following approaches:

1 Existing and wanted customers – the goal is to retain these customers; the strategy is to generate customer loyalty
2 Potential and wanted customers – the goal is to recruit these customers; the strategy is to promote the business to this group
3 Potential and unwanted customers – the goal is to maintain the current position of not attracting these customers; the strategy is to ignore them

Hospitality, Leisure & Tourism Series

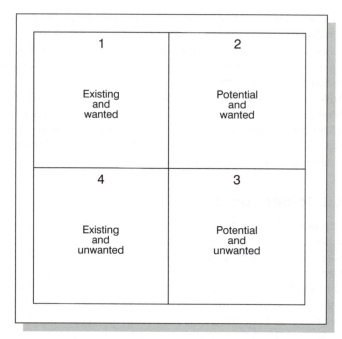

Figure 12.1 Customer categories

4 Existing and unwanted – the goal is to discourage these customers; the strategy is to down-manage their expectations.

In order to make these strategies work it is necessary to understand how and why each category makes the choice of where to visit, and what they look for when they do. There are some basic tools to help you do this, and we will look at two of the key ones now. These are:

1 *Segmenting* customers into groups
2 *Targeting the occasions* that are important to the customer segments in your unit.

Segmentation

The activity of segmenting customers is based on the principle that not all customers want the same things – that they are different in what they buy, and how and why they buy it. As a result it is not feasible to treat all customers the same, to offer them the same products and services in the same way. This is especially so in a service business such as branded licensed retailing. In fact, in this context it could reasonably be suggested that the ideal customer segment would be a segment of one – that is, each customer should be treated individually and given an experience of products and services that is unique. Referring back to Chapter 1, this would be a personalized product and service that was very much relationship-dependent. However, there are many reasons why this is not a feasible approach for branded licensed retail unit operations, not least of which is the time, effort and cost involved in delivering it. The limited opportunity to personalize product and service is one of the key factors that differentiates these branded licensed retail units from the local pub. The 'local' has far fewer customers who will use the business in the course of a week, and these customers are less transient – that is, they spend longer in this one location, rather than moving round from unit to unit, whether during a single night out or the course of a week. In addition, the customers of a 'local' are less subject to the vagaries of fashion than are the customers of larger branded businesses. They are not constantly bombarded with new and improved offers, and indeed businesses, from an ever-changing and growing list of competitors. All this is likely to make them more loyal, returning more often, over a longer period of time. These circumstances make it more feasible for licensees in 'locals' to get to know customers on an individual basis and to give them the personal attention they demand – knowing regulars' names and what they drink, or even making sure they have their own glass.

Accepting, therefore, that it is not possible to treat all customers individually but it is not desirable to treat them all the same, a compromise has to be found. Segmenting customers offers this compromise. It involves putting customers into groups called *market segments*. A market segment is a group of consumers who have similar characteristics (variables) that help us to either understand their current needs/behaviour or to predict their future needs/behaviour.

To be useful in management terms these segments should be large enough to deal with separately and yet still small enough for the members to have similar needs and requirements.

Your role in segmenting markets

As a unit manager, segmentation will have dual relevance for you:

1 The brand within which you are operating will be carefully designed to appeal to a clear market segment or segments. There will be particular groups of customers who have been identified as key targets for the brand to attract. It is also likely that there will be a useful profile of these segments and their specific needs and requirements. You should be fully aware of this, and have it as a key focus for your management decision-making. An important responsibility of unit managers is to deliver products and services to brand standards as specified, and this is much easier to do when you understand how these specifications were derived and how they are intended to appeal to particular customers. If you are not familiar with this, you need to become so immediately!

2 You will need to be able to apply the ideas at the local level for your particular unit. The overall brand focus ignores local market conditions. It cannot realistically be expected to take account of these, as units will operate across the country in very different local conditions. The best brands will have a clear level of consistency from unit to unit and region to region, in terms of delivering brand standards to customers. There will, however, be some decision-making autonomy for unit managers in how best to deliver these standards to their own particular customers. You must therefore be able to recognize and understand the particular segments in your market and their relative importance.

Making it work

The earlier outline of segmentation and the reason it is necessary highlights the two key elements of successful segmentation. These are:

1 Being able to put customers into groups that can be readily and accurately identified and understood
2 Being able to make reasonably accurate judgements about them and their likely behaviour on the basis of these groups.

Success in achieving these objectives is dependent on the choice of criteria by which the segments are defined. These criteria for defining groups are called segmentation variables. In order for the segment to be effective, the variables you choose must display relevance, visibility, measurability, viability and accessibility.

Relevance ● ● ●

The variables that are identified as distinguishing the group must be relevant in understanding or predicting customer buying behaviour. They must also suggest that the likely behaviour of the group is compatible with the behaviour required from your customers.

For example, age is clearly linked with the consumption of certain products and at certain times; however, age is not necessarily linked to average spend. Also, evidence suggests that students are not as price-sensitive or as design/style-conscious as people usually assume (Table 12.1).

Variable	Myth	Reality
Relevance	Students require cheap products	Students are only price-sensitive on very specific occasions
	Students are trendy/design-conscious	Students want somewhere where they feel at home and are not afraid to 'put their feet on the seats'

Table 12.1 Relevance: myths and realities

Visibility ● ● ●

The segment must be clearly distinguishable from the rest of your customers. The common characteristics should clearly mark it out as different to other possible groupings, and they should be readily identifiable.

For example, you may want to communicate with high-income professional workers – but can you identify them, or will you have to look for other characteristics that might signal this? Again, you may be able to identify all those who wear Nike trainers in your unit, but does this really single them out as different to those in Adidas? The fact that they wear trainers/sportswear may actually be the thing that is important to their potential attitudes and behaviour.

Measurability • • •

It should be possible to put some kind of quantitative measure to the segment. Preferably, this means real numbers of customers or the amount spent. It is more likely, however, that you will have to measure segments in relative or percentage terms – you may say that a particular group makes up 25 per cent of your lunchtime and 40 per cent of your evening trade, or that this group is likely to spend up to twice as much as another group. Measurability is important when it comes to prioritizing and deciding where to focus your effort.

For example, can you actually measure the spend of particular groups or (even more useful) their spend on particular products or at a particular time of the day? It might seem that the majority of your food customers at lunch time are workers from the immediate surrounding area, but can you actually measure this – is it an absolute, or relative?

Viability • • •

Viability relates directly to measurability. Is the segment large enough or potentially lucrative enough to warrant consideration? What kind of activity does a particular segment justify? What sort of effort will be needed to secure appropriate returns from a particular group?

There is evidence that some members of the older market are becoming increasingly affluent and willing to spend more on eating and drinking. Attracting this particular niche of the older market could be profitable, but it is still largely ignored – possibly because this is an example of a group that actually spends more but would appear to spend less.

There may well be a population of women shoppers in the vicinity of your unit – but how many? And how many of these are without children and in the market for eating/drinking in your kind of environment?

Accessibility • • •

A segment is only worthwhile if it is accessible. In other words, can you effectively get your message across to this segment, and can it easily access your products and services?

For example, how do you prepare and communicate messages that seek to communicate with a particular social class? If you can't do this effectively, then they do not make an effective segment. Increasing the service speed of lunchtime food may make your product more accessible to some groups of consumers.

Table 12.2 provides a review of the most widely used segmentation variables and their possible value as a tool for segmenting markets for units in the licensed trade. When considering the value of each variable it is important to remember that different variables may be more relevant for some brands than others, and may well have differing value in different circumstances. Take the variable of family, for example. This is one of the key variables if you have a unit with children's facilities and child-friendly service. Targeting families with children of the correct age is vital, and this becomes a variable that you must be able to recognize and use. However, you may also have a promotion that aims to increase sales on mid-week tea times; the 'early doors' slot. It is quite likely that the same people coming with their families at weekends may also be the people who will boost your sales in this slot. However, whether they have families or not is of far less relevance to their behaviour in these circumstances than is their place of work and transport method, and the fact that the benefits of companionship and community should be important to them when choosing a pub to visit.

Customer occasions

Relationship with segmentation

Understanding your customers is made more complex by the fact that individual customers have differing requirements depending on when they visit or their reasons for visiting. This means you cannot rely solely on identifying market segments and their needs. You may usefully make some assumptions about the needs, expectations and likely behaviour of customers in different segments, but customers from one particular market segment may have different needs and requirements on different occasions. Introducing the concept of customer occasions can therefore increase the value of your market understanding, giving you a better understanding of your customers and a sense of local market conditions and needs.

The idea of occasions has been considered to be a part of market segmentation. Some marketing theorists have included it (or something similar) as one of the segmentation variables by which markets can be grouped. While this is a valid way of thinking, we believe occasions to be distinct from the process of market segmentation. As you will see in our discussion of occasions, they share some similar ideas with segmentation but are much broader and cover a wider range of information, making them a potentially more powerful concept.

It is possible to identify a number of different occasions for which customers may use pubs, bars and restaurants, and the majority of larger operators in the industry have done this in some shape or form. There are many different variations of the occasions sought, and many different names used to describe them. Some occasions may never be relevant to certain types of outlet (the food-oriented occasions, for example), and some occasions may differ from brand to brand. However, the following is a distillation of customer occasions as defined for the licensed retail sector:

- big night out – circuit or venue
- pre-club

Table 12.2 Overview of segmentation variables – personal characteristics

Key	Variable	Measures	Relevance	Visibility	Measurability	Viability	Accessibility
Demographics	Age	<6, 6–11 years etc.	G	VG	VG	Av	VG
	Sex	M/F	G	VG	VG	VG	VG
	Family	No. of children	VG	G	G	VG*	Av
	Income	<£10 000, £10 000–£15 000 etc.	G	P	VG	G	P
	Occupation		P	Av	Av	G	G
	Lifestage		G	P	P	VG	P
	Education	To GCSE, A level, degree, masters	AV	P	G	G	G
	Religion		Av	Av	G	G	G
	Race	Afro-Caribbean, Asian, Arab, White	P	G	G	G	G
	Social class	A, B, C1, C2, D, E	G	Av	Av	G	Av
Geographic	Nationality	Country of origin	Av	P	Av	P	Av
	Climate	Hot or cold, wet or dry	P	P	P	Av	P
	Locality	Specific region, town or area	P	P	Av	P	G
Geo-demographic	Residential	Combinaton of locality, housing types and demographics	G	G	G	G	Av
Psychographics	Lifestyle	Can be generic or specific to the product	VG	Av	Av	G	G
	Personality	Extrovert/introvert, stable/unstable, tough/tender minded	G	P	P	Av	P
Behavioural	Benefits	As sought by customers – speed, value, comfort, status etc.	VG	Av	P	VG	G
	Usage	One-off, regular, habitual, special occasion	G	VG	G	G	VG
	Loyalty	No loyalty to complete loyalty	G	VG	G	G	VG

* Viability is usually concerned with a segment being large enough to make it worthwhile. In the licensed trade sector, there is an issue about whether some segments are too big to be viable targets.
Av, average; G, good; VG, very good; P, poor.

- pit stop
- socializing
- taking part/activities
- finding company
- the match
- being fed
- family day out
- a meal out.

In defining these occasions so that they become useful for management decision-making, a number of attributes and characteristics can be identified. Definition of customer occasions using these attributes will clarify the occasion and help to specify what must be delivered to customers. This concentrates on the customers' requirements and expectations and their experience/perception of the occasion. The following are used:

1 *Concept definition*. This is a broad overview of the occasion. It covers the key points that distinguish this occasion from others and gives a feeling of what the occasion is about.
2 *Key benefits/core values*. These define the values customers associate with this occasion and the key benefits they seek when they experience it. Benefits/values describe how customers wish to feel when they are taking part in this occasion.
3 *Projected customers*. This profiles the types of customers most likely to take part in this occasion.
4 *Critical success factors*. This identifies the key elements of the offer that must be delivered to ensure that customers get the benefits they seek.
5 *Complementary/contradictory occasions*. This identifies other occasions that fit with this one and those that don't – specifically in the same unit at the same time.
6 *Competition*. These are other brands and independent offers that compete for this occasion by offering customers similar values and benefits. They do not necessarily have to be branded licensed retail units or even pubs; they can be any leisure offer that meets these customers' requirements.

It is worth looking at an example of an occasion in detail to illustrate what is meant by each attribute and to give some guidance as to how it can be used to define the occasions (Box 12.1). From this definition it is then possible to identify the key operational elements of the occasion and consider how they influence the management of the unit to ensure the occasion is delivered effectively.

Box 12.1 *Big night out – venue*

1 *Concept definition*: Usually happens in town/city centres or other accessible urban centres with a concentration of outlets and occasionally in key destination pubs (although the reliance on driving is in conflict here). The outlets have a lively and friendly atmosphere communicated by both fellow customers and staff. Customers will tend to stay in one outlet for the evening and may go on after this

to eat at a curry house, Chinese restaurant, or pizza place for example. The occasion is based on socializing with existing friends and not on meeting new people. Customers tend to be out for 'a few drinks' rather than just for 'a drink'. It is often a regular get together for what may be a fixed or fluctuating group.

2 *Key benefits/core values*: The core values of this occasion are 'letting you hair down with people you know' in a fun and comfortable environment. Customers will seek to feel:
- relaxed but lively
- comfortable, not pressurized or stressed
- unconcerned with their appearance or behaviour
- entertained and invigorated
- free from the usual routine.

3 *Projected customers*: This occasion usually interests customers in the 18–40 years age group, perhaps with a bias to the older end. Customers usually partake of the occasion in groups known to each other. In many cases these groups are based on work, sporting/activity or study colleagues. They may be single or mixed-gender groups – neither gender predominates. They may well travel from a reasonable distance for this occasion and the group may come from different locations – a factor that makes a convenient central location important. They will probably have some previous experience of the unit, which reduces the risk of going somewhere that does not meet their requirements. This risk reduction is a key element of the consumer decision process for this occasion. (As a point of interest, this familiarity could be where brands derive a marketing advantage for these customers. Customers for this occasion usually buy this familiarity by going to the same pub, and may actually be persuaded that the familiarity of a brand is worth valuing.)

4 *Critical success factors*:
- informal atmosphere – a buzz
- speedy service and minimal waiting by customers
- variety and quality of drinks available
- consistency of offer and experience
- friendly welcome and recognition of group (if regular)
- seats/space to congregate
- convenience of location key factor in choice.

5 *Complementary/contradictory occasions*:
- Complementary occasions include big night out; circuit; pre-club; the match; socializing
- Contradictory occasions include finding company; family day out; eating out (special meal out).

6 *Competition*:
- It's A Scream
- Rat & Parrot
- Bar Oz
- O'Neils
- Comedy clubs.

Making the occasion happen

Having defined the occasion by the nature of the customer experience expected and required, it is now possible and necessary to add in the operational elements that are needed to ensure that this experience is effectively delivered to customers. These can be grouped under seven key headings:

1 Location/site
2 Product
3 Service
4 Design
5 Facilities
6 Staffing
7 Promotion.

If these are applied to our example, we may well come up with the list of key operational elements shown in Box 12.2.

Box 12.2 *Key operational factors: big night out – venue*

The key to this type of occasion is in the production of an upbeat but relaxed atmosphere – lots of fun and entertainment, supported by staff who are outgoing and friendly.

1 *Location/site*: The venue should be located in town/city centres or prominent urban locations near other sympathetic leisure and retail offers. The site must be easily accessible, with public transport and parking. Larger sites are generally used, with trading area in excess of 1200 square feet.

2 *Product*: A good range of products is required. These must be high quality products, with a number of sophisticated/premium items offered. Innovation in product range and menus is valuable for maintaining interest, but this should not be at the expense of the key core brands and items. These key core items/brands must be clearly specified, and may include premium-packaged lagers, cask ales, and wine by the glass. A focus on availability and quality of product must be maintained to ensure that high standards are consistently delivered; lapses in quality are particularly dangerous for this occasion. Constant review of sales profiles and mix to maximize product offer is vital.

3 *Service*: Preparation for service is key – the back bar and fridges must be fully stocked, cellar arrangements made to allow for quick changeover at peak service times, and sufficient glass clearing and washing capacity ensured, etc. Constant monitoring of service levels is necessary to maximize service speed and accuracy, during the session, and on a day-to-day and week-to-week basis. Staff levels, roles and training are important in building service speeds and up-selling. Staff who enjoy the atmosphere and can communicate with customers on their own terms are important, so recruitment and selection are particularly significant.

4 *Design*: Design needs to ensure that floor space is used effectively, to maximize space for groups both standing and sitting. In addition, booths or smaller individual areas are useful for groups. The exterior should give clear clues as to the offer, but avoid obtrusive branding. Internal decoration should balance modern and traditional, be durable, and suggest a welcoming and fun feel.

5 *Facilities*: Music is important, and could be provided in a number of ways – by a DJ or a managed music system, for example. In addition, a public entertainment licence could be useful, as could the capability to acquire a late drinks licence as needed, particularly on the busy weekend nights or when there are key holiday events. Games, entertainment, karaoke and machines (AWP/SWP) can be part of the atmosphere. Seating and furniture are key elements of the facilities – there must be sufficient seating to allow groups to sit together and it must be comfortable enough to encourage customers to spend longer in the unit.

6 *Staffing*. Employ staff who are compatible with customers and who are lively and outgoing without being 'loud'. Also ensure there are always sufficient staff present to avoid service hold-ups. Training, development and incentives will help to focus the service and atmosphere factors. In town centre locations, it is likely that door staff will be required.

7 *Promotion*: Promotional activities should be geared to the average spend and to encouraging repeat purchase/longer stays, as well as contributing to the development of the atmosphere. This could include the creative use of prominent point of sale displays and staff trained to promote 'star' lines. Headline nights allow for customers and staff to focus on a particular event or musical style, for example. It is also useful to develop links with the local Students' Union or specialist sports clubs and societies, and with work-centred groups. Further detailed consideration will be given to developing promotional activity in the following chapter.

Remember that Box 12.2 is an outline of the key operational factors for making this occasion a success; it is not a complete checklist for operation.

It is apparent from this outline that these operational elements split into two clear categories. The first of these are those elements that are designed and/or delivered as part of the brand and are not within the control of unit managers. These clearly include the site/location elements, the majority of design and some of the facilities. The second group includes the elements that we are most concerned with – those that are within the direct control of the manager. These include the product and service elements associated with quality, and the promotion and staffing elements. It is important for unit managers to understand both categories, even if their influence is primarily limited to one.

Active learning point:

1 For a unit or brand known to you, identify the key customer occasions.
2 Take one of the occasions and describe it using the attributes identified earlier.
3 What are operational elements of managing this occasion? Does your unit/brand meet these?

Brand/unit	Occasion definition
Concept definition	
Key benefits/core values	
Projected customers	
Critical success factors	
Complementary/contradictory occasions	
Competition	

Brand/unit	Key operational elements
Location/site	
Product	
Service	
Design	
Facilities	
Staffing	
Promotion	

Occasions and customers

You have now developed an understanding of how to recognize and profile customers accurately, and classify the reasons why they may visit your pub. What will become apparent is that there are a number of different segments in your market, and that these have a number of different occasions when they may visit the unit. Unfortunately it is not as simple as matching one occasion to one segment, as this will vary as well. The key to a complete understanding of the market is to identify which occasions are important to which segments and when.

As examples, consider the following scenarios.

1 25-year-old male of low disposable income and social class D, in the young family lifestage, with stable and introvert tendencies and a high degree of loyalty, may have the following profile of pub usage over a weekend:

- After work on Friday with workmates, mid-afternoon/early evening looking to have a break between work and home and to gear up for the weekend – *pit stop*.
- Saturday evening with his partner, out celebrating a special occasion and looking to have a big night out as baby sitters are hard to organize – *big night out – circuit or pre-club*.
- Sunday lunchtime, looking to get out of the house and to socialize with his mates in the rugby team and to relive his Saturday night exploits over a couple of pints. He may be getting ready to watch the Sunday game on the big screen. He wants a relaxed and leisurely drink – *finding company or the match*.

It is quite feasible that he may choose to visit the same pub for any or all of these occasions. We can see, though, that he wants something very different on each occasion even though he is still the same person. The occasion does not change his segmentation variables, and we need to understand this individual's different occasions to be able to satisfy him effectively.

2 Now consider the following occasion that happens in one pub. There may be a number of different people wishing to experience the *taking part* occasion:

- Older couples and individuals who want an escape from the routine and the opportunity to see some friendly faces.
- Younger males, social groups C2, D, E, looking for competition and a chance to show off.
- Females aged 30–40 years, possibly in large groups, looking for 'a laugh' and not interested in being pestered by men.

It is immediately apparent that, although wishing to *take part*, these segments want something very different, and satisfying them may well be dependent on offering the correct activity. The first group may well enjoy a quiz, although this is unlikely to appeal to the third group.

It is therefore a combination of occasion and segment that gives the most powerful understanding of the market and their needs. There may well be so many different occasions and segments in your pub that you are unable to cater directly for each of them. This is not a major problem. What you have to be able to do is identify the key ones and when they most often occur by asking the following questions:

- What are the key customer profiles, and which occasions does each like?
- What customer occasions do we offer, when, and what kind of customer is each likely to attract?

From this you can make the necessary management decisions to ensure that the delivery of your product and service is matched to these occasions and segments as closely as possible.

Box 12.3 provides an example.

Box 12.3 *Rat & Parrot*

Scottish and Newcastle's Rat & Parrot has been one of the more successful brands to emerge since the development of branded licensed retail units began. Over this period of time it has undergone constant review and revision, but this process has been characterized by a clear understanding of the brand, its customers and occasions. This can be seen by the following definitions and profiles from the early stages of its development.

Target customer:
- Morning – mix of local workers (junior/middle management), other locals, shoppers and possibly tourists; aged up to 40 years; 60 per cent male.
- Lunch – as morning, but slightly broader mix including secretarial and administrative staff and more shoppers/tourists; aged up to 50 years.
- Evening – local business people and other locals to begin with, giving way to younger, sophisticated and aspirational customers. Age range drops to 24–30 years and there is a more even split between male and female, with more same-sex groups than couples.

Occasions:
- Morning – breakfast/coffee and/or snack, taking a quick break.
- Lunch – meeting over lunch, relaxed and safe.
- Evening – a night out with a lively atmosphere; either circuit or venue options.

Value/selling proposition:
A continental-style pub/bar with a safe and aspirational atmosphere, which offers an excellent product range and service to give a sophisticated meeting place for stylish and fun people like us.

Critical success factors:
- Design – open frontage with clear vision and a continental feel; modern but with some familiar pub features; transforms throughout the day.
- Product – quality and premium brands key; up-to-date and fashion products; key focus on product display and merchandising.
- Service – consistently high quality, with table service where possible; professional yet friendly at bar servery.
- Location – prime sites amongst related leisure/retail sites, such as fashion clothing.

Site:
Town and city centre sites with high pedestrian footfall, close to business centres and retail outlets; must be on the circuit and preferably near transport links. One-room sites, minimum 1500 sq ft trading space, with a corner site preferable.

This brand definition, while perhaps a little lacking in terms of detailed understanding of customer needs, still offers a number of very useful insights into the key factors for managing the operation to satisfy the customer groups. These have been presented as key attributes of the offer, and are detailed in Table 12.3.

It is also possible to see from this example that the occasion discussed earlier (big night out – venue) fits very closely with this definition of the Rat & Parrot brand (although it was not taken from there!).

Understanding the market and customers for your business can be accomplished by the application of the ideas of segmentation and occasions. However, this activity will only be as successful as the quality of the information you are able to use to carry it out. There must, therefore, be an effective way to capture information about customers and their requirements.

Element	Attribute	Priority	Brand standard	Operational standard	Avoid
Product	Drink	1	Quality choice and display; offer latest products	Cocktails, coffee, aspirational soft drinks, wine (glass and bottle)	Focus on 'value' products
	Food	1	Sophisticated and aspirational choice; plate service. Evening availability (8.00 pm at least)	Priced in line with direct competition	Widely available dishes
	Price	2		Premium priced, in line with competition	Discount promotions
Design	Outside	1	Attractive; open and inviting – European; clear branding	Planting and seating	Scottish and Newcastle branding and merchandise
	Lighting	2	Quality fittings; dimmers and changes in time periods		
	Décor	1	Mix of soft/hard furnishings; traditional materials with modern design		Too feminine/soft – have rats and parrots!
	Layout	2	Standing room around the bar; clear and sufficient seating areas	Seating/standing split; comfortable seating	Separate eating and drinking areas; bar seating
Facilities	Toilets	2	Good ventilation; quality finishes and clean	Music and enough female cubicles	
	Music	1	Correctly profiled; zoned	Profiled mid-ground when jukebox not being used	Live music/discos
	Air quality	1	Essential to be smoke-free	Temperature control; no smoking areas	
Activities	Promotions	3	Chalkboards; quality branded point of sale	Strong aspirational brand links; added value	Heavy point of sale or posters; price promotions
	Machines	3			Loud noise level or obtrusive; extensive range, pool or TV
Service	Staff	1	Fast, friendly staff	Similar to evening customers; waiting table service until at least 8 pm; uniforms	

Table 12.3 Key attributes of the offer – Rat & Parrot

Capturing information

What information?

Clearly, the information collected must relate to segments and occasions.

Segments: information is required on the variables identified as important, such as where customers live, how old they are, how often they visit, customers working in the local area, etc.

Occasions: these depend on the pub and the occasion, but the following list of questions could be considered to gain information:

1 Where have your customers been *before* visiting the unit?
2 Where are your customers going directly *after* visiting the unit?
3 How long do customers take to make the decision to visit the unit?
4 What mode of transport do they use?
5 How often do they visit the unit?
6 How often do your customers visit the area?
7 What competition do your customers also use?
8 Do they come in groups, couples, or singly?
9 What is the average party size?
10 Do customers use the pub as a meeting place?
11 What are the flow patterns of customers in your pub?
12 How long do customers stay?
13 What style of clothing do your customers wear?
14 What is the male:female ratio?
15 How do customers interact with bar staff?
16 How many customers bring children with them?

It is useful to gather this information about customers based on particular days and even different sessions – it may well be very different on a Friday night to a Saturday night, for example.

How to collect it?

Some of the information you need may well exist already. For example, it may come from within the company (databases, brand definitions and standards, and possibly information gathered previously by regional or unit managers for this unit) or from outside the company (local libraries and council offices, Business Link and Chambers of Commerce, and market research reports). There may also be informal local links and networks that you could tap into – Leeds has a Small Independent Bars Association, for example, although it's doubtful how welcoming they would be of representatives of branded licensed retail units!

On the whole, the information that is available already is likely to be more general and to focus on the easier to measure segmentation variables such as demographic or geographic characteristics. Information more specific to particular units, or concerned with customers' attitudes, requirements and expectations, is more likely to have to be collected specifically. This information can be collected in two ways; formally or informally (Table 12.4).

	Strengths	Weaknesses
Formal	Potentially more accurate and reliable; broader coverage of topics with more information	More costly, complex and time consuming
Informal	Less expensive (in terms of time and money); easier to do (no special requirements)	Limited in terms of information that can be gathered; potentially less reliable; potentially intrusive

Table 12.4 Collecting information

There may well be occasions when formal information gathering methods are appropriate and it is beneficial to use techniques such as customer surveys or customer focus groups. For example, when asking about future requirements or collecting names and addresses, a simple formal approach may be most effective.

Always remember two basic points when considering formal approaches:

1 It is often a good idea to link this kind of technique with an incentive or reward to encourage customers to actually supply the information you want.
2 Be careful with the use of questionnaires, particularly for measuring customers' satisfaction. They are much more difficult to complete properly than they appear, and they can produce low value or even misleading results.

However, because of the drawbacks mentioned above, informal methods are most likely to provide a good deal of the customer information necessary for pubs, bars and restaurants. Information collected in this way will usually give sufficient qualitative detail to be valuable, and can be reliable if it is checked and corroborated – with other customers, with staff, with regional mangers or with other unit managers, for example.

Informal techniques that could prove useful for collecting information include:

1 Observation – walking round the unit, working the bar, CCTV!
2 Chatting with customers
3 Discussing things with staff
4 Reviewing sales records (see Chapter 10).

It has been said that the best way to find out what your customers think of you is to listen in to their conversations, and the best place to do this is in the ladies toilet; however, we cannot recommend this as a strategy as there are too many potential difficulties!

When it comes to storing this information, there may be value in considering the development of a simple database that can allow easy access to the information and perform simple tasks such as grouping and categorizing information.

Active learning point

Thinking back to your customer segments and occasions, list all the information you need to find out about your customers in order to define them clearly and accurately.

1 Is the information readily available?
2 How could you collect this information?

Conclusion

This chapter has further considered the competitive nature of the market for branded licensed retail operations and established the need for your unit to be able to compete effectively in this market by establishing a competitive advantage of some kind. To do this requires that you understand the position of your unit in the marketplace with particular reference to your customers.

The chapter goes on to explain the need to understand your customers – both existing and potential – and emphasizes the importance of this understanding to all facets of your business. The main focus of the chapter is concerned with two important tools that you can use to develop a comprehensive and useful understanding of your customers. These are *market segmentation* and *customer occasions*.

Both these tools are explained in detail in terms of their important characteristics, the value that they offer and the ways in which they can be used most effectively in pubs, bars and restaurants. In addition, the relationship between segmentation and customer occasions is discussed and concludes that the tools, while effective in their own right, make a much more powerful contribution to supporting management decision making if used in conjunction with one another.

The final section of the chapter covers the information you need to know about customers in order to be able to use the tools effectively and briefly discusses the formal and informal approaches for collecting this data.

Whatever kind of business you operate the single most important element of that business is its customers. Every decision you make concerning the management of the unit must focus on the customer and their needs. For your decision to be fully effective it must be based on a sound understanding of all your customers and their needs and expectations. This chapter has developed the understanding and introduced tools to enable you to do this.

Reflective practice

Answer these questions to check your understanding of the chapter.

1 Why is an understanding of the nature of your customers so important?
2 How does an understanding of customers help you to secure competitive advantage?
3 What is market segmentation? Identify and describe the three most important market segments for your unit or a unit known to you.
4 Describe the factors that determine whether or not a market segment is worth targeting.
5 What is a customer occasion, and why can a knowledge of customer occasions assist in management decision-making?
6 What information is it necessary to know about customers in order to identify the segments and occasions appropriate to a particular unit? How would you go about collecting this information?

Further reading

Lewis, R., Chambers, R. and Chacko, H. (1995). *Marketing Leadership*. Van Norstrand Reinhold.

Purdy, W. (1997). *A Guide to Retail Business Planning*. ING Business Resources.

Smith, I. (1997). *Meeting Customer Needs*. Butterworth-Heinemann.

Let's keep in touch

After working through this chapter, you should be able to:

- clarify priorities for action based on an understanding of unit operating environment

- choose appropriate promotional tools for particular business goals or problems

- implement the chosen promotion to achieve maximum impact

- evaluate the impact of the promotion undertaken.

Marketing – promoting your business

In Chapter 12 we considered the customers that make up your market, both existing and potential, and discussed what information you needed to know about these customers, including their individual characteristics and the segment(s) they could be grouped into, their specific requirements from your product, and the occasions they are likely to seek from your unit.

This chapter extends the marketing discussion to the environment in which your business operates, considering competitors, the local community and the local environment. It then goes on to discuss developing promotional activity.

Understanding the competitors

As we discussed earlier, the business environment for branded licensed retail units is increasingly competitive, and you must manage the unit to take account of this competition. There are two elements of competition you need to understand:

1 Direct competitors – that is, businesses within the same locality that offer similar goods and service and cater for similar customer occasions to your unit. These include other branded licensed retail units, but also independent pubs and bars and some restaurants.
2 Competitors who might meet similar customer needs in a different way. Here the customer may visit another type of leisure/retail business as a substitute for a branded licensed retail units. The occasion of *taking part* may well be met by a visit to ten-pin bowling or a pool hall for example.

Increasingly there is a third area of competition that must be considered, and that is customers meeting their needs with home-based leisure activities. A number of the occasions identified can be met by customers at home, such as *the match* and *socializing*.

In the first two cases, it is important that you are aware of what your competitors offer in terms of the attributes that most influence customer choice. You should have a clear idea of the important attributes from your knowledge of customer segments and occasions. Competitor analysis needs to consider both the product attribute aspects of the competitors' offers and the quality levels delivered to customers.

It may be difficult to understand what it is that customers prefer about the home option, and even harder to change this. The focus of your effort should therefore be on the business competitors.

It is useful to conduct a regular competitor audit comparing your main competitors against your own assessment of your unit. This should highlight where you hold advantages over the competition that can be exploited, or areas in which your competitors have the advantage and where you should consider possible remedial action. The criteria by which each unit is judged must be as clear and objective as possible to make comparison valid. Table 13.1 provides an example of an audit form, which uses a scoring system (e.g. 10 = excellent, 5 = average, 1 = poor).

Understanding the local community

Although some branded licensed retail businesses will serve customers who come from a wide area, most serve a local community. It is important to build up a picture

Use a scoring system e.g. 10 = Excellent, 5 = Average, 1 = Poor

Name of competitor _____

Attribute	Competitor's score	Own score	Nature of advantage/ disadvantage	Possible action
Visibility and location – how effective is it?				
Access – how easy is it to use the unit? Car parking?				
Drinks range				
Menu and range				
Service style?				
Additional offers (specials, music, AWP/SWP)				
Facilities (standards, baby changing areas, high chairs, disabled toilets, disabled access)				
Seating (numbers, tables and variety)				
Pricing and special offers				
General cleanliness (external, internal, toilets)				
Promotional activities (external signage, internal notices, special discounts)				

Table 13.1 Unit and competitor evaluation form

of your trading area so that potential opportunities can be identified. You will find this information useful when you come to develop a SWOT (strengths, weaknesses, opportunities and threats) analysis. Table 13.2 is a suggested local community audit form.

Understanding the local environment

In addition to information about competitors and the community, you need a clear understanding of developments in the local environment. There may be economic trends that create either opportunities or threats for your unit. This may be, for

	Name	Level of involvement (current/potential)
Local MP, MEP		
Councillors/Chief Officers/Mayor		
Key local charities		
Schools, colleges and universities in the area		
Services. Police, Fire Brigade		
Local sponsorship		
Business community – Chambers of Commerce		
Education business partnerships		
Local press, radio, TV media		
Key local employer organizations		
Major sports or other venue		

Table 13.2 Suggested local community audit form

example, a new business locating in the area, or existing operations closing down. Likewise, changes in the local housing market may also create changes to the customer base. There may be political or legislative factors – throughout the 1990s and early 2000s, Leeds Council has pursued policies that have led to a massive growth in the numbers of pubs and bars in the city centre.

Table 13.3 lists some issues that may be worth considering when analysing the local environment.

The SWOT analysis

Having developed a thorough understanding of the environment and market within which you operate, it is necessary to know how your unit is positioned within this. A thorough and honest analysis of the strengths, weaknesses, opportunities and threats with regard to your unit is therefore valuable. This analysis brings together much of the information already gathered – sales analysis, customer profiles, local community, competitors and local environmental issues. The example given in Table 13.4 is one way of completing this process. The benefit of this model is that it does help you to identify the priorities for action.

Issues to evaluate	Yes	No	Comments
Are there any factories, shops or offices in the area that are likely to close down and negatively impact on your sales?			
Are there any planned factories, shops or offices in your area that are likely to increase your sales?			
Are there are any planned new facilities that might bring more customers to the area, thereby increasing sales?			
Are there any planning restrictions that might impact on your business?			
Are there any minor traffic changes that might impact on your business – e.g. double yellow lines			
Are there any major traffic plans that will result in new roads that might impact on the business?			
Are there any local council policies that might impact on your business – opening hours, noise control etc.?			

Table 13.3 Suggested local environment audit

Factor	Is this a strength or weakness?	Priorities – high, medium or low?
Service quality audit – customer contacts and mystery customer reports plus inter unit audit (e.g. service times are too slow)		
Sales or costs targets – may relate to increasing sales of priority products or reducing costs (e.g. increase lunch sales or decrease wage sales)		
Merchandising – exploring all external and internal promotional activity (e.g. improve back bar displays)		
Visibility – the awareness of the location of the unit and issues related to poor visibility (e.g. improve the visibility from the north)		
Access – ability of all potential customers to gain access to the unit (e.g. no wheelchair ramp)		
Facilities – full range of spaces available and facilities, or needs to be competitive (e.g. children's play area, insufficient seating)		
Customers – the current customer profile and usage occasions (e.g. high number of shoppers, the need to look for other customer groups, office workers)		
Local trading area business generators – surrounding facilities that can bring customers into the area (e.g. local swimming pool nearby)		
Local community links – police, fire brigade and other community groups who support the unit (e.g. excellent links with local police)		
Competition – current provision and quality issues, exploiting common promotions or weaknesses in service (e.g. competitor bar running major promotion)		
Environment – issues likely to affect the local trading conditions, fewer or more potential customers (e.g. new housing development near completion)		

Table 13.4 Suggested SWOT analysis and action priorities

Active learning point

Choose a unit that is familiar to you, in an area that you know well, and use Tables 13.3 and 13.4 to review your unit and competitors, the local community and environment.

1 Classify the information as a strength, weakness, opportunity or threat for the business.
2 From this analysis, what are the key priorities for action?

SWOT high priority actions

It is unlikely that you will have the time, resources (or energy!) to do everything that has been identified from the SWOT analysis – certainly not in the short term. There may well also be possible actions that are in conflict with each other. As a result of this, you need to be able to prioritize the activities you wish to take. You can do this by applying the general objectives discussed earlier and setting clear and specific goals for your business.

Business development objectives have been classified as seeking to improve profitability through either increasing turnover or improving margins. When we take into consideration the likely span of control of unit managers, then these objectives may well cover the following aspects.

Turnover:

1 Get new customers
   • referrals – customers who are friends of existing customers, who are referred to you by existing customers, or are perhaps already customers of another outlet in the same brand
   • strangers – customers who have no previous connection to the unit.
2 More spend from existing customers
   • more visits per year or other time period appropriate for the target market
   • higher spend per visit – either a longer stay per visit (which assumes greater consumption per visit) or additional products purchased (such as snacks, accompaniments for food, AWP games etc.).

Margin:

1 Improved sales mix – trade up to products with greater GP margins
2 Added value to existing products.

Customer loyalty is also a key long-term business goal, although engendering loyalty may not change business performance in the short term. It is not likely to have an immediate impact on any of the goals mentioned above. However, it may well have such an impact in the long term and it will certainly help to maintain business performance and give an effective platform on which to build.

Being explicit and precise about the objectives you are seeking to achieve will help you to prioritize which activities to focus on. Prioritization of actions from the SWOT is also based on:

• which activities can be achieved with least effort
• which will be most likely to yield the quickest returns.

From this analysis you should be able to identify the immediate priority actions, which can be built into an effective marketing plan.

Marketing plan

Traditionally, in a marketing plan the achievement of your objectives would be accomplished by the manipulation of the full range of the marketing mix. In the case of licensed retailing units, we can consider the marketing mix to consist of:

1 Product
2 Price
3 Place
4 People
5 Promotion.

Our focus in this chapter is solely on the *promotion* element of this mix, and if we examine the mix in a little more detail we can see why this is so.

1 *Product*: As a unit manager you have an influence over the quality of food, drink, service and environment received by your customers. However, you are not able to influence the actual nature of the product, the variety or mix of goods offered or the service used to deliver these to customers to any great extent.
2 *Price*: Unit managers are not in a position to influence the prices charged in their unit – certainly not without reference to head office, and not in the short term.
3 *Place*: Your unit is where it is, and there is very little chance of you moving it! There is perhaps the possibility of alternative means of distributing the product to your customers with home delivery and email ordering. Again, however, these are likely to require head office involvement, and take time to introduce.
4 *People*. The people in the business are a key area of influence for unit managers, and this has been discussed at great length throughout the book.
5 *Promotion*: This leaves promotion as the one remaining area of the marketing mix over which you can exert influence to improve the performance of your business.

What is promotion?

Promotion is the act of communicating with your customers in order to achieve a particular objective or set of objectives.

Setting the objectives for any communication is the first stage in the process of designing and carrying out effective promotional activity. This entire process is outlined in Figure 13.1.

This process will form the basis of the rest of this chapter. We will examine each stage, and consider its implementation in pubs, bars and restaurants.

Promotional objectives

Promotional objectives are concerned with influencing customers to behave in a different way – in line with the business objectives discussed earlier. However, using communication to persuade customers to behave differently is a complicated process and involves four clear stages. These can be described by a simple model called the AIDA model (Figure 13.2):

1 *Awareness*. Customers must first know about your unit; they must have awareness. This doesn't mean some vague notion that your pub exists somewhere around the corner from the nearest Rat & Parrot or Yates'; it means that they know what your

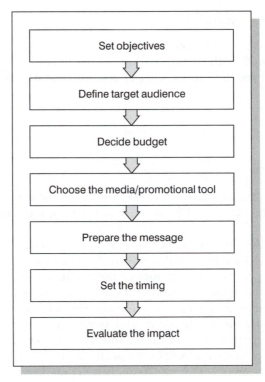

Figure 13.1 Developing promotional activity

pub is about and where it is, and have some idea about the sort of experience they can expect if they visit.

2 *Interest*. Once they have awareness, then they must develop an interest in your pub. You role is to find what interests customers and tell them about it.

3 *Desire*. Having let people know that you exist and generated an interest in your business, it is now necessary to develop that interest into a desire to experience the pub. In reality, once potential customers know the facts about your pub, it is a

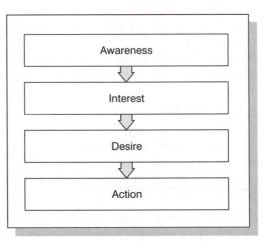

Figure 13.2 The AIDA model

fairly simple job for them to decide if they have any desire to visit or not, so the development from interest to desire is a very small one.

4 *Action*. It may actually be a bigger jump for customers to get from a wish to visit your pub to actually doing so. Customers may have a routine that does not involve your pub. Their friends may not be as interested, or it may take a bit of extra effort that they are not prepared to spend. Whatever their reason for not visiting, you have got to persuade them to take the action of actually walking through your door and spending money in your pub.

Getting customers to visit your pub is not the end of promotion. Research by some of the larger licensed retailers has shown that up to 65 per cent of customers in city centre pubs and bars do not know what they are going to drink as they approach the bar, and the figures for food are even higher. These people are ready to be influenced, and it is your job to see that it happens to your benefit. This time you have a much shorter period to influence customers' product awareness, interest, desire and action – up to a minute at the most in the case of drinks, and a little longer when it comes to food. The principles are the same in both cases, but the actual tools used may well be very different. In broad terms then, promotional objectives usually relate to either persuading people to visit your pub or to behave in a certain way once they are there.

Stage	Communication objectives
1 Awareness	Customers learn facts – they acquire knowledge and understanding • Provide information clearly and appropriately
2 Interest	Customers want more facts and some opinions, and are stimulated to think about your offer • Stimulate a desire to find out about the product
3 Desire	Customers now feel well disposed to the pub; they have a preference for it in comparison to other pubs, it is the best product for them • You now want the audience to feel favourable to the product. • Communicate positive messages and associations; use emotional appeals
4 Action	Changing the customer's positive disposition into purchase behaviour • The buyer may need more information or an incentive to act at this stage, e.g. promotional prices

Table 13.5 Steps toward purchase

The steps towards customer purchases are summarized in Table 13.5.

Influencing customers' behaviour through their awareness, interest, desire and action is a communication objective that you have to achieve; doing this will help you to achieve the business goals identified earlier. For any of these business goals . . .

• attracting new customers
• getting existing customers to spend more
• improving the mix of products they buy

... it is necessary that customers are aware of and interested in your offer, have a desire to experience it, and translate this desire into the required action.

If, for example, your business objective is to increase turnover by getting more of your drinking customers to eat in your pub, then you must make sure they are aware of the food you offer. Get them sufficiently interested to want to try it, and finally actually motivate them to take the plunge and give it a go.

Occasionally there may be a need or opportunity to run a promotion with specific goals that are not covered by those identified above – for example, moving old stock that is nearing its sell-by date. These are no different in the way they are developed and run.

Active learning point

Think back to the key customer occasions and their core customers you identified in Chapter 12.

1 What are the likely promotional objectives for these occasions and customers?
2 How will these promotional objectives contribute to improving business performance?

The target audience

In the example above, you are trying to influence the customers who already drink in your pub. In this case you have a clear and unambiguous understanding of who you want to communicate with – of your target audience.

This will be determined by your objectives.

The simplest breakdown of your target audience is whether it consists of existing or new customers. Beyond that, you may want a particular group of customers. These groups could be identified on the basis of how likely they are to be influenced to behave in a way that matches your objectives:

• customers who are most likely to spend more
• customers who are most likely to buy more expensive products
• customers who are most likely to be persuaded to spend longer in the pub each time they visit.

For example, lunchtime customers who work locally need quick service. They often also want to make themselves feel better, give themselves a little treat, which is a less widely acknowledged need. They may not be fully aware of your range of sophisticated sandwiches. Alternatively, they may have simply never considered the option of having a large cappuccino with their lunch instead of a small fruit juice. Both of these present opportunities to get them to buy more expensive products.

In any case, what you have to be able to do is clearly identify the likely customers and use this information to define your target audience. The details of your target audience will be used in two ways:

1 To decide on what is the correct message to appeal to them
2 To choose the best channels for getting this message to them.

In Chapter 12 we developed detailed criteria by which you can group and understand your customers. From this, you should already know the details necessary to identify and reach the target audience for any communication.

Decide the budget

You may have a clearly defined promotional budget within which to plan, or you may have no designated budget or source of funds for promotional activity and have to clear all promotional activity through the correct channels before carrying it out. In either case, the key thing about budgeting any promotional communication is to understand the relationship between the cost of the activity and the extra revenue generated.

This can be framed using two questions:

1 How much extra revenue must be generated to cover the cost of a promotion?
2 How much will a promotion cost in order to generate a certain extra level of income?

A simple way of assessing the financial requirements of any promotional activity is to use the ideas of cost–volume–profit analysis (see Chapter 9 for examples), and a brief example shows quite clearly why this is necessary.

A reasonably busy bar has quiet Wednesday nights, averaging only £800 in takings. In order to improve this, they decide to advertise a new DJ. The total cost of this for the first promotion is £250, and the expected increase in sales is £500. If the gross profit margin is 60 per cent, this means an increase in profit of £300. However, there is also an extra £50 cost for two more members of staff, taking total extra costs to £300, wiping out all the additional profit. What at first glance seems a successful promotion nets the business nothing.

This is a very simplified calculation, and there are more sophisticated ways of carrying out this analysis of projections; if you wish to know more, please check out the further reading section at the end of the chapter.

There are two further guiding principles for the budgeting of promotions:

1 The decision-making depends on the accuracy of the forecast outcomes of the promotional activity. Therefore a key factor in budgeting for promotions is the analysis of results from previous activity to make your forecasts of outcomes as accurate as possible.
2 Set a maximum limit for the cost of the promotion – the top price you will pay for entertainment or an advertisement, the maximum number of cases of beer to be sold cheaply etc. This way you can be sure that the calculations you make on the costs and returns of promotional activity remain as accurate as possible.

Choose the promotional tool

There are a number of choices that you can make regarding the promotional tool you use to communicate with your audience, and these are illustrated in Figure 13.3.

Each of these alternatives can be judged against four key criteria:

1 Effectiveness against particular promotional objectives
2 Target audience reached
3 Credibility as perceived by audience
4 Cost.

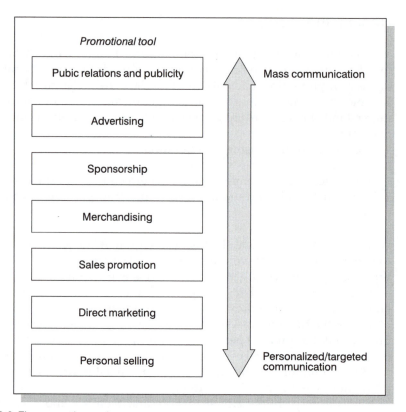

Figure 13.3 The promotions mix

Table 13.6 compares the promotional tools available for branded licensed retail units.

Strengths and weaknesses

So which promotional tools should you use? The answer to this question is (as expected) it depends! Each circumstance has to be dealt with individually. The specific business objectives, the target audience – location, size and current relationship to product – and the resources available will determine what you can and should do. However, it is possible to draw some general conclusions about promotional activity in licensed retailing regarding both what is more or less appropriate, and how such activities might be made more effective.

1 *Public relations and publicity*:
- Public relations presents particular problems in terms of the lack of focus and control of the message.
- Public relations is still a valuable tool and one that offers real benefits; however, it is difficult for pubs, bars and restaurants to secure publicity, and it would be a mistake to devote too much time and resources to it.
- You should always be searching for potential public relations opportunities from your customers, staff and the unit itself.

- Make sure the necessary networks are in place with local media etc., so that when opportunities arise you can respond to them immediately.

2 *Advertising*:
- Advertising remains relevant for licensed retailing, but it needs to be treated with caution. There are often other tools that could achieve the same outcomes more effectively or at cheaper cost.
- The cost of advertising emphasizes the importance of clear objectives and means for measuring their achievement.
- For maximum effectiveness customers need repeated exposure to advertising, so repetition and development in concerted campaigns rather than one-off adverts is recommended.
- Any advertising you carry out must be creative in order to stand out from the mass of other adverts around it and communicate simple messages in a striking and believable way – in short, if you can't do it well, then don't do it!

3 *Sponsorship*:
- There are potential benefits to be gained from sponsorship for all licensed retailing businesses, but it has greater relevance possibly for those operations that are more community-based.
- Events, activities and groups to be sponsored must be carefully chosen; they should match the values of the unit and the brand, and offer real value in outcomes.
- Sponsorship is a good vehicle for other promotional activity – information built into public relations activities, sales promotions linked to the sponsored events and so on.

4 *Merchandising*:
- This is one of the key promotional tools for all pubs, bars and restaurants, and you should make a concerted effort to understand and maximize all merchandising opportunities in your unit – merchandising does not begin and end with the back bar. Consider toilets, entrances, the siting of AWPs etc.
- Understand and apply the general principles of the brand's approach in all areas; in addition, think about how you can use merchandising to support other promotional activity – sales promotions in particular.
- Support is often available from suppliers; this can be useful, but be careful and don't use it indiscriminately – it is often generic and not appropriate for particular customers, objectives or even brands as a whole.

5 *Sales promotion*:
- Sales promotion is a very effective tool for influencing behaviour and is highly suitable for licensed retailing units, in particular for promoting specific items or product categories. However, it is costly and tends to be overused in the industry. It needs to be recognized that achieving promotion objectives does not always need the give-aways usually associated with sales promotion, especially in high added-value branded units.
- It should be undertaken with care in order not to undermine the value of particular products or the customers' perception of the unit overall.

Table 13.6 Comparison of promotional tools available for branded licensed retail units

Promotional tool	Objectives	Target audience	Credibility	Cost
Public relations: The generation of publicity, usually free, by communicating newsworthy activity through any media channels. The activity concerned need not necessarily be about your actual product or what you offer to customers, as long as it can be positively connected to your business	*Awareness and interest.* People get to know about and feel well disposed to your business	Both existing and new customers. Usually a fairly local area, but with a good breadth of coverage in that area. The nature of the event and the reporting channels will influence the segments reached	Probably the highest levels of credibility of any of the communication tools. The message is seen as being independent and with no ulterior motive	There are no direct costs as such, but the costs of putting on the events and/or establishing the contacts should not be ignored
Advertising: This is a highly visible and mass-market method of communicating. Virtually any media can be used – flyers and brochures, TV and radio, papers and magazines, buses, billboards etc. It offers an opportunity for eye-catching and memorable images and messages to be presented. With easily understood products like ours, customers spend less time thinking about the advertising they see or concentrating on complicated messages	*Awareness and interest.* Advertising generates familiarity with your product. It is good at getting across a feeling or image, and encouraging customers to feel the same way	Advertising can reach all target audiences and communicate effectively with large numbers. It is less effective for targeting specific groups of customers or particular occasions	Credibility is limited. People's awareness of advertising today creates difficulties for using this medium in pubs, bars and restaurants in two ways: (1) People will take a lot of persuading to trust what we say; (2) The messages have to be ever more sophisticated if they are to stand up to, and be different from, the mass of other advertising messages	Advertising is costly. Even the most basic print ads are expensive, and these are usually the cheapest form of advertising
Sponsorship: A longstanding part of the pub promotional mix, sponsorship is providing support for activities or organizations outside your normal area of operation. These are usually small-scale local activities, and may include sports teams, arts groups, community projects and so on. In return, you get recognition and association with the activity	*Awareness and action.* It is usually associated with awareness and interest rather than customers 'doing'. At the local level, though, it can influence customers' purchase behaviour. Sponsored teams are far more likely to spend money in your pub at other times as well as match days	Sponsorship can range from being targeted through to very general events with broad appeal. In all cases, the event/group should have the same target audience as the one you want to reach	It can be very credible as long as it's not too obvious. It allows customers to form their own perceptions without telling them what to think. Again, credibility can depend on the event sponsored	This varies tremendously depending on the popularity of the event/group. It can seem expensive because it is difficult to measure the impact it has
Merchandising: Non-personal communication that takes place in-house, usually at the point of sale. In most cases, it is the visual presentation of information or products in a way that is appealing to the eye. It is likely that you will have booklets detailing the principles and brand specifics of merchandising, a lot of which have been developed from supermarket ideas. Usually merchandising is about the products on sale in the pub, not the pub itself	*Awareness, interest, desire and action.* It has got the ability to achieve all these goals, although it is primarily about stimulating people to purchase. Constantly changing merchandising can maintain customers' interest. It can also be used to manage the behaviour and flow of customers around the pub	The audience is largely restricted to existing customers within the pub. Displays can be made appealing to different target groups. There is a possibility to appeal to external customers through appealing signage and such like	It is often not seen as promotional activity by customers and therefore the credibility is increased, although this depends on the neutrality of displays and copy – the more overt the 'buy me' message, the less the chance for credibility	Costs can be high with complex designs etc., but effective merchandising can be accomplished quite cheaply – by product and bar displays, for example

	Action		Credibility	Cost
Sales promotions: These are usually temporary activities, changed regularly to maintain interest. They can be run in-house or externally, and they usually involve an incentive for customers to act – often in the form of savings. Sales promotions tend to rely on other promotional tools to raise customers' awareness of their existence	**Action**. Sales promotions are clearly designed to stimulate action from our target market – product trial or repeat purchase, for example. They are largely short-term focused, and as such do not greatly influence customers' loyalty or even their perceptions of the business as a whole. There can be a spin-off benefit of creating interest if well presented	They work equally well for new or existing customers, but they must at least have an interest already. There is a danger that sales promotion may attract offer-conscious rather than product-conscious customers	Credibility depends on the perceived value of the offer to the customers and their ability to redeem it, so pick offers that are important to customers – don't just use sales promotion to sell off slow-moving products!	It can be costly, as there are the fixed costs of raising awareness of the promotion and the variable costs of the offer itself
Direct marketing: Direct marketing is any promotion that has a mechanism to encourage and facilitate direct response – for example, a coupon in the paper or given out in the pub. Direct mail is just one aspect of direct marketing	**Action**. As the name implies, direct marketing seeks to stimulate purchase as a response. It does not work for building awareness, as people will not give the time or attention to products or businesses they are not familiar with. It is effective at communicating long and complex messages	One of the key benefits of direct marketing is its ability to target a particular audience – right down to specific individuals. It is more likely to target existing customers as it is easier to get the necessary details and we are unlikely (at unit level anyway) to purchase mailing lists for use	Two words – JUNK MAIL! There can be big problems with the credibility of this method. If done properly and targeted effectively, the messages can be very persuasive. Direct marketing, especially mail, is not generally associated with the licensed retail sector, and therefore retains better credibility	The cost is high, but value can be good because of good response rates that can be measured more accurately than any other method
Personal selling: Any direct communication from staff to customers with the intention of persuading customers to buy is considered to be selling. Staff in pubs, bars and restaurants are likely to use a very simplified approach to personal selling, which is often only used to support other promotional activity such as sales promotion and merchandising	**Action**. Personal communication from staff to customers can actively influence all the objectives. However, when considering selling specifically, the aim is purely to secure the purchase, now	A very narrow target audience of existing customers, currently in the unit. Often only those who are already in contact with staff	Credibility can be very high, depending on the capability of the staff member concerned. Again, it is more credible where it is less overt	The only pre-cost is in training and developing staff to be able to sell properly. Any staff incentives must be costed, but these are based on additional sales

- The timing is important – it should last long enough to maximize the benefits, but not so long that it bores customers or becomes a core expectation of the product rather than a promotion.
- The key to long-term benefit from sales promotion is gained by developing those customer behaviours encouraged by the promotion into repeat behaviours and loyalty.

6 *Direct marketing*:
- This is an under-used tool in licensed retailing, and it has a great deal to offer. The highly personalized approach may seem less appropriate to some branded city venues with transient clientele, for example, but it still has benefits to bring to all types of unit.
- It is an important tool for getting closer to your customers and encouraging loyalty in pubs that are getting too big to develop and too big for staff to know regular customers through the informal networks used in the past.
- To make it work to its full potential requires a long-term programme – collecting and managing data about customers and using this to drive your promotional activity.
- Owing to the direct response element, the evaluation of its impact is built into direct marketing.

7 *Personal selling*:
- This tool should be encouraged and used in every branded retail outlet, the aim being for it to become a natural part of how every staff member serves customers. The more natural it is, the more effective it will be.
- Staff training is the key to this, ensuring that the selling is effective but unobtrusive. This will then add to customer satisfaction as well as sales.
- Every contact between staff and customers is an opportunity for selling – longer contacts giving greater opportunities.
- Personal selling offers clear opportunities for incentives and rewards, and this is an especially effective approach to getting it established.

Active learning point

In a unit known to you, identify a particular business problem that needs to be solved or a business objective to be met.

1 Which promotional tool is most likely to achieve this, and why?
2 Given the specific circumstances of the business, what are the likely difficulties of implementing this, and how could they be overcome?

Prepare the message

Preparation of the message is focused on how you want people to respond to it – in other words, what change do you want to bring about in your audience? The message may be to:

- increase or improve their knowledge (awareness)
- change their feelings or beliefs (interest and desire)
- persuade them to act in a certain way (action).

Putting together effective promotional messages is a skill that akes lots of time and practice to develop. There are some basic guidelines that you can follow whenever you need to prepare communications with your customers:

1 Decide what to say
2 Decide how to organize what you are saying
3 Decide how to present it.

Decide what to say ● ● ●

This may include some or all of the following:

1 **Features of the product**. Include basic facts about what the product is or what it does. These help customers to understand the product better, to make it more tangible – for example, 'Our bar is big, bright and busy'.
2 **Clear benefits or solutions to customers' needs**. Explain to the audience what the product will do for them and what they will get out of it – for example, 'We can serve you your lunch in 10 minutes or you will get your money back'.
3 **Differentiate the business from its competitors**. Explain clearly what it is that makes you better than X or different from Y – for example, 'We have the best range of bottled beers in Basingstoke – ten more than any other bar in town'.
4 **Explicit actions you want customers to take and the reason they should take them** – for example, 'Bring this coupon with you between 5 and 7pm on a Monday, Tuesday or Wednesday night, and you can have the first drink on us'.

Decide how to organize what you are saying ● ● ●

What you put at the beginning and the end are important – start with a bang and introduce the main benefits first, or leave these to the end so they linger in people's minds. A similar question arises if you are encouraging customers to act – should this be early or later in the message?

Should you mention only positive things about the pub, or should you acknowledge drawbacks? Recent research has shown that, with sophisticated audiences, messages that don't suggest everything is perfect are more powerful – for example, 'We try harder'.

It would seem logical to conclude the message with a confirmation of the key points that make it so attractive. Again, however, it has been shown that messages that allow the customer to draw their own conclusions can be more powerful.

Decide how to present it ● ● ●

In the examples above, words (copy) were used to get the message across. Some of these messages could be communicated equally well with the use of images and illustrations – for example, a simple picture would show 'our bar is big, bright and busy', probably more effectively and certainly more poetically than using the words.

There are numerous non-verbal cues that can make the message easier to understand or more powerful – merchandizing can be almost all images and colour

Hospitality, Leisure & Tourism Series

etc., and people will still get the message – 'the eye line is the buy line', and so on.

Obviously, not all these factors are equally important to every promotional tool. There is little chance to put information at the beginning or the end of merchandising, or to conclude it for that matter.

However you combine these factors, the outcome should be the same – a message that is clear and easy to understand, grabs the audience's attention and maintains their interest, is believable and convincing, and therefore elicits the desired response in your customers.

Evaluate the impact

As with the evaluation of any activity, the key purpose of evaluating promotional communication is to find out whether the objectives have been achieved. For promotional activity, this means assessing the impact on:

- the target audience – that is, the customers' knowledge, attitudes and beliefs resulting from the promotion, and any specific actions taken
- the business performance – that is, the changes in the key financial measures relevant to a particular promotion (turnover and margin).

Impact on the target audience • • •

Evaluation through sophisticated and costly consumer research is not necessary at unit level. Your proximity to your customers means that you have an advantage over brand managers and agencies when it comes to evaluation. You can collect valuable information by talking informally to customers. Try asking a few simple questions such as those listed in Table 13.7.

Impact on business performance • • •

The primary focus of this evaluation is the specific goal(s) of the promotion, but you should also be aware of the possible side effects – impacts on areas not directly related to the activity. For example, there may be a reduction in draught beer sales while you are running a promotion for bottled beers.

Make sure that you make full use of the built-in evaluation measures offered by some direct marketing and sales promotion tools.

The financial data presented by your EPOS systems will provide valuable data for evaluating the impact of promotions. This, linked to the sales analysis ideas discussed in Chapter 10, will probably provide a sufficiently detailed and accurate evaluation. The sorts of things you will be concerned with are:

- sales volumes – in total, and for specific products and product categories
- the value of transactions
- the sales mix
- the timing of sales
- sales from particular members of staff.

Question	Yes	No	Comments
Are you aware of the promotion we just ran on ?????			
Do you know about ???? as a result of the promotion? • What do you know?			
Were you interested by the promotion?			
Did the promotion change the way you feel about ?????			
Did you respond in any way to the promotion? • If so, why did you respond? • If not, why not?			
Was the promotion good value?			
Would you like to see similar promotions in the future?			

Table 13.7 Informal evaluation

There are a few general principles of evaluation that can improve the reliability of your findings:

1 Evaluation requires both 'before' and 'after' measures to assess any change
2 Always be aware of and record other variables that could have affected the impact of the promotion
3 Wherever possible, build evaluation into the activity itself – the use of coupons and codes, for example.

Evaluation is not the final act of promotion, but should be the beginning of the next round of promotions, building into a cyclical process in which you reflect upon the success of your actions, learn from this, and improve the next activity as a result.

Example of promotional activity – Whitbread's *Business Builder* pack

Box 13.1 provides an example of company support for unit promotional activities.

Box 13.1   *The Business Builder*

A number of companies provide detailed support for unit promotional activity. At one extreme is the prescriptive 'what to do and when' approach, with a calendar of events and a generic pack of posters, drip mats and tent cards to go with it. At the other extreme is the company that leaves units to get on with it as they see fit, and provides resources and/or advice as and when requested. Somewhere between these two extremes is the approach taken by the Business Builder pack from Whitbread. This is presented as a 'Springboard to Success', and claims to contain:

> . . . everything you could ever need to run a successful promotion in your outlet.

The pack consists of a menu of promotional activities and the materials needed to run them. In addition, there is advice and material in support of advertising, merchandising and signage, and guidance on how to build a marketing database and use it to run a direct mail campaign.

The Business Builder pack is run as a mail order catalogue for promotions, and there is also guidance for managers in how to choose the right promotion for their business. The pack covers a number of sections that take unit managers through planning, implementing and evaluating promotional activity. These include:

- identifying customer segments and occasions
- ideas for promotions (split into drink, food and machines)
- other promotional communications activity (usually external to the unit)
- how to run the promotions
- evaluation processes
- the legal implications
- a calendar of events that could form the basis of promotional activity.

The *Business Builder* pack appears to have two benefits that recommend it in the context of the approach to marketing and promotion followed in this text:

1 It provides a number of 'road-tested' promotional activities and some clear guidelines about other elements of the promotional mix, all of which are well thought out and appropriate to the needs of unit level activity.
2 Perhaps more importantly, it requires managers to follow the full process for developing promotions if they are to utilize the pack. Before ordering a pack, managers must identify their objectives and match these to a particular promotion. This identification of objectives is linked to the use of '*The Business*' operational guidebook and the section on marketing planning. Here, promotional objectives such as encouraging extra spend and rewarding existing customers are discussed. Managers must also:

- identify how much the promotion is likely to cost
- set a date for the promotion
- identify the expected additional revenue (perhaps a slightly simplistic approach to budgeting, but better than nothing)

- plan how it will be implemented
- evaluate the promotion.

To encourage compliance with this last stage of the process, managers are required to pay a fee for the resources, and this is refunded when the evaluation is received at head office.

The promotions

Each promotion is presented in a format that gives clear guidance about how it ought to be run. This includes:

- the promotion objectives
- a description of the key points of the promotion
- guidance about when to run it
- the mechanics of planning the promotion – consulting with regional managers etc.
- a checklist of the manager's actions to make it happen
- an evaluation form.

This approach offers managers some say in decisions about promotions for their unit, and there is more opportunity available should they wish it. A 'pick 'n' mix' element to the pack gives managers guidance on how to make their own kits, and access to the resources in order to be able to do this – as long as they use the building blocks prescribed by the company. Whilst this is a step in the right direction, it stops short of truly empowering managers and allowing them to design and deliver communications appropriate to their audience – which could then be evaluated and brought into the company programme when deemed successful.

Conclusions

This chapter has developed the discussion from Chapter 12. It is clear that the increased competition in the sector has raised the need for individual units to seek out ways of achieving local competitive advantage. The marketing elements of this book argue that this can only ever be achieved on the basis of comprehensive understanding of the market and operating environment of the business.

This chapter has presented an overview of the information required for a full understanding of the environment in which your business operates. The unit manager with this breadth of knowledge is rare indeed, and it offers a genuine basis for actions to gain the competitive advantage sought. These actions can be identified and prioritized through the use of the SWOT analysis tool. As a unit manager, you have the scope to use this knowledge to build on the brand and identify the elements that can be offered to customers not already enjoying it.

It is recognized that there are many possible strategies for creating the advantage you seek. However, there are good reasons, based on span of authority and responsibility, why promotional activity is presented here as a key strategy.

The discussion of the development process for effective promotions, the characteristics of each promotional tool and the requirements for successful implementation and evaluation provides clear guidance for the use of promotional communication in branded units within the licensed retail sector. Like many of the activities discussed in this book, the greatest long-term impact can be gained from treating this as an iterative process in which you are constantly reflecting the effectiveness of your promotional activity and adjusting future activity on the basis of this reflection.

Reflective practice

1 How can SWOT analysis help you identify the possible actions required for the future development of your unit? When preparing a SWOT analysis, what information do you need to consider regarding the local community and local environment?
2 Thinking back to the key customer occasions you identified in Chapter 12, what promotional activities are appropriate for each one? Why are they appropriate – considering objectives and target audience? What are the particular challenges of implementing them for each occasion?
3 Evaluate critically the role of promotional activity in achieving local competitive advantage.
4 Discuss the need for promotional activity to be designed as a coherent strategy or as individual promotions with discrete objectives.
5 What are the three most relevant promotional tools for a unit known to you? Explain your decision. How could they be implemented to improve business performance?
6 Where are the potential conflicts between promotion at unit level and that at brand level? How can unit promotion reflect the need of the brand overall?

Further reading

Bacon, M. (1997). *DIY Direct Marketing*. J Wiley & Sons.
Lewis, R., Chambers, R. and Chacko, H. (1995). *Marketing Leadership*. Van Norstrand Reinhold.
Maitland, I. (1999). *Perfect PR*. International Thompson Publishing.
Shaw, M. (2000). *Hospitality Sales: A Marketing Approach*. John Wiley & Sons.
Williams, J. (1983). *The Manual of Sales Promotion*. Innovation Ltd.

CHAPTER 14

Improving the chance of reaching your destination

After working through this chapter, you should be able to:

- understand the need to produce and work to a unit business plan

- gather the information and background detail needed for the plan

- write up and present an effective business plan

- work to the plan, making the necessary adjustments needed.

Preparing a unit business plan

Although you may be working for a large branded licensed retailer, and managing a unit that is already covered by the plan for the overall business, it is useful to prepare a business plan for your unit. For independent business in freehold, tenanted, leased or franchised business, a business plan is essential. As the above statement indicates, business plans assist managers to plan the direction of the business, compare performance with the plan, and take corrective action.

Preparing a business plan allows you to:

- think about the mission and key objectives of the business, and the actions needed to achieve the objectives
- identify the information needed to understand the customers and competition
- develop a competitive business strategy for the unit
- plan all the activities needed to make the strategy work
- forecast the results of the unit and plan to overcome difficulties
- keep track of the business and take corrective action where needed.

It therefore helps you understand the business and the planning process. It is this process that is important to your role as unit manager, because the licensed retail sector is fast moving and dynamic, and a plan gives you a sense of direction and purpose. It gives you a basis to make changes and amendments as circumstances unfold. As part of a group, the business plan shows how your unit will contribute to the overall goals and objectives of the company.

Describing the business

The business planning process starts with a clear description of the business, the management and team, and core business activities.

Mission statement, objectives and actions

The mission statement and objectives are important because they help to give everyone in the unit focus and a sense of purpose. They also help everyone to consider problems and difficulties to be overcome. Figure 14.1 illustrates the pyramid of goals.

The mission statement • • •

In large organizations this will be provided by head office, but as unit manager you will need to understand the statement and encourage team members to understand their contribution to achieving the mission. A good mission statement provides an organization with a focus, and helps to concentrate managerial staff and employees on the key activities and to prevent them from trying to do too many things. In particular, the mission statement should cover the following points:

1 What business you are in, and what your purpose is
2 What you want to achieve over the next one to three years
3 How you will achieve this – your values and standards.

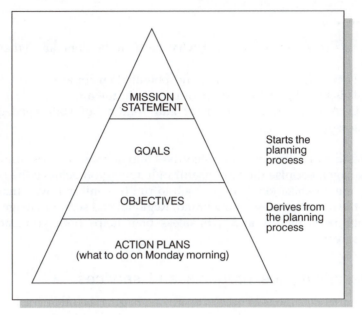

Figure 14.1 The pyramid of goals

Mission statements should neither be too bland, nor so general that is difficult to know what business you are working in.

Goals • • •

Define the specific goals to be achieved over the next three years. They have to be written in specific and measurable terms – for example:

1 To increase sales by 20 per cent over three years
2 To reduce employee turnover by 10 per cent each year
3 To increase customer satisfaction scores by 5 per cent within one year.

By defining the key goals you are providing a set of targets so that you are more likely to achieve the overall purpose of the business. They provide you with a measurable set of pointers that guide actions over the forthcoming period.

Objectives • • •

Objectives are the specific activities that you need to undertake in order to achieve the objectives set. They are the 'how' statements that will make the objectives happen. For example:

1 Identify complementary customer occasions, so as to attract new customers to the business
2 Target businesses that might undertake joint products with my products and services
3 Direct promotional material and special offers to customers that use the unit in quiet periods.

Hospitality, Leisure & Tourism Series

Actions ● ● ●

In this case you are showing what needs to be done and when. For example:

1 This week, survey existing and potential customers
2 This month, visit all competitor units in the area
3 In August, start recruitment and training of staff needed for the Christmas season.

The identification of goals, objectives and actions are most important to you as unit manager, because they are useful in helping you achieve the overall mission as set by the organization. It is your job to run the unit in a way that makes it contribute to the overall success of the brand. Regional and senior managers will be monitoring your performance, and a business plan helps both you and them to overview progress.

Describing the products and services

Even in situations where you are managing a unit of a branded licensed retail organization, it is worthwhile focusing on the key products and services that you are supplying to customers. Licensed retail operations often involve the sale of a mixture of food and beverage items. These need to be analysed:

- by meal types – e.g. set meals or snacks
- by types of drinks – e.g. alcoholic or soft drinks
- through other income streams – e.g. from machines.

Where accommodation is also offered for sale, the analysis should include room sales and types. Table 14.1 is a typical product and services analysis sheet.

The analysis should also consider the primary customer occasions the business is servicing, and identify potential complementary occasions that might be tapped as a source of sales growth.

This statement of the key product and service together with a statement relating to product and service quality and some targets for its management is a crucial

Product/service	Description	Percentage of sales
1		
2		
3		
4		
5		

Table 14.1 Product and service analysis

planning tool. Chapter Seven provides an overview of different approaches to quality management. But this statement with clear objectives is an important aspect of the way you plan a manage the business. Also flowing from your analysis of the customer occasions at the core of your business it is also possible to list the key critical success factors so that you focus on those aspects of the product and service offer most important to meeting customer expectations.

You and your team

Careful consideration of the experience, training and development and skills available within the management team and the employees is a valuable starting point for considering the skill needs of the unit. Clearly, the plan can help you to:

- identify potential strengths in the team
- highlight key skills and experiences that can be used for projects and special initiatives
- focus on skill shortages and development needs for the future
- plan employees' and managers' career development.

Increasingly, licensed retail units are concerned with availability of key staff at all levels. The right management team skills and experience necessary to run and develop a multi-million pound business are, of course, vital. In addition, the inability to attract, recruit and train employees is further compounded in many licensed retail organizations by high levels of staff turnover, which often represents a key weakness and substantial additional cost to the business. A clear commitment to building a strong team and increasing staff retention needs to be a key part of your overall strategy and objectives, and your analysis of the team. When writing your business plan, consider the following:

1 Explain the thinking behind the company's mission statement, and show how you will work to achieving the mission in your unit
2 List your goals for the unit, both long- and short-term
3 List the objectives and actions you need to take to achieve the goals
4 Describe your products and service as if to a new employee
5 How do your goods and services differ from those of competitors?
6 Are there possible complementary occasions through which you could attract new customers?
7 What relevant skills and talents are available to you?
8 What are the shortages of skills and talents, and how do you plan to fill the gaps?
9 What are current levels of staff retention and staff turnover?
10 What are the current levels of financial performance – cost levels, sales growth, profit levels etc., and targets for the future?

Market research

Many branded licensed retail operators commission research on the brand, customers, competitors and markets, and you will usually have access to this national information. However, you need to understand these issues as they relate to your particular unit and the community in which it is located. The following issues need to be considered in the business plan:

1 The core customers the unit is servicing
2 The types of customers who are attracted to the business
3 The activities of competitors
4 The general conduct of the market in which you operate.

An ongoing analysis of these issues helps you keep the plan in focus and allows you to react to any changes that come up – for example, the unforeseen opening of a competitor unit or the closure of a major local employer may have adverse impacts to which you need to react.

Customers • • •

This text suggests that each brand represents a series of tangible and intangible benefits in products and services to customers. These can best be understood through an analysis of the 'occasions' on which customers visit the establishment.

The key starting point of your plan is to consider the various customer needs you are servicing through the business, and the factors that are critical for success. This needs to be developed further by an analysis of the customers themselves, and the following points should be considered:

1 *Socio-economic group.* How do customers comprise the key socio-economic groups? Issues to do with income, status and employment can have important consequences, particularly if you build up a picture of key employers for whom your customers work.
2 *Life cycle position.* A description of the life cycle positions of key customer groups also helps you to analyse the number of potential customers in your locality, and their needs and concerns regarding businesses like yours.
3 *Gender.* The mixture of male and female customers has a number of consequences for the product and services you offer. Healthy eating options on the menu, the provision of non-smoking areas, and security are issues that may be important where a substantial number of customers are women.
4 *Geographical location.* What kind of area do customers mostly live in? What are the main housing types and locations, and are there other similar areas that might yield customers? What developments are there in these areas that might impact on your business?
5 *Lifestyle.* Are there issues about environmental awareness or health consciousness, or appeals that can be made to those concerned with material rewards? In some units, a series of healthy options might attract customers to use the unit more frequently.
6 *Personality.* What personality types dominate the customer base? Are there additional opportunities to attract similar customers, or a different sort of customer at different times?

These matters need your careful consideration, because over recent decades the emergence of licensed retail brands has depended upon changes in the population and their spending power. Here are just a few examples of such changes:

1 More women are working and having careers interrupted, but not stopped, by having children
2 There are more dual-income households
3 There are more single households
4 There are more elderly people, living longer, and with higher incomes
5 There has been a general increase in the number of people eating out
6 More people are concerned about healthy eating.

These changes have resulted in some additional opportunities – for example, retired customers can be attracted to use restaurants and pubs during the late afternoon and early evening through special offers. More women with independent income means that more women are able to go out to eat and drink on their own. More health consciousness and growth in vegetarianism means that most menu offers have to include vegetarian and healthy eating options, and increasing numbers of non-smoking customers are demanding smoke-free atmospheres or no smoking areas in restaurants and bars.

Key customer occasions and critical success factors

The key occasions that motivate customers to make the decision to visit a bar, pub or restaurant are outlined in an earlier chapter. The following acts as a reminder of the key customer occasions most appropriate to licensed retail operations in general. The list provided is not exhaustive, and your business may well be meeting other customer needs that are not included here. Your business plan needs to list the core customer occasions and the potential complementary occasions that might yield more customers. The basic list of key occasions consists of:

- big night out – circuit or venue
- pre-club
- pit stop
- socializing
- taking part
- finding company
- the match
- being fed
- family day out
- a special meal out.

In addition, your business plan needs to list the critical success factors that are at the heart of customer expectations of a successful visit to the unit.

Competitors • • •

Research on local competitors provides an important source of information on which to plan your own activities. Many retail licensed markets are dominated by 'me-too brands' – that is, brands that are aiming at similar market segments and offering to satisfy similar customer needs on similar customer occasions. You need to know their current strengths and weaknesses so that you can learn from their strengths and attack their weaknesses.

Remember the points made earlier; that there are both immediate and second-order competitors for your customers' spend. Concentrate initially on the immediate, first-order competitors, but you need also to think about the other competitors who are meeting similar customer needs to your business. Your business may well have its own features in relation to customers that will add to the following list of key concerns. The important point is that the issue you investigate needs to be relevant to your business and the customer needs it is aiming to serve. Table 14.2 is a typical competitor analysis sheet.

Factor	Competitor	Own unit
Visibility and access		
Menu and range		
Service style		
Additional offers		
Facilities		
Seating		
Opening hours		
Pricing and special offers		
General cleanliness		
Promotional activities		
Estimated sales revenue		
Average check size or transaction value		
Internal competitor audit		

Table 14.2 Competitor analysis

When drawing up your business plan you need to have an honest accurate picture of the strengths and weaknesses of competitors, and this will then inform your plan. Where can you build genuine competitive advantage? What actions and targets are required to gain the competitive edge needed? Flowing from the initial research, you need to be constantly tracking competitors and exploring issues beyond the immediate customers, good and services offered. Usually you are competing in the same labour markets and in the same local environment, so you may also need to explore wage rates and incomes, and competitors' links with local employers, schools, local government, planning offices, etc.

The local environment • • •

Your business plan must also consider the local environment, because this provides a context of opportunities and threats that will impact on the business. Contacts with relevant government authorities can help you identify useful data regarding the economic, political, social and legal environment. Again, these items flow from your marketing analysis, but here are some issues you might like to consider:

- local population demographic profile – trends and changes
- general level of economic activity – employment, incomes, changes and future trends
- local offices or factories – major employers that may impact on your business, perhaps either closing or expanding
- any planned traffic changes or other planning decisions that might have an impact
- the general approach of the planning authorities to your type of business?

The key is scanning the future for potential factors that will impact on the business you are in. Do these factors potentially generate more customers or fewer? As Wellington once said, 'The value of recognizance is knowing what is over the hill'. In fast moving licensed retail businesses, you have to be aware of changes before they occur. By scanning environmental developments you will be in a strong position to benefit from increased numbers of customers, or ready to deal with problems. Consider the following:

1 What is the geographical area from which customers are likely to be drawn? Consider numbers, locations, housing stock, etc.
2 What are the customer needs, expressed in customer occasions, which will provide your core customers? Identify potential customer occasions.
3 Consider the critical success factors for each of these customer groups, and differences between groups.
4 Are the markets you aim to draw from increasing or declining?
5 Are there any potential changes in customer tastes or habits that might either increase or reduce sales?
6 List the competitors with whom you compete directly.
7 List competitor opportunities to satisfy the same customer needs.
8 Highlight the strengths and weaknesses of competitors' approach to serving these customers.
9 Match these with the strengths and weaknesses of your business.
10 Describe the local economic and social context in which your business is located.
11 Identify local firms who might be used to form alliances.
12 Identify the key threats and opportunities posed by the local environment.

Competitive business strategy

You should now be in a position to formulate a competitive business strategy that will help you plan your tactics and actions over the short, medium and long term. As a unit manager, you need to think of the short term as within the next year, medium term as between one and two years, and long term as three years plus.

Working within a branded environment, the business strategy in terms of the overall direction of the business will be decided and shaped at head office. Your role as unit manager is to understand the strategy and interpret it within the local context. Broadly, there are three types of strategy that organizations follow, and these are briefly described below:

1 *Overall cost leadership*. This strategy is usually employed by large firms who can take advantage of reduced costs through economies of scale. The size of the business allows the firm to work on reduced costs due to lower production and distribution costs, greater purchasing power with suppliers, and reduced advertising and selling costs.
2 *Differentiation*. This strategy of differentiation, through quality, good design and image, creates brand loyalty and a willingness to pay a price premium. In some cases, the 'label' is the key benefit to the customer. TGI Friday Restaurants are in part attempting to gain competitive advantage in this way.
3 *Focus*. Here, a company focuses on a particular narrow market segment that is too specialized to attract competitors. By focusing in such a way, the firm makes the market its own. In some cases, being the only supplier of a particular licensed service to a particular local market can have elements of this, although in many cases the entry barriers for licensed firms are too low to make it a realistic national strategy.

The overall business strategy brings together the various elements of the mission and objectives, market research and marketing strategies, the market place, and the marketing mix, leading to the overall plan. The service marketing mix must be stated in your business plan, and you need to give it the local flavour that will help you action the overall brand strategy.

Pricing

As shown in Chapter 13, pricing is one of the elements of the marketing mix. In branded situations you have to work with national brand selling price strategies. Here are a few key pointers to pricing:

1 The selling price shapes customer perceptions – higher prices can communicate a perception of higher quality
2 Price is associated with concept of value, but customers use perception of the benefits to assess whether price paid represents good value
3 Many competitive markets are price sensitive, and small changes in price can result in large changes in customer demand

4 It is possible to adopt approaches where prices are held constant but bonus offers and the promotional mix increase sales.

Your business plan needs a clear statement about the pricing strategy of the brand and how you will use this in local campaigns.

Advertising and promotion

You need to communicate with your local market – both current and potential customers. Advertising is paid for, and consists of messages in the form of, say, local press advertising, whilst promotion covers those activities that will help to generate sales.

Your marketing plan needs to consider how you will promote sales through an array of different activities. Here are some examples that you might consider:

1 Local newspapers and 'free sheets' are often effective in that they reach target markets and are increasingly able to tailor their messages to specific localities. These are most effective when tied to an 'editorial' piece – for example, a story about your unit that is of local interest.
2 Leaflets dropped through letter boxes or sent by post to targeted postcode areas are also useful in that you can direct your messages to the people most likely to use your establishment.
3 Links with complementary firms – cinemas, theatres and other leisure venues – can provide joint offers such as pre-theatre dinners or money-off vouchers to attract customers to your business.

Your business plan needs to show how you will promote the business over the period:

1 What are the aims and objectives of promoting the business?
2 How much is the promotion worth?
3 Which methods will you use?
4 What benefits do you expect to receive?
5 How will you check the results?

Place

Your business plan needs to consider the nature of the premises, as these provide both tangible and intangible benefits to customers. As we saw, issues that may be benefits or limitations include the approach and external appearance, signage, cleanliness, visibility to the inside, external décor and car parking facilities.

Internally, the overall atmosphere, cleanliness, décor, music, toilet provision, non-smoking areas, availability of children's play areas, etc. are also issues that need to be considered, because capital expenditure may be required to meet changed customer expectations.

Often it is said that location is the key to success in licensed businesses, but difficulties can be overcome with the right attention to service, customer expectations and promotional activity.

Your business plan should include an analysis of the facilities so that you can analyse and act upon the strengths and weaknesses they pose for meeting and exceeding customer expectations. Consider the following:

1 What are the key cost elements that your business has to incur to make an operating profit?
2 What is the overall price strategy?
3 How do your prices compare with your competitors?
4 Are there differences amongst customers in their price sensitivity?
5 What are your key objectives for advertising and promotional activities?
6 What methods will you use to achieve the objectives and why?
7 How will the results be monitored and evaluated?
8 Are the premises adequate for future needs?
9 What development work is needed and why?

Operations

Operations is the name given to the activities required to make the strategy happen. In licensed retail operations these activities cover the production and service of food and drink, and in some cases accommodation. Your business plan needs to show in detail how the products and service will be supplied to customers, and the following is a suggested format:

1 Start with an indication of what it is you are selling in broad terms, although an appendix could include the full product range.
2 From this, go on to indicate the opening hours of the unit and the sales mix at different times of day.
3 Provide an organizational plan that shows the organization of the unit and indicates the key job roles required to produce the goods and services. This will indicate the management posts involved and broad statements of responsibilities. Again, the appendix can be used to provide job descriptions (showing the duties and responsibilities) and person specifications (showing the skills and qualities) for each job title.
4 Indicate how the individuals will be managed, rewarded and motivated. Consider issues to do with group and team work in the management of particular customer groups and customer occasions. In other words, how will you manage the critical success factors?
5 Following this, you should indicate your approach to customer complaint handling and the responsibilities for dealing with customer satisfaction.
6 Your business plan needs to consider the management of materials and cash involved in the operation.
7 In most licensed retail operations there are strict legal responsibilities associated with food hygiene, health and safety, licensing, and other responsibilities to customers and staff. Your plan should show how these matters are handled and managed.

The operational plan lays down a blueprint for the key issues that are priorities in building a successful unit that is likely to deliver satisfied customers and employees.

Forecasting results

The ultimate aim of a unit offering licensed retail products is to deliver a profitable operation that will make a positive contribution to the company's financial performance, and forecasting results is an important part of the business plan.

Sales forecasts

The sales forecast is arguably the most important set of figures to arise from the planning process. Sales forecasts help to establish the targets that you will use throughout the year, and to provide a set of unit profit and loss accounts.

Your estimate of sales from various income streams – meals, non-alcoholic and alcoholic beverages, machines, accommodation etc. – will need above all else to be based on sound reasoning. As part of a branded multi-unit operation you will have previous trading experience on which to build, even in a new unit. In many cases, however, you will be managing a unit that has been trading for some time. The following is a checklist of issues to bear in mind when calculating and justifying the sales forecasts:

1 How big is the market, bearing in mind the customer profile you will be wanting to attract and the local population within the unit's catchment area? Is the overall market growing or shrinking, and at what rate? Avoid unsubstantiated statements – you need to be convinced that the targets are achievable.
2 How many customers are there who are likely to buy from you, and how much do they spend on average per visit? Are there seasonal variations, or variations between customer types? Licensed retailers can get some information about the area, customer types, traffic flows, footfalls etc. from both the local authority and research organizations.
3 The desired income approach is appropriate for these operations, and your aim is to achieve the forecast. By a thorough analysis of potential sales you can make adjustments if sales slip for some reason.
4 Are there product life-cycle issues to consider? Some licensed retail operations – pubs, for example – are working in markets where customer visits are in decline, although there are growing opportunities in the restaurant sector.

Finally, how long a period should your sales forecasts cover? In fast moving retail markets it is unusual to plan more than three years ahead, and most operate a twelve-month cycle.

Operating profit statement

The operating profit statement sets out to match income with expenditure over the appropriate time period of your business plan. It is the way in which profit and loss can be calculated for the period.

Sales income • • •

This shows the projected total budget sales income for each month over the year. The figure includes the total projected income from all the unit's revenue-earning activities – sales of meals, snacks, alcoholic and non-alcoholic drinks, machines, accommodation etc. – by each month as it is likely to occur. Therefore, you must consider potential variations month by month. Traditionally, licensed retail operations experience low sales in January after peaks in December.

Cost of sales • • •

To show a trading profit, it is necessary to deduct the costs of the materials purchased to produce the goods sold. Thus the cost of all the food, drinks and other materials used to produce the goods sold are deducted from the sales revenue. The trading profit is the balance after these costs have been deducted. Usually these costs are represented as an average and calculated as a percentage, although there may be major differences between the profitability of different income streams and products.

Labour costs • • •

These again relate to the costs of producing the products and services associated with the sales revenue generated. Thus the total direct labour costs of kitchen, bar, restaurant, and accommodation are calculated as a means of arriving at a gross profit – that is, the surplus after the costs directly associated with generating the sales revenue have been taken into account. Again, the costs of labour can be calculated as a percentage, although there are differences between departments and sections depending on the labour intensity and the use of supplies that require different amounts of handling by staff.

Table 14.3 is an extract from accounts for a licensed retail operation such as yours.

The gross profit shows you how much income will be generated after the immediate costs of producing the products and services sold. However, these are not the only unit-based expenses. Managers' salaries and other administration costs, as well as rent, rates, lighting and electricity, unit-based advertising, staff uniforms and other expenses will need to be taken into account to show the profit contribution that your unit makes to the overall business.

Table 14.4 shows an example from the same organization, demonstrating how the operation profit can be calculated.

Clearly a branded licensed retail unit is different from an independent business, because it is unusual for these organizations to produce unit-specific balance sheets. However, each business will be considered as a business investment, and the return on capital employed might be an issue that company's accounts want to consider.

Writing up, presenting and working with your business plan

The business plan is both a document to be presented to colleagues that shows how you plan to manage the unit, and a document that you will use throughout the year

Year xxxx	Chelmsford £
Sales:	
• Drinks	650 000
• Food	300 000
Total	950 000
Cost of sales:	
• Drinks	260 000
• Food	75 000
Total	335 000
Trading profit	615 000
Staff wages (hourly paid)	175 000
Gross profit	440 000

Table 14.3 Extract from gross profit budget for The Wise Owl, Chelmsford

Year xxxx	Chelmsford £
Sales:	
• Drinks	650 000
• Food	300 000
	950 000
Cost of sales:	
• Drinks	260 000
• Food	75 000
	335 000
Trading profit	615 000
Staff wages (hourly paid)	175 000
Gross profit	440 000
Lease and local tax	90 000
Electricity and gas	20 000
Management and administration	54 000
Promotional activity	18 000
Maintenance	36 000
Other consumables	36 000
Depreciation	30 000
Pub profit contribution	156 000

Table 14.4 Extract from gross profit budget for The Wise Owl, Chelmsford

Hospitality, Leisure & Tourism Series

to work from and assess your progress. The business plan therefore needs to be presented in a professional manner and easily accessible.

Presentation of the written document

The business plan needs to conform to professional standards in the way it is written and presented:

1 A simple business folder with a spiral binding will be sufficient
2 It must be word processed (typed)
3 The layout should be more like a report than a memo or essay
4 The page layout should use wide margins and be pleasing on the eye.
5 The document should be printed on single sided A4 paper and paginated
6 Tables, figures and graphs aid understanding and are a quick way of communicating information, but these should also be explained and discussed in the text.

Remember, an appendix should be used to provide useful background information; all information that is essential to the plan must be included in the text.

Layout and content

There is no formally accepted business plan format, and a business plan for a unit that is part of an multi-unit organization is different to one for an independent business. The balance sheet section and the justifications that an independent business is required to include are not needed in a document for a multi-unit organization.

The front cover of the document should clearly state the name of the business and the date of the business plan. It is important that it is clear that this is the latest version of the plan.

The second sheet behind the front cover should include:

1 The current trading position of the restaurant, past successes, and a general appraisal of performance over recent years
2 The products and services currently being sold, and the unit's ranking compared with competitors
3 The customers and the potential customer base in the area, and the reasons why they use the unit
4 The unit aims and objectives in the short term, and the strategies to be employed in achieving them
5 A summary of forecast sales and profits.

The table of contents

The table of contents is valuable because it helps readers to find their way around the document and focus on the issues of immediate concern. Remember, you will be using this document, so you need to be able to turn to the sections that are of interest at a specific time.

There are a number of ways of numbering pages and sections. It is most appropriate to use a system that gives every section a new number, with subsections broken down by decimal points.

Although there are likely to be variations between different businesses, the following is an example to work from that might be useful as basis for designing your own document.

Sample table of contents • • •

Section
Executive summary

1   The unit and management
    1.1   History and overview of progress to date
    1.2   Current mission
    1.3   Objectives and actions needed
    1.4   The team

2   Products and services
    2.1   Products and services
    2.2   Current sales mix

3   Market and competition
    3.1   Description of customers
    3.2   Customer occasions, needs and benefits
    3.3   Market segments
    3.4   Market size in the area
    3.5   Location of customers and flows
    3.6   Marketing projects over the period
    3.7   Competition

4   Competitive business strategy
    4.1   Pricing policy
    4.2   Promotional plans
    4.3   Premises
    4.4   Competitor responses

5   Operations
    5.1   Critical success factors
    5.2   Quality management and control
    5.3   Organization structure
    5.4   Employee management and motivation

6   Forecasts and results
    6.1   Sales forecasts
    6.2   Operational budget

Appendix

The writing of the plan may have to go through several stages – at a minimum, there will be a first draft that you will show to and discuss with colleagues, and a second draft that will be the final document. It is important that the final draft is clear and well written, free from spelling and grammatical errors. The document has to be detailed enough to show that you have thought through the issues and recorded your thinking at the time, but it must not be overly long. Part of the editing process is to ensure that the information that is needed is in the document and that you have not over-written parts.

Working with the business plan

The business plan should be used throughout the year to monitor and keep track of progress. The assumptions and calculations built into the plan made sense to you and your colleagues at the time, so you need to think critically about how you will use the plan to guide your trading performance. Consider:

1 Sales analysis – hourly, daily, weekly and monthly sales audits can keep track of issues such as the sales mix, sales of most profitable lines, average transaction values, numbers of transactions, party sizes, irregular flows in the times customers use the business, etc.
2 Promotional plans and activities – the impact of particular offers, bonuses, national and local initiatives, and their relative success
3 Customers – regular users and customer retention, location and reasons for coming to the unit, demographic profiles, complaints and comments of satisfaction, customer focus groups, mystery customer reports
4 Employees – staff retention and labour turnover, staff satisfaction surveys, costs of training, benefits from training and development, sales analysis and up-selling opportunities, labour costs and investment in human capital
5 Competitor activities – make records of their initiatives that impact negatively on your sales, and how they respond to your initiatives
6 Cost control and profitability – ensuring that you record the costs of the materials and labour needed for the production of goods and services is essential in developing the basis for profitable performance.

Conclusion

There are differences between a business plan prepared by a unit manager of a branded licensed retail operation and a traditional business plan, because the former are rarely used in support of a request for finance – as would be the case with an independent business. However, there are times when a business plan might be used to justify an increased investment in the unit. In the main, however, business plans in multi-unit branded licensed retail operations do not involve calculations that consider the investment benefits of the business, so it is unusual for this type of business plan to consider the balance sheet and the various ratios associated with return on capital employed, etc.

The business plan provides a detailed map of how the unit will develop and will undertake its activities. It is essentially a tactical account of the unit and the issues that need to be managed in order for it to meet the brand's commitment to customer satisfaction, sales and profitability growth, and continued success in the community in which it is located.

Although there are no hard and fast rules about how this type of business plan should be presented, it is important that you undertake the research necessary, as described in this chapter, in as thorough a manner as possible. The more you invest in making rational decisions based on a sound understanding of the most relevant information, the more likely it is that your plan will form a sound basis for arriving at your desired objectives.

Further reading

Barrow, C., Barrow, P. and Brown, B. (1998). *The Business Plan Workbook*. Kogan Page.

CHAPTER 15

Seeing the wood for the trees – case study

Learning objectives

After working through this chapter, you should be able to:

- analyse the key features of licensed retail service

- identify problems and their causes in licensed retail operations

- show how problems in licensed retail operations are inter-related

- suggest improvements to licensed retail service operations.

Silverwood Pub Company

The case study outlined in this section is designed to help you practise an analysis of licensed retail unit management in a context that is based on a real-life situation. Although the situation and characters have been embellished to provide levels of analysis, the basic details and figures provided are taken from a hospitality retail operator. The preceding chapters give you a range of tools and ideas that can be applied to overcome the difficulties experienced here.

Background

The Silverwood Pub Company was established as a result of the changes precipitated by the Monopolies and Mergers Commission report of the late 1980s. Originally the pubs in the estate had been part of a larger company that had been owned by a brewer retailer operating on a national level. They were bought from the licensed retailer, who operated city-centre bars and had this small number of suburban properties that were medium-sized 'traditional' pubs offering food and drink. The licensed retailer had been advised to divest the properties because they were not consistent with the rest of the estate and the core business. The Silverwood Pub Company was formed by three former employees of the brewery pub company, who used their senior managers' redundancy money to buy the properties from the larger company. At the time of the incident described here, the company has grown to thirty pubs operating in two areas in the UK. A further twelve pubs are either under development or at various stages of planning and will commence operations within the next twelve months.

Brand attributes suggest value for money, consistent quality and traditional pub qualities. Drinks tend to major on traditionally brewed beers, although wine sales are becoming increasingly important. The food menu on offer in all pubs is adequate in size but limited to fewer than fifteen main menu items, although it is supplemented by a 'children's menu' and an ongoing programme of special offer products. These latter products help to overcome the 'menu fatigue' that is inherently a problem in this type of business.

Key customer occasions include *being fed*, *pit stop*, and *family day out*. Some of the larger units have a 'kids' area' and specialize in children's parties. On average, regular customers visit the pubs 6.5 times per month. Sixty per cent of customers are regular users, with a further 20 per cent visiting pubs more than once per quarter. The average spend per transaction is in the region of £3.41, and each transaction accounts for 1.4 customers in the bars. In the restaurants these amounts increase to an average of £10.60 per transaction, with an average of 2.4 customers per transaction.

The two areas are loosely 'north' and 'south', with little difference in the mix of pubs in the two areas. In reality, all the pubs are located in the suburbs of four major cities, along the motorway corridors between Sheffield and Nottingham, and Leeds and Manchester. The company is a fast moving licensed retailer, and considers that restaurants with sales of less than £400 000 per annum are too small.

Table 15.1 illustrates the sales and transactions in the twelve restaurants concerned, at the time of the incident.

A minority of the kitchen and restaurant staff are employed on 35-hour full-time contracts, but most of the staff are employed part-time on an hourly basis. Typically,

Hospitality, Leisure & Tourism Series

Unit	Average weekly sales (£)	Average weekly transactions	Average transaction (£)
North1	15 953	4347	3.67
North2	33 434	8235	4.06
North3	17 699	5601	3.16
North4	26 767	7044	3.80
North5	26 321	6051	4.35
North6	20 962	5027	4.17
South1	30 013	8446	3.55
South2	14 535	4895	2.96
South3	30 457	8515	3.57
South4	18 162	5513	3.29
South5	27 919	7386	3.77
South6	27 150	7536	3.60

Table 15.1 The twelve pubs at the time of the incident

they work 16–20 hours per week. Rates are £4.20 per hour. Where staff shortages occur, agency staff are employed from a contractor and are charged at £12.00 per hour.

The company states that training staff to perform tasks in the 'one best way' is an essential feature of delivering the company's highly standardized and uniformity-dependent offer to customers. Production and service operations are tightly defined and are subject to detailed training programmes. Staff are supposed to be trained against these standards, and a management development programme supports manager training for each stage of the management hierarchy up to unit management.

The key elements of the Silverwood approach to training are:

- all staff are trained (full- and part-time employees)
- training is competence based
- ultimately, training aims to develop a flexible workforce capable of undertaking all jobs
- much staff training involves learning to do the job in the 'one best way'
- competencies are defined for each job
- completed training is rewarded through pay increases
- training is delivered through a 'training team' (staff members trained to train)
- staff appraisals are also used to monitor ongoing employee performance.

Unit managers are accountable for training, and are monitored through the 'training log' and training audits to ensure that crew training is being administered correctly and completed to plan. The Human Resource and Training (HRAT) computer system enables both unit managers and regional executives to monitor training in each restaurant.

Staff training • • •

All staff should be trained according to the company's standard procedures. Although there are some exceptions, particularly in jobs such as 'hostess' or 'maintenance' staff, the standard approach to training involves functional flexibility – in other words, staff are generally trained to do the full range of production and service tasks in the pub. Although some employees have personal preferences and skills that mean they do specialized jobs either in the kitchen, restaurant or bar, most employees seem to like the variety that this approach to training allows.

Monitoring and development • • •

Appraisals play an important role in both defining the standard performance for each of the restaurant's key tasks and providing a standard against which ongoing performance can be monitored. Each restaurant has its own computer, which is used to record the individual training record and, subsequently, the training record for each member of staff. The computer-generated staffing schedule also uses information from these records. This assists managers in planning the duty roster for the forthcoming week. The system identifies the skills needed for each shift period, matches the result against the skill levels of each individual, and makes a recommendation for the manager's action. Clearly, the training approach allows flexibility in staffing options. The HRAT programme identifies training and staffing priorities.

Regional monitoring of each pub's training log shows how many employees have been fully trained, and identifies the priorities for training. This regional record also shows the state of training in each unit. Consequently, each pub can be evaluated against the management of staff training and performance monitoring. Information on the training activity of each pub is used to provide a 'training grade', and it is expected that these grades will be above 90 per cent.

For the purposes of this study, the training grades were used to identify pubs that appear to be meeting and exceeding the company's training standards, and those that are operating below the expected standards.

In summary, the Silverwood Pub Company is in many ways a benchmark organization for the provision of training amongst UK licensed retail organizations. Their systematic and detailed approach, together with the universality of training for all employees and line management accountability for training, is an example that could be adopted by others.

The immediate situation

You have been recently appointed to the post of Area Manager for the Sheffield area, responsible for the six restaurants in the area. The post has been vacant for nine months and has been directly managed by the Operations Director, Graham Fastbuck. You have just completed a three-week induction programme.

Graham Fastbuck was appointed from one of the major UK pub chains – a competitor of Silverwood Pub Company – in preparation for the rapid expansion of the chain. The Board of Directors were keen to appoint a British executive who had a proven record in the UK marketplace. Since being appointed, Fastbuck has indeed tightened up on controls within the Company. He viewed the more autonomous management style that was in place before he joined as 'anarchy'. He has fixed stringent budgets for each unit, monitors the budgets with the managers and supervisors concerned at monthly meetings, and uses these meetings to 'jolly up' individuals whose actual costs vary from budgeted performance.

Fastbuck approves items on the menu, and likes to ensure that the dishes developed match his expectations. Where appropriate he will make alterations to planned recipes. He does not like food with strong flavours. Fastbuck approves all selling prices to be paid by customers in all pubs, and makes all other marketing decisions about both unit promotional material and general brand marketing strategy.

Fastbuck has attempted to delegate the selection and recruitment of staff at operative level to the Recruitment and Training Officer, Val Pole. She recruits all the staff in the South area. Unit managers inform her of their needs, and she appoints staff accordingly. Fastbuck recruits all unit managers personally; he likes to ensure that those entering the management team are 'the sort of people who will fit in'. Particularly, he values people who are prepared 'to get things done and make things happen', people like himself, 'with a bit of get up and go'.

Fastbuck recognizes the importance of good communications. He holds weekly meetings with senior managers in the business, when he tells them his decisions and gives them their instructions for the week. He makes sure that he personally visits each of the units once per month, and is thereby available to hear staff grievances during his tour of inspection.

Despite all of Fastbuck's efforts, operational accounts show a stubborn resistance to cost reduction and are currently showing a considerable budget variance. In addition, there are some worrying performance indicators in the South area and, despite his direct intervention over the past nine months, the situation appears to be getting worse.

Other members of the management team

Val Pole, Recruitment and Training Officer, has been in this post for almost two years. She was one of the first appointments that Fastbuck made on becoming Operations Director. Val was the Personnel Officer at AVCO Engineering prior to her appointment. Fastbuck said that her expertise was 'just what the Silverwood Pub Company needed'.

Since joining the business she has certainly made an impact on the selection and recruitment of staff in the South region. This work has grown over the past couple of years, and recently she has attempted to persuade management that she needs an Assistant Recruitment Officer to help with this work in the North region, although Ann Jackson (Operations Manager in the North Region) has been resistant to Val and Graham's attempts to centralize recruitment in her area. The new post would attract a salary of £18 000 per annum.

Val takes her job seriously, and values a systematic and organized approach to recruitment. She designs all advertisements, and shortlists and selects all operative staff herself. Given the growth in selection and recruitment activities, Val has not been able to spend much time on training activities over the last twelve months; however, this is just as well, because the training budget has been cut to save money.

Three clerical assistants also work in Val's section. They help with record keeping, wages calculations, and the administration needed for staff recruitment/separations etc.

Val feels that she certainly earns her £27 000 salary each year. She prides herself on being able to carry through her ideas and make them stick. She had to overcome a lot of resistance from the unit managers when she first arrived and centralized the recruitment of staff, but she didn't mind stepping on a few toes, and eventually got her own way. Val has a reputation for being fair with staff in the business, but can be sarcastic with people she considers to be less committed to the job than herself.

Terry Ball, Property Development Manager, has worked in the licensed retail sector for over thirty years. He has been an Operations Manager with one or other of the industry's brands since 1979. In fact, he was asked to set up the current Silverwood Pub Company until Fastbuck was appointed and the business reorganized in preparation for the coming wave of expansion.

Although he is close to retirement, Terry has been an innovator and force for change, particularly in the early years. He organized much of the provision, bringing in an empowered management style that delegated much decision-making to the unit managers. As an 'old hand', Terry has always valued the part that a high quality provision can contribute to business performance. Throughout his time working in the UK branded restaurant business he has always said, 'Consistent quality is the key to customer loyalty'.

Over the last couple of years, Terry has become increasingly fond of telling people that he is looking forward to retirement. He doesn't like all the changes that have taken place; Silverwood Pub Company just isn't the same place to work, with 'too many bloody accountants in charge'. At one time he argued against the changes, which he felt were not in the interests of staff and customers, but nowadays he doesn't let things get to him – life's too short. He tends to go along with Fastbuck's decisions, he doesn't take sides, and likes to remain neutral when some of the units managers come to him with complaints or disagreements. He is happy that his job involves site visits to progress the new pub openings, so he spends a lot of time out of the office and tries to avoid Fastbuck's company.

John Marsh, Distribution Manager, has worked in licensed retailing for five years. He is responsible for the team of drivers who take product ingredients and packaging to the pubs. Supplies are distributed in vans. Recent legislation has laid down strict requirements on food temperatures during transportation, so John places high value on maintaining good relations with his staff. He often feels as though he is torn between loyalty to his management colleagues and to the staff in his section. He likes to avoid conflict and tries to soothe feelings when conflicts occur within his team. Often he uses humour to maintain friendly relationships.

Ann Jackson, Operations Manager North Region, has responsibility for the six restaurants in the Manchester region. Over the next year, another nine pubs will be opened in her region. Work is organized through the unit managers. She has resisted Fastbuck's attempts to impose more centralized control in her area, and there have been several very heated discussions about the way to run the business. Up to this point Fastbuck has been unwilling to dismiss her, although he hopes that she will buckle under his pressure and resign from her post.

Ann has some five years experience working in the Silverwood Pub Company. She joined after completing a HND in Hotel, Catering and Institutional Management.

Hospitality, Leisure & Tourism Series

Ann has been in her current post for just over two years, and during that time she has shown herself to be concerned with ensuring that decisions are taken after seeking out the opinions and ideas of other people in her region. When conflicts have arisen, she has attempted to discover the underlying causes and resolve them. She has sometimes upset Fastbuck because she has frequently argued against his policies and has personally been prepared to change her mind when convinced by other people's arguments. Fastbuck has privately described her as 'a bit of a wimp', and a mistake in his normally accurate selection process. That said, Ann's subordinates generally like working for her and value her sense of humour even under pressure – and there has certainly been plenty of that. There have been difficulties caused by Fastbuck's insistence on financial performance measures as the only indicator of business success. She has argued that customer and employee satisfaction should also be taken into account. In line with this, she has recently calculated that staff turnover incurs a direct cost of £500 per head.

She has recently further angered Fastbuck by telling him she will be taking maternity leave in three months, although she does plan to return. Fastbuck told Terry Ball that this was one of the problems of recruiting women to senior management positions.

You, Operations Manager South Region, have recently been appointed to this post after having worked as an Area Supervisor in one of the other pub chains. You have been in post for three weeks. Your predecessor was in post for approximately eighteen months, and has now taken up a similar job in a competitor organization in Derby. The post has been vacant for nine months because Fastbuck wanted to run these restaurants directly himself, and the opportunity to save the salary enabled him to save on the Administration and Management budget.

The immediate incident

On the Monday morning of your fourth week, you are summoned to the Managing Director's office. She tells you that Graham Fastbuck has been suspended prior to a disciplinary hearing relating to a matter of gross misconduct. He is not expected to return to work. She also gives you the impression that Fastbuck's removal has been at insistence of the Board of Directors. They have been particularly concerned that the South Region's performance has suffered since Fastbuck took over.

She asks you to take over as Operations Director temporarily; she expects that it will be two or three months before the company will be able to begin to find a replacement. Whilst mindful of the need to observe equal opportunities policies, she gives you the clear impression that you might be offered the post on a permanent basis, providing you make a good job of running the business.

She wants your assessment of the chain's problems in a couple of weeks. She says she wants you to prepare for a meeting in which you will be expected to identify the causes of the problems and highlight the actions needed to improve business performance. You will need to start by making an analysis of the management reports provided (Tables 15.2–15.5).

Management reports

Unit	Average weekly sales (£)	Average weekly transactions	Average transaction (£)	No. of staff	Staff working over 35 hours	Percentage of staff working over 35 hours	Average hours worked
North1	15 953	4347	3.67	35	9	25.7	23.68
North2	33 434	8235	4.06	71	17	24.3	23.68
North3	17 699	5601	3.16	33	9	27.2	23.93
North4	26 767	7044	3.80	54	8	11.3	20.16
North5	26 321	6051	4.35	46	7	15.2	22.17
North6	20 962	5027	4.17	41	7	17.1	23.83
South1	30 013	8446	3.55	72	12	16.6	19.43
South2	14 535	4895	2.96	34	11	32.3	27.3
South3	30 457	8515	3.57	70	3	4.3	17.04
South4	18 162	5513	3.29	47	9	19.1	21.3
South5	27 919	7386	3.77	44	11	25.0	22.2
South6	27 150	7536	3.60	49	7	14.3	21.57

Table 15.2 Pub sales information

Units	Overall training grade	Average staff numbers	Fully rotatable staff	Fully trained staff	(%)	Training team	Outstanding OCLs	Employee satisfaction with training (%)
North1	92	35	21	15	71	6	8	64
North2	91	71	46	35	76	5	9	56
North3	93	33	15	10	67	3	7	66
North4	85	54	27	13	48	3	15	63
North5	85	46	26	15	58	6	15	80
North6	93	41	33	20	61	3	7	71
South1	76	72	38	19	50	8	26	55
South2	80	34	26	8	31	4	19	36
South3	74	70	39	16	41	4	26	46
South4	80	47	27	13	48	3	23	39
South5	72	44	26	13	50	3	27	38
South6	54	49	35	13	37	5	36	44

Table 15.3 Training in the pubs

Hospitality, Leisure & Tourism Series

Units	Headline rate (%)	Rate after temporary staff (%)	Temporary staff leavers	Leavers after temporary staff	Cost of staff turnover in restaurant
North1	42.07	42.07	0	14	
North2	52.57	46.88	4	33	
North3	74.09	74.09	0	23	
North4	60.06	60.06	0	38	
North5	74.03	67.35	3	33	
North6	78.8	43.01	15	18	
Average North		55.57			
South1	128.1	118.6	7	87	
South2	158.0	152.4	2	55	
South3	175.0	166.1	5	93	
South4	128.4	126.0	1	54	
South5	176.1	155.5	9	68	
South6	169.7	118.2	27	62	
Average South		139.46			

Table 15.4 Staff turnover in the pubs

Units	Mystery customer	Quality	Service	Cleanliness
North1	96.7	100.0	92.0	98.3
North2	92.9	96.8	92.1	95.6
North3	89.1	96.4	83.6	88.0
North4	91.2	93.6	88.9	90.7
North5	88.5	90.7	82.9	95.1
North6	94.7	96.8	92.1	95.6
South1	85.5	96.8	74.4	84.5
South2	86.7	93.1	80.9	85.4
South3	86.7	88.4	84.1	86.9
South4	92.7	96.2	87.4	96.7
South5	81.9	87.4	72.8	82.7
South6	83.4	87.4	76.0	82.7

Table 15.5 External customer satisfaction ratings

Units	Overall	Your job	Performance and training	Pay and work	Management and leadership	Customers	Communication	Competition
National average	57	49	57	57	59	65	53	58
North1	65	51	64	67	64	79	62	64
North2	64	52	56	62	75	76	54	65
North3	65	53	66	64	76	68	56	63
North4	68	59	63	68	72	80	60	66
North5	81	74	80	74	84	86	80	84
North6	66	51	71	64	66	83	58	68
South1	51	44	55	62	46	64	42	46
South2	33	23	36	39	37	23	35	31
South3	43	26	46	46	41	49	41	46
South4	35	33	39	34	34	42	27	37
South5	38	25	38	35	46	40	32	40
South6	49	43	44	53	57	49	46	47

Table 15.6 Employee satisfaction survey results (expressed as a percentage)

Index

Hospitality, Leisure & Tourism Series

Hospitality, Leisure & Tourism Series

Hospitality, Leisure and Tourism Series 2002

07506 53345
**Business Development
in Licensed Retailing**
(Lashley & Lincoln)

07506 54317
In Search of Hospitality
(ed. - Lashley & Morrison)

07506 5659X
**Financial Management
for Hospitality
Decision Makers**
(Guilding)

07506 52446
Empowerment
(Lashley)

07506 47728
**Franchising Hospitality
Services**
(ed. - Lashley & Morrison)

07506 47965*
Events Management
(Bowden et al.)

07506 45563
Stats To Go
(Buglear)

07506 4480X
**Strategic Questions in
Food and Beverage
Management**
(Wood)

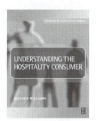

07506 52497
**Understanding the
Hospitality
Consumer**
(Williams)

07506 46160
**Hospitality Retail
Management**
(Lashley)

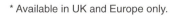

* Available in UK and Europe only.

**BUTTERWORTH
HEINEMANN**

An imprint of Elsevier Science
www.bh.com